"Very ably condensed all the essentials . . . amazing that a slim volume can contain so much . . . has clarity of vision and sympathy of understanding . . . style is plain and well suited to the western reader."

—Dr. Khwaja Ahmad Faruqi,
Professor and Chairman, Department of Urdu Studies, University of Delhi, Delhi, India

△ Dr. John Alden Williams lectures on Islamic history at the Institute of Islamic Studies, McGill University, Montreal. A graduate of the University of Arkansas and Princeton University (Ph.D.), Dr. Williams has also studied at the American University (Beirut) and the University of Munich.

In addition to being a National Woodrow Wilson Fellow, he has received Fulbright and Rockefeller grants for study in various centers of Islamic civilization. He has also received a post-doctoral grant to study Islamic art and architecture from The American Center for Research in Cairo.

Islam is one of six volumes in a comprehensive series published originally by George Braziller at a retail price of $24.00. Each of these volumes will be issued as complete and unabridged paper-bound reprints by Washington Square Press. See the reverse of this leaf for a full listing.

GREAT RELIGIONS OF MODERN MAN

Richard A. Gard, *General Editor*

BUDDHISM

Edited by Richard A. Gard

CHRISTIANITY: CATHOLICISM

Edited by George Brantl

CHRISTIANITY: PROTESTANTISM

Edited by J. Leslie Dunstan

HINDUISM

Edited by Louis Renou

ISLAM

Edited by John Alden Williams

JUDAISM

Edited by Arthur Hertzberg

Islam

Edited by
John Alden Williams

WASHINGTON SQUARE PRESS
POCKET BOOKS • NEW YORK

ISLAM

WASHINGTON SQUARE PRESS edition published April, 1963
4th printing........................August, 1972

A new edition of a distinguished literary work now made available in an inexpensive, well-designed format

L

Published by
POCKET BOOKS, a division of Simon & Schuster, Inc.,
630 Fifth Avenue, New York, N.Y.

WASHINGTON SQUARE PRESS editions are distributed in the U.S. by Simon & Schuster, Inc., 630 Fifth Avenue, New York, N.Y. 10020 and in Canada by Simon & Schuster of Canada, Ltd., Richmond Hill, Ontario, Canada.

Standard Book Number: 671-47886-9.

ACKNOWLEDGMENTS

The editor wishes to thank the following for permission to reprint the material included in this volume:

George Allen & Unwin Ltd.—for selection from F. Rahman, *Prophecy in Islam.*

American Oriental Society—for selection from W. Klein, *Al-Ibānah 'An Usūl Ad Diyānah.* Used by courtesy of the publishers, American Oriental Society.

A. & C. Black Ltd.—for selection from E. G. Browne, *A Year Amongst the Persians.*

Bollingen Foundation—for selections from *Ibn Khaldûn: The Muqaddimah.* Trans. from the Arabic by Franz Rosenthal. Bollingen Series XLIII. By permission of Bollingen Foundation, New York.

P. R. E. Browne & E. M. A. Browne—for selection from E. G. Browne, *Literary History of Persia.*

Cambridge University Press—for selection from R. A. Nicholson, *Divani Shamsi Tabriz;*—for selection from E. G. Browne, *Literary History of Persia;*—for selection from A. J. Wensinck, *The Muslim Creed;*—and for selections from R. A. Nicholson, *Studies in Islamic Mysticism.*

Islamic Research Association (Bombay)—for selection from A. A. A. Fyzee, *A Shī'ite Creed.*

Luzac & Company Ltd.—for selections from Margaret Smith, ed., *Readings from the Mystics of Islam;*—for selection from A. J. Arberry, *Immortal Rose;*—and for selection from W. E. Miller, trans., *Al-Bābu-l-Hādī 'Ashar.*

THE MACMILLAN COMPANY (New York)—for selections from A. J. Arberry, *The Koran Interpreted;*—for selections from A. J. Arberry, trans., *Sufism;*—and for selections from Montgomery Watt, *The Faith and Practice of Al-Ghasali.*

RICHARD J. MCCARTHY, S. J.—for selection from *Kitab Al-Lum'a.*

MOUTON & CO. N. V. (The Hague)—for selection from Marshall G. Hodgson (trans.), *The Order of the Assassins.*

JOHN MURRAY (London) and THE GROVE PRESS—for selection from Sardar Sir Jogendra Singh, *The Persian Mystics.*

OXFORD UNIVERSITY PRESS (London)—for selections from Alfred Guillaume, *The Life of Muhammad.*

ROUTLEDGE & KEGAN PAUL LTD.—for selections from *Ibn Khaldûn: The Muqaddimah.*

S. P. C. K.—for selections from Constance E. Padwick, *Muslim Devotions.*

CONTENTS

Islam

THE OPENING

In the Name of God, the Merciful, the Compassionate.

Praise be to God, the Lord of the Worlds,
The Merciful One, the Compassionate One,
Master of the Day of Doom.

Thee alone we serve, to Thee alone we cry for help.
Guide us in the straight path
The path of them Thou hast blessed.
Not of those with whom Thou art angry
Nor of those who go astray.

The *Fātiḥa*, the "Lord's Prayer" of Islam, is the opening sūra of the Qur'ān. It is recited for each new beginning.

CHAPTER ONE

THE QUR'ĀN: THE WORD OF GOD

The departure point of the Islamic religion, the central article of faith from which all else flows, may be stated as follows: God (the only God there is: *al-Ilāh*, *Allah* in Arabic; *El*, *Elohim*, *Jahweh* in Hebrew; *Khudā* or *Yazdān* in Persian, *Tanri* in Turkish, *ὁ Θεός* in Greek, *Deus* in Latin, *God* in plain English) has spoken to man in the Qur'ān.

This divine communication is seen as the final stage in a long series of divine communications conducted through the prophets. It began with Adam, the first man, who was also the first prophet, because he was the first to whom God revealed Himself.

After Adam, God continued to address men through prophets, to warn them that their happiness lay in worshiping Him and submitting themselves to Him, and to tell them of the terrible consequences of disobedience. In each case, however, the message was changed and deformed by perverse men. Finally, in His mercy, God sent down His final revelation through the seal of His prophet, Muhammad, in a definitive form which would not be lost.

The Qur'ān, then, is the Word of God, for Muslims. While controversies have raged among them as to the sense in which this is true—whether it is the created or uncreated Word, whether it is true of every Arabic letter or only of the message as a whole, that it *is true* has never been questioned by them.

The Qur'ān was revealed in Arabic. It is a matter of faith in Islam that since it is of Divine origin it is inimitable, and since to translate is always to betray, Muslims have always deprecated and at times prohibited any attempt to render it in another language. Anyone who has read it in the original is forced to admit that this caution seems justified; no translation, however faithful to the meaning, has ever been fully successful. Arabic when expertly used is a remarkably terse, rich and forceful language, and the Arabic of the Qur'ān is by turns striking, soaring, vivid, terrible, tender and breathtaking. As Professor Gibb has put it, "No man in fifteen hundred years has ever played on that deep-toned instrument with such power, such boldness, and such range of emotional effect."[1] It is meaningless to apply adjectives such as "beautiful" or "persuasive" to the Qur'ān; its flashing images and inexorable measures go directly to the brain and intoxicate it.

It is not surprising, then, that a skilled reciter of the Qur'ān can reduce an Arabic-speaking audience to helpless tears, that for thirteen centuries it has been ceaselessly meditated upon, or that for great portions of the human race, the "High-speech" of seventh-century Arabia has become the true accents of the Eternal.

The selections which follow here have been taken from Professor Arberry's translation, the only one in English which has succeeded in suggesting the extraordinary qualities of the original.[2]

1. *God Speaks to Man*

The first words of the "Sūra (chapter) of the Clot" are the first which were revealed to Muhammad. The section which follows the "Sūra of the Clot" here is the opening portion of the second and longest chapter of the Qur'ān, the "Sūra of the Cow." It thus forms a sort of introduction to the Book as a whole.

Recite: In the Name of thy Lord who created,
created Man of a blood-clot.

Recite: And thy Lord is the Most Generous,
who taught by the Pen.
taught Man that he knew not.

No indeed; surely Man waxes insolent,
for he thinks himself self-sufficient.
Surely unto thy Lord is the Returning.

What thinkest thou? He who forbids
a servant when he prays—

What thinkest thou? If he were upon guidance
or bade to godfearing—
What thinkest thou? If he cries lies, and turns away—
Did he not know that God sees?

No indeed; surely, if he gives not over,
We shall seize him by the forelock,
a lying, sinful forelock.
So let him call on his concourse!
We shall call on the guards of Hell.

No indeed; do thou not obey him,
and bow thyself, and draw nigh. (96:1–19)

Alif Lam Mim

This is the Book, wherein is no doubt,
a guidance to the godfearing
who believe in the Unseen, and perform the prayer,
and expend of what We have provided them;
who believe in what has been sent down to thee
and what has been sent down before thee,

and have faith in the Hereafter;
those are upon guidance from their Lord,
those are the ones who prosper.

As for the unbelievers, alike it is to them
whether thou hast warned them or hast not warned them,
  they do not believe.
God has set a seal on their hearts and on their hearing,
  and on their eyes is a covering,
and there awaits them a mighty chastisement.
And some men there are who say,
"We believe in God and the Last Day";
  but they are not believers.
They would trick God and the believers,
and only themselves they deceive,
  and they are not aware.
In their hearts is a sickness,
and God has increased their sickness,
and there awaits them a painful chastisement
for that they have cried lies.
When it is said to them, "Do not corruption in the land,"
they say, "We are only ones that put things right."
  Truly, they are the workers of corruption
  but they are not aware.
When it is said to them, "Believe as the people believe,"
they say, "Shall we believe, as fools believe?"
  Truly, they are the foolish ones,
  but they do not know.
When they meet those who believe, they say, "We believe";
but when they go privily to their Satans, they say,
  "We are with you; we were only mocking."
God shall mock them, and shall lead them on
  blindly wandering in their insolence.
Those are they that have bought error
  at the price of guidance,
and their commerce has not profited them,
  and they are not right-guided.

The likeness of them is as the likeness of a man
who kindled a fire, and when it lit all about him
God took away their light, and left them in darkness
  unseeing,
  deaf, dumb, blind—
  so they shall not return;
  or as a cloudburst out of heaven
in which is darkness, and thunder, and lightning—
  they put their fingers in their ears
against the thunderclaps, fearful of death;
  and God encompasses the unbelievers;
the lightning wellnigh snatches away their sight;
whensoever it gives them light, they walk in it,
and when the darkness is over them, they halt;
  had God willed, He would have taken away
their hearing and their sight.
Truly, God is powerful over everything.
O you men, serve your Lord who created you,
and those that were before you; haply so
  you will be godfearing;
who assigned to you the earth for a couch,
and heaven for an edifice, and sent down
out of heaven water, wherewith He brought forth
fruits for your provision; so set not up
  compeers to God wittingly.
And if you are in doubt concerning that We have
sent down on Our servant, then bring one sūra
like it, and call your witnesses, apart from
  God, if you are truthful.
And if you do not—and you will not—then
fear the Fire, whose fuel is men and stones,
  prepared for unbelievers.

Give thou good tidings to those who believe
and do deeds of righteousness, that for them
await gardens underneath which rivers flow;
whensoever they are provided with fruits therefrom

they shall say, "This is that wherewithal
we were provided before"; that they shall be
given in perfect semblance; and there
for them shall be spouses purified; therein
they shall dwell forever. (2:1–25)

Blessed be He in whose hand is the Kingdom—
He is powerful over everything—
who created death and life, that He might try you
which of you is fairest in works; and He is
the All-mighty, the All-forgiving—
who created seven heavens one upon another.
Thou seest not in the creation
of the All-merciful any imperfection.
Return thy gaze; seest thou any fissure?
Then return thy gaze again, and again, and thy gaze comes
back to thee dazzled, aweary.
And we adorned the lower heaven with lamps, and made
them
things to stone Satans; and We have prepared for them
the chastisement of the Blaze.

And for those who disbelieve in their Lord
there awaits the chastisement of Gehenna—
an evil homecoming! (67:1–7)

The story of the Garden of Eden is similar to that contained in Genesis; however, the doctrine of Original Sin is not accepted in Islam. Adam's fall is not seen as a sin, but an error in judgment, and has not tainted the human race with its consequences. From the Creation, man has made a contract to serve God.

Alif Lam Mim Sad

A Book sent down to thee—
so let there be no impediment in thy breast
because of it—

to warn thereby, and as a reminder to believers:
Follow what has been sent down to you from your
Lord, and follow no friends other than He; little
  do you remember.
How many a city We have destroyed! Our might came
upon it at night, or while they took their ease
  in the noontide,
and they but cried, when Our might came upon them,
  "We were evildoers."
So we shall question those unto whom a Message was sent,
  and We shall question the Envoys,
And We shall relate to them with knowledge; assuredly
  We were not absent.
The weighing that day is true; he whose scales are heavy—
  they are the prosperers,
and he whose scales are light—they have lost their souls
  for wronging Our signs.

We have established you in the earth
and there appointed for you livelihood;
  little thanks you show.
We created you, then We shaped you,
then We said to the angels: "Bow yourselves
to Adam"; so they bowed themselves,
save Iblis—he was not of those
  that bowed themselves.
Said He, "What prevented thee to
bow thyself, when I commanded thee?"
Said he, "I am better than he; Thou
createdst me of fire, and him Thou
createdst of clay."
Said He, "Get thee down out of it;
it is not for thee to wax proud here,
so go thou forth; surely thou art
  among the humbled."
Said he, "Respite me till the day
  they shall be raised."

Said He, "Thou art among the ones
that are respited."
Said he, "Now, for Thy perverting me,
I shall surely sit in ambush for them
on Thy straight path;
then I shall come on them from before them
and from behind them, from their right hands
and their left hands; Thou wilt not find
most of them thankful."
Said He, "Go thou forth from it, despised
and banished. Those of them that follow
thee—I shall assuredly fill Gehenna
with all of you."

"O Adam, inherit, thou and thy wife,
the Garden, and eat of where you will,
but come not nigh this tree, lest you be
of the evildoers."
Then Satan whispered to them, to reveal
to them that which was hidden from them
of their shameful parts. He said, "Your Lord
has only prohibited you from this tree
lest you become angels, or lest you
become immortals."
And he swore to them, "Truly, I am for you
a sincere adviser."
So he led them on by delusion; and when
they tasted the tree, their shameful parts
revealed to them, so they took to stitching
upon themselves leaves of the Garden.
And their Lord called to them, "Did not I
prohibit you from this tree, and say
to you, 'Verily Satan is for you
a manifest foe'?"
They said, "Lord, we must have wronged ourselves,
and if Thou dost not forgive us, and

have mercy upon us, we shall surely be
among the lost."
Said He, "Get you down, each of you
an enemy to each. In the earth a sojourn
shall be yours, and enjoyment
for a time."
Said He, "Therein you shall live, and
therein you shall die, and from there you
shall be brought forth." (7:1–24)

And when thy Lord took from the Children of Adam,
from their loins, their seed, and made them testify
touching themselves, "Am I not your Lord?"
They said, "Yes, we testify"—lest you should say
on the Day of Resurrection, "As for us, we
were heedless of this,"
or lest you say, "Our fathers were idolaters
aforetime, and we were seed after them.
What, wilt Thou then destroy us for the deeds
of vain-doers?"

So We distinguish the signs; and haply
they will return.

And recite to them the tidings of him to whom
We gave Our signs, but he cast them off,
and Satan followed after him, and he became
one of the perverts.
And had We willed, We would have raised him up
thereby; but he inclined towards the earth
and followed his lust. So the likeness of him
is as the likeness of a dog; if thou attackest it
it lolls its tongue out, or if thou leavest it
it lolls its tongue out. That is that people's likeness
who cried lies to Our signs. So relate the story;
haply they will reflect.
An evil likeness is the likeness of

the people who cried lies to Our signs, and
  themselves were wronging.
Whomsoever God guides,
  he is rightly guided;
and whom He leads astray—
  they are the losers.
We have created for Gehenna
  many jinn and men;
they have hearts, but understand
  not with them;
they have eyes, but perceive
  not with them;
they have ears, but they hear
  not with them.
They are like cattle; nay, rather
  they are further astray.
Those—they are the heedless.
To God belong the Names Most Beautiful;
  so call Him by them,
and leave those who blaspheme His Names—
they shall assuredly be recompensed
  for the things they did. (7:172–180)

The Qur'ān repeatedly reminds man that he is surrounded with the evidences of Divine handiwork; it expresses astonishment that he can nevertheless be so blind as not to remember the Creator.

God's command comes;
so seek not to hasten it.
Glory be to Him!
High be He exalted above that they associate with Him!
He sends down the angels with the Spirit of His command
upon whomsoever He will among His servants, saying:
Give you warning
that there is no God but I;
so fear you Me!

He created the heavens and the earth in truth;
high be He exalted above that they associate with Him!
He created man of a sperm-drop; yet, behold,
he is a manifest adversary. And the cattle—
He created them for you; in them is warmth, and uses
various, and of them you eat, and there is beauty
in them for you, when you bring them home to rest
and when you drive them forth abroad to pasture;
and they bear your loads unto a land that you
never would reach, excepting with great distress.
Surely your Lord is All-clement, All-compassionate.
And horses, and mules, and asses, for you to ride,
and as an adornment; and He creates what you know not.

God's it is to show the way;
and some do swerve from it.
If He willed, He would have
guided you all together.

It is He who sends down to you out of heaven water
  of which you have to drink,
and of which trees, for you to pasture your herds,
  and thereby He brings forth
for you crops, and olives, and palms, and vines,
  and all manner of fruit.
Surely in that is a sign for a people who reflect.
And He subjected to you the night and day, and
the sun and moon; and the stars are subjected
  by His command.
Surely in that are signs for a people who understand.
And that which He has multiplied for you in the earth
  of diverse hues.
Surely in that is a sign for a people who remember.
It is He who subjected to you the sea, that you
  may eat of it
fresh flesh, and bring forth out of it ornaments
  for you to wear;

and thou mayest see the ships cleaving through it;
  and that you may seek
of His bounty, and so haply you will be thankful.
And He cast on the earth firm mountains, lest it
  shake with you,
and rivers and ways; so haply you will be guided;
and waymarks; and by the stars they are guided.
  Is He who creates as
he who does not create? Will you not remember?
If you count God's blessing, you will never number it;
surely God is All-forgiving, All-compassionate.

  And God knows what you keep secret
  and what you publish.
And those they call upon, apart from God,
created nothing, and themselves are created,
dead, not alive, and not aware when
  they shall be raised.
  Your God is One God.
And they who believe not in the world to come,
their hearts deny, and they have waxed proud.
  Without a doubt God
knows what they keep secret
  and what they publish;
He loves not those that wax proud. (16:1–22)

2. *He Speaks Through the Prophets*

Abraham: The Patriarch Abraham, ancestor of the Semites, is seen in the Qur'ān as the prototype of the Muslim; it is implied that he arrived at monotheism by pure reason before the revelation came. With his first-born, Ishmael, he built the Temple of the Ka'ba at Bekka, or Mecca, and instituted the rites of pilgrimage. While he has been claimed by both the Jews and the Christians, he did not belong to either of these religions, it is said; he was simply a man who submitted himself to God: a Muslim.

And mention in the Book Abraham;
surely he was a true man, a Prophet.
When he said to his father, "Father,
why worshippest thou that which neither
hears nor sees, nor avails thee anything?
Father, there has come to me knowledge
such as came not to thee; so follow me,
and I will guide thee on a level path.
Father, serve not Satan; surely Satan
is a rebel against the All-merciful.
Father, I fear that some chastisement
from the All-merciful will smite thee,
so that thou becomest a friend to Satan."
Said he, "What, are thou shrinking
from my gods, Abraham? Surely, if thou
givest not over, I shall stone thee;
so forsake me now for some while."
He said, "Peace be upon thee!
I will ask my Lord to forgive thee;
surely He is ever gracious to me.
Now I will go apart from you
and that you call upon, apart from
God; I will call upon my Lord,
and haply I shall not be, in calling
upon my Lord, unprosperous."
So, when he went apart from them
and that they were serving, apart
from God, We gave him Isaac and
Jacob, and each We made a Prophet;
and We gave them of Our mercy,
and We appointed unto them
a tongue of truthfulness, sublime. (19:41–50)

Say: "God has spoken the truth; therefore follow
the creed of Abraham, a man of pure faith
and no idolater."
The first House established for the people

was that at Bekka, a place holy, and a guidance
  to all beings.
Therein are clear signs—the station of Abraham,
and whosoever enters it is in security.
It is the duty of all men towards God to come
to the House a pilgrim, if he is able to
  make his way there.
As for the unbeliever, God is All-sufficient
  nor needs any being. (3:95–97)

And they say, "Be Jews or Christians and
you shall be guided." Say thou: "Nay, rather
the creed of Abraham, a man of pure faith;
  he was no idolater."
Say you: "We believe in God, and
  in that which has been sent down on us
and sent down on Abraham, Ishmael,
Isaac and Jacob, and the Tribes,
and that which was given to Moses and Jesus
and the Prophets, of their Lord; we
make no division between any of them, and
  to Him we surrender."
And if they believe in the like of that you
believe in, then they are truly guided; but if
they turn away, then they are clearly in schism;
God will suffice you for them; He is
  the All-hearing, the All-knowing;
the baptism of God; and who is there
that baptizes fairer than God?
  Him we are serving. (2:135–138)

Moses: Moses is one of the most frequently mentioned of the prophets; he was sent to rescue the children of Ishmael's nephew Israel from Egypt. However, the Children of Israel became proud and disobeyed God; they regarded themselves as a Chosen People and wronged their brethren, and when God sent prophets to warn them, they refused to listen and put His messengers to death. They are People of the Book, since God gave them the scriptures, but they have perverted their revelation.

So when Moses had accomplished the term
and departed with his household, he observed
on the side of the Mount a fire. He said to his
household, "Tarry you here; I observe a fire.
Perhaps I shall bring you news of it,
or a faggot from the fire, that haply
you shall warm yourselves."
When he came to it, a voice cried from the right bank
of the watercourse, in the sacred hollow,
coming from the tree: "Moses, I am God, the
Lord of all Being.
Cast down thy staff." And when he saw it
quivering like a serpent, he turned about
retreating, and turned not back. "Moses,
come forward, and fear not; for surely thou
art in security.
Insert thy hand into thy bosom, and it will
come forth white without evil; and press to thee
thy arm, that thou be not afraid. So these
shall be two proofs from thy Lord to Pharaoh
and his Council; for surely they are an
ungodly people."
Said he, "My Lord, I have indeed slain
a living soul among them, and I fear that
they will slay me.
Moreover my brother Aaron is more eloquent
than I. Send him with me as a helper
and to confirm I speak truly, for I fear they
will cry me lies."
Said He, "We will strengthen thy arm by means
of thy brother, and We shall appoint to you

an authority, so that they shall not reach you
because of Our signs; you, and whoso follows you,
shall be the victors."
So when Moses came to them with Our signs,
clear signs, they said, "This is nothing but a
forged sorcery. We never heard of this among
our fathers, the ancients."
But Moses said, "My Lord knows very well
who comes with the guidance from Him, and shall
possess the Ultimate Abode; surely the evildoers
will not prosper."
And Pharaoh said, "Council, I know not that you
have any god but me. Kindle me, Haman,
a fire upon the clay, and make me a tower, that I
may mount up to Moses' god; for I think that he is
one of the liars."
And he waxed proud in the land, he and his hosts,
wrongfully; and they thought they should not be
returned to Us.
Therefore We seized him and his hosts, and cast them
into the sea; so behold how was the end
of the evildoers!
And We appointed them leaders, calling to the
Fire; and on the Day of Resurrection they
shall not be helped;
and We pursued them in this world with a curse,
and on the Day of Resurrection they shall be
among the spurned.
And We gave Moses the Book, after that We had
destroyed the former generations, to be examples
and a guidance and a mercy, that haply so
they might remember. (28:29–43)

Children of Israel, remember My blessing
wherewith I blessed you, and that I
have preferred you above all beings;
and beware of a day when no soul for another

shall give satisfaction, and no intercession
shall be accepted from it, nor any counterpoise
be taken, neither shall they be helped.

And when We delivered you from the folk of Pharaoh
who were visiting you with evil chastisement,
slaughtering your sons, and sparing your women;
and in that was a grievous trial from your Lord.
And when We divided for you the sea
and delivered you, and drowned Pharaoh's fold
  while you were beholding.
And when We appointed with Moses forty nights
then you took to yourselves the Calf after him
  and you were evildoers;
then We pardoned you after that, that haply
  you should be thankful.
And when We gave to Moses the Book
and the Salvation, that haply
  you should be guided. (2:40–53)

And when Moses sought water for his people,
so We said, "Strike with thy staff the rock";
and there gushed forth from it twelve fountains;
all the people knew now their drinking-place.
"Eat and drink of God's providing, and
mischief not in the earth, doing corruption."
And when you said, "Moses, we will not endure
one sort of food; pray to thy Lord for us, that He
may bring forth for us of that the earth produces—
green herbs, cucumbers, corn, lentils, onions."
He said, "Would you have in exchange what is meaner
for what is better? Get you down to Egypt;
you shall have there that you demanded."
And abasement and poverty were pitched upon them,
and they were laden with the burden of God's anger;
that, because they had disbelieved the signs of God
and slain the Prophets unrightfully; that,

because they disobeyed, and were transgressors.
Surely they that believe, and those of Jewry,
and the Christians, and those Sabaeans,
whoso believes in God and the Last Day, and works
righteousness—their wage awaits them with their Lord,
and no fear shall be on them, neither shall they sorrow.
(2:60–62)

Jesus: John and Jesus are seen as members of the righteous family of 'Imrān, among the Children of Israel. Jesus holds a place unique among the prophets in Islam. He is born of a virgin "purified above all women," he is the promised Messiah, "The Word of God and a Spirit from Him," an almost superhuman figure who spoke from the cradle and worked great wonders by the power of God; but the central doctrines of Christianity are set aside. The idea that he is the Son of God is sternly rejected, the doctrine of the Trinity is held to contradict God's Oneness, and since Jesus did not die on the cross and there was no collective guilt of man for which he could atone, there was no Atonement and no Resurrection. While also People of the Book, the early Christians are held to have deliberately falsified the scripture he brought, and to have worshiped the Messiah blasphemously. Later generations have been perhaps sincere but certainly misguided, so that a new revelation became necessary. As for Jesus, God took him to Himself when the Jews rejected him, and will justify him before the end of the world.

And when the angels said,
"Mary, God has chosen
thee, and purified
thee; He has chosen
thee above all women.

Mary, be obedient to
thy Lord, prostrating
and bowing before Him."
(That is of the tidings
of the Unseen, that We
reveal to thee; for thou
wast not with them, when
they were casting quills
which of them should have
charge of Mary; thou
wast not with them, when
they were disputing.)
When the angels said,
"Mary, God gives thee good
tidings of a Word from Him
whose name is Messiah,
Jesus, son of Mary;
high honoured shall he be
in this world and the next,
near stationed to God.
He shall speak to men
in the cradle, and of age,
and righteous he shall be."
"Lord," said Mary,
"how shall I have a son
seeing no mortal has touched me?" "Even so,"
God said, "God
creates what He will.
When He decrees a thing
He does but say to it
'Be,' and it is." (3:42–47)

So she conceived him, and withdrew with him
to a distant place.
And the birthpangs surprised her by
the trunk of the palm-tree. She said,
"Would I had died ere this, and become

a thing forgotten!"
But the one that was below her
called to her, "Nay, do not sorrow;
see, the Lord has set below thee
a rivulet.
Shake also to thee the palm-trunk,
and there shall come tumbling upon thee
dates fresh and ripe.
Eat therefore, and drink, and be
comforted; and if thou shouldst see
any mortal,
say, 'I have vowed to the All-merciful
a fast, and today I will not speak
to any man.' "
Then she brought the child to her folk
carrying him; and they said,
"Mary, thou hast surely committed
a monstrous thing!
Sister of Aaron, thy father was not
a wicked man, nor was thy mother
a woman unchaste."
Mary pointed to the child then;
but they said, "How shall we speak
to one who is still in the cradle,
a little child?"
He said, "Lo, I am God's servant;
God has given me the Book, and
made me a Prophet.
Blessed He has made me, wherever
I may be; and He has enjoined me
to pray, and to give the alms, so
long as I live,
and likewise to cherish my mother;
He has not made me arrogant,
unprosperous.
Peace be upon me, the day I was born,

and the day I die, and the day I am
raised up alive!"
That is Jesus, son of Mary,
in word of truth, concerning which
they are doubting.
It is not for God to take a son
unto Him. Glory be to Him! When he
decrees a thing, He but says to it
"Be," and it is.
Surely God is my Lord, and your
Lord; so serve you Him. This is
a straight path. (19:22–36)

And when Jesus perceived their unbelief, he said,
"who will be my helpers unto God?"
The Apostles said: "We will be helpers of God,
We believe in God; witness thou that we [are Muslims].[3]
Lord, we believe in what Thou hast sent down,
And we follow thy Messenger.
Inscribe us with those who witness to the truth."
(3:52–53)

Then (his enemies) devised against him,
And God devised.
And God is the best of devisers! (3:54)

And for their unbelief, and their uttering
against Mary a mighty calumny,
and for their saying, "We slew the Messiah,
Jesus son of Mary, the Messenger of God"—
yet they did not slay him, neither crucified him,
only a likeness of that was shown to them.
Those who are at variance concerning him surely
are in doubt regarding him; they have no knowledge
of him, except the following of surmise;
and they slew him not of a certainty—
no indeed; God raised him up to Him; God is
All-mighty, All-wise.

There is not one of the People of the Book
but will assuredly believe in him before his
death, and on the Resurrection Day he will be
  a witness against them. (4:154–159)

People of the Book, go not beyond the bounds
in your religion, and say not as to God
but the truth. The Messiah, Jesus son of Mary,
was only the Messenger of God, and His Word
that He committed to Mary, and a Spirit from
Him. So believe in God and His Messengers,
and say not, "Three." Refrain; better is it
for you. God is only One God. Glory be
to Him—that He should have a son!
To him belongs all that is in the heavens
and in the earth; God suffices
  for a guardian.
The Messiah will not disdain to be a servant
of God, neither the angels who are near
  stationed to Him. (4:171–172)

Muhammad: Muhammad is the chosen instrument by which God sent the Eternal Message in its definitive form, "the prophet" par excellence. The Qur'ān addresses him directly, to assure him that he is not insane, and to encourage him against men's doubts; it solemnly confirms as true the visions he has seen. Finally, it is suggested that the truth of his message may be seen from the faith of the Muslims.

Nun

By the Pen, and what they inscribe,
thou art not, by the blessing of thy Lord,
  a man possessed.
Surely thou shalt have a wage unfailing;
surely thou art upon a mighty morality.

So thou shalt see, and they will see,
  which of you is the demented.

Surely thy Lord knows very well
those who have gone astray from
His way, and He knows very well
  those who are guided. (62:1–7)

By the Star when it plunges,
your comrade is not astray, neither errs,
  neither speaks he out of caprice.
This is naught but a revelation revealed,
taught him by one terrible in power,
  very strong; he stood poised,
  being on the higher horizon,
then drew near and suspended hung,
two bows'-length away, or nearer,
then revealed to his servant what he revealed.
His heart lies not of what he saw;
what, will you dispute with him what he sees?

Indeed, he saw him another time
by the Lote-Tree of the Boundary
nigh which is the Garden of the Refuge,
When there covered the Lote-Tree that which covered;
  his eyes swerved not, nor swept astray.
Indeed, he saw one of the greatest signs of his Lord.
(53:1–18)

Qaf

Nay, but they marvel that a warner has come to
them from among them; and the unbelievers say,
  "This is a marvellous thing!
What, when we are dead and become dust? That
  is a far returning!"
We know what the earth diminishes of them;
  with Us is a book recording.
Nay, but they cried lies to the truth

when it came to them, and so they are
  in a case confused.
What, have they not beheld heaven above them,
how We have built it, and decked it out fair,
  and it has no cracks?
And the earth—We stretched it forth, and cast on it
  firm mountains,
and We caused to grow therein of every joyous kind
  for an insight
and a reminder to every penitent servant.
  And We sent down out of heaven
  water blessed,
and caused to grow thereby gardens
  and grain of harvest
and tall palm-trees with spathes compact,
  a provision for the servants,
and thereby We revived a land that was dead.
  Even so is the coming forth.

Cried lies before them the people of Noah
  and the men of Er-Rass, and Thamood, and
Ad and Pharaoh, the brothers of Lot, the
men of the Thicket, the people of Tubba'.
Every one cried lies to the Messengers,
  and My threat came true.

What, were We wearied by the first creation?
No indeed; but they are in uncertainty
  as to the new creation.

We indeed created man; and We know
what his soul whispers within him,
and We are nearer to him than the
  jugular vein. (50:1–17)

And We sent Noah, and Abraham,
and We appointed the Prophecy and
the Book to be among their seed; and

some of them are guided, and many of
them are ungodly.

Then We sent, following
in their footsteps, Our
Messengers; and We sent,
following, Jesus son of
Mary, and gave unto him
the Gospel.
And We set in the hearts of those who
followed him tenderness and mercy.

And monasticism they invented—We
did not prescribe it for them—only
seeking the good pleasure of God; but
they observed it not as it should be
observed. So We gave those of them
who believed their wage; and many of
them are ungodly.

O, believers, fear God, and believe
in His messenger, and He will give you
a twofold portion of His mercy, and
He will appoint for you a light whereby
you shall walk, and forgive you; God is
All-forgiving, All-compassionate;
that the People of the Book may know
that they have no power over anything
of God's bounty, and that bounty is in
the hand of God; He gives it unto
whomsoever He will; and God is of
bounty abounding. (57:26–29)

Muhammad is the Messenger of God,
and those who are with him are hard
against the unbelievers, merciful
one to another. Thou seest them
bowing, prostrating, seeking bounty

from God and good pleasure. Their
mark is on their faces, the trace of
prostration. That is their likeness
in the Torah, and their likeness
in the Gospel: as a seed that puts
forth its shoot, and strengthens it,
and it grows stout and rises straight
upon its stalk, pleasing the sowers,
that through them He may enrage
the unbelievers. God has promised
those of them who believe and do deeds
of righteousness forgiveness and
a mighty wage. (48:29)

3. *He Reveals Himself*

Since the Qur'ān is God's Word, the surest knowledge man can have of Him is to be found there, and it is by pondering on the Book as a whole rather than by abstracting or paraphrasing what it says that the Muslim arrives at knowledge of God. In themselves, the verses seem to be contradictory. Thus God appears as utterly transcendent, far above ever being an object of knowledge, and at the same time "nearer to man than his jugular vein." But both statements about Him are equally true. He sustains men and is merciful; He teaches and guides them, but if they disbelieve He "leads them further astray." Muslims who argue for predestination as well as those who seek to preserve man's free will have each been able to find support in the Qur'ān for their views. While God has personal qualities, no Muslim would refer to Him as personal (*shakhsī*).[4]

Man is invited to believe, but in the end God is unknowable, except insofar as He has chosen to reveal Himself; the way to Him lies through His Book and devoted service to Him, and He enlightens and guides whom He will.

God—
there is no god but He, the
Living, the Everlasting.
Slumber seizes Him not, neither sleep;
  to Him belongs
all that is in the heavens and the earth.
Who is there that shall intercede with Him
  save by His leave?
He knows what lies before them
  and what is after them,
and they comprehend not anything of His knowledge
  save such as He wills.
His Throne comprises the heavens and earth;
the preserving of them oppresses Him not;
He is the All-high, the All-glorious.

No complusion is there in religion.
Rectitude has become clear from error.
So whosoever disbelieves in idols
and believes in God, has laid hold of
the most firm handle, unbreaking; God is
  All-hearing, All-knowing.
God is the Protector of the believers;
He brings them forth from the shadows
  into the light. (2:255–257)

God is the Light of the heavens and the earth;
the likeness of His Light is as a niche
  wherein is a lamp
  (the lamp in a glass,
the glass as it were a glittering star)
  kindled from a Blessed Tree,
an olive that is neither of the East nor of the West
whose oil wellnigh would shine, even if no fire touched it;

Light upon Light;
(God guides to His Light whom he will.)
(And God strikes similitudes for men,
and God has knowledge of everything.)
in temples God has allowed to be raised up,
and His Name to be commemorated therein;
therein glorifying Him, in the mornings and the evenings,
are men whom neither commerce nor trafficking
diverts from the remembrance of God
and to perform the prayer, and to pay the alms,
fearing a day when hearts and eyes shall be turned about,
that God may recompense them for their fairest works
and give them increase of His bounty;
and God provides whomsoever He will, without reckoning.

And as for the unbelievers,
their works are as a mirage in a spacious plain
which the man athirst supposes to be water,
till, when he comes to it, he finds it is nothing;
there indeed he finds God,
and He pays him his account in full; (and God is swift
at the reckoning.)
or they are as shadows upon a sea obscure
covered by a billow
above which is a billow
above which are clouds
shadows piled one upon another;
when he puts forth his hand, wellnigh he cannot see it.
And to whomsoever God assigns no light,
no light has he. (24:35–40)

God knows the Unseen in the heavens and the earth;
He knows the thoughts within the breasts.
It is He who appointed you viceroys in the earth.
So whosoever disbelieves, his unbelief shall be
charged against him; their unbelief increases
the disbelievers only in hate in God's sight;

their unbelief increases the disbelievers only
  in loss. (35:38–39)

God is He that looses the winds, that stirs up clouds,
and He spreads them in heaven how he will, and shatters them;
then thou seest the rain issuing out of the midst of them,
and when He smites with it whomsoever of His servants
  He will, lo, they rejoice,
although before it was sent down on them before that
  they had been in despair.

So behold the marks of God's mercy,
how He quickens the earth after it
was dead; surely He is the quickener
of the dead, and He is powerful
  over everything.
But if We loose a [hot] wind, and they see [the earth]
  growing yellow,
  they remain after that unbelievers.

Thou shalt not make the dead to hear,
neither shalt thou make the deaf to hear the call
  when they turn about, retreating.
Thou shalt not guide the blind out of their error
  neither shalt thou make any to hear
except for such as believe in Our signs, and so surrender.

God is He that created you of weakness, then He appointed
after weakness strength, then after strength He appointed
weakness and grey hairs; He creates what He will, and
  He is the All-knowing, the All-powerful. (30:48–54)

  That then is God your Lord;
  there is no god but He,
  the Creator of everything.
  So serve Him,
  for He is Guardian over everything.
The eyes attain Him not, but He attains the eyes;
  He is the All-subtle, the All-aware. (6:102–103)

4. *He Commands*

It is in the Revelation that God makes known His sovereign will; what He has chosen for men and what He has forbidden.

O believers, eat of the good things
wherewith We have provided you, and give thanks
to God, if it be Him that you serve.
These things only has He forbidden you:
carrion, blood, the flesh of swine,
what has been hallowed to other than God.
Yet whoso is constrained, not desiring
nor transgressing, no sin shall be on him;
God is All-forgiving, All-compassionate.

Those who conceal what of the Book God has sent down
on them, and sell it for a little price—they shall eat
naught but the Fire in their bellies; God shall not
speak to them on the Day of Resurrection
neither purify them; there awaits them
  a painful chastisement.
Those are they that have bought error at
the price of guidance, and chastisement at
the price of pardon; how patiently they
  shall endure the Fire!
That, because God has sent down the Book
with the truth; and those that are
at variance regarding the Book
  are in wide schism.

It is not piety, that you turn your faces
  to the East and to the West.
  True piety is this:
to believe in God, and the Last Day,
the angels, the Book, and the Prophets,
to give of one's substance, however cherished,
  to kinsmen, and orphans,

the needy, the traveller, beggars,
  and to ransom the slave,
to perform the prayer, to pay the alms.
And they who fulfill their covenant
when they have engaged in a covenant,
  and endure with fortitude
  misfortune, hardship and peril,
these are they who are true in their faith,
  these are the truly godfearing.

O believers, prescribed for you is
retaliation, touching the slain;
freeman for freeman, slave for slave,
female for female. But if aught is pardoned
a man by his brother, let the pursuing
be honourable, and let the payment be
with kindness. That is a lightening
granted you by your Lord, and a mercy;
and for him who commits aggression
after that—for him there awaits
  a painful chastisement.
In retaliation there is life for you,
men possessed of minds; haply you
  will be godfearing. (2:172–179)

O believers, prescribed for you is
the Fast, even as it was prescribed for
those that were before you—haply you
  will be godfearing—
for days numbered; and if any of you
be sick, or if he be on a journey,
then a number of other days; and for those
who are able to fast, a redemption
by feeding a poor man. Yet better
it is for him who volunteers good,
and that you should fast is better for you,
  if you but know;

the month of Ramadan, wherein the Koran
was sent down to be a guidance
to the people, and as clear signs
of the Guidance and the Salvation.
So let those of you, who are present
at the month, fast it; and if any of you
be sick, or if he be on a journey,
then a number of other days; God desires
ease for you, and desires not hardship
for you; and that you fulfil the number, and
magnify God that He has guided you, and haply
you will be thankful. (2:183–185)

Permitted to you, upon the night of
the Fast, is to go in to your wives;
they are a vestment for you, and you are
a vestment for them. God knows that you have been
betraying yourselves, and has turned to you
and pardoned you. So now lie with them,
and seek what God has prescribed for you.
And eat and drink, until the white thread
shows clearly to you from the black thread
at the dawn; then complete the Fast
unto the night, and do not lie with them
while you cleave to the mosques. Those are
God's bounds; keep well within them. So God
makes clear His signs to men; haply they
will be godfearing.
Consume not your goods between you
in vanity; neither proffer it
to the judges, that you may sinfully
consume a portion of other men's goods,
and that wittingly. (2:187–188)

And fight in the way of God with those
who fight with you, but aggress not: God loves
not the aggressors.

And slay them wherever you come upon them,
and expel them from where they expelled you;
persecution is more grievous than slaying.
But fight them not by the Holy Mosque
until they should fight you there;
then, if they fight you, slay them—
such is the recompense of unbelievers—
but if they give over, surely God is
All-forgiving, All-compassionate.
Fight them, till there is no persecution
and the religion is God's; then if they
give over, there shall be no enmity
save for evildoers.
The holy month for the holy month;
holy things demand retaliation.
Whoso commits aggression against you,
do you commit aggression against him
like as he has committed against you;
and fear you God, and know that God is
with the godfearing.

And expend in the way of God;
and cast not yourselves by your own hands
into destruction, but be good-doers; God
loves the good-doers.

Fulfil the Pilgrimage and the Visitation
unto God; but if you are prevented,
then such offering as may be feasible.
And shave not your heads, till the offering
reaches its place of sacrifice. If any
of you is sick, or injured in his head,
then redemption by fast, or freewill offering,
or ritual sacrifice. When you are secure,
then whosoever enjoys the Visitation
until the Pilgrimage, let his offering
be such as may be feasible; or if he

finds none, then a fast of three days
in the Pilgrimage, and of seven when
you return, that is ten completely;
that is for him whose family are not
present at the Holy Mosque. And fear
God, and know that God is terrible
in retribution. (2:190–196)

Prescribed for you is fighting, though it be
hateful to you.
Yet it may happen that you will hate a thing
which is better for you; and it may happen that you
will love a thing which is worse for you; God knows,
and you know not.

They will question thee concerning
the holy month, and fighting in it.
Say: "Fighting in it is a heinous thing,
but to bar from God's way, and disbelief in Him,
and the Holy Mosque, and to expel its people
from it—that is more heinous in God's sight;
and persecution is more heinous than slaying."
They will not cease to fight with you,
till they turn you from your religion,
if they are able; and whosoever of you
turns from his religion, and dies disbelieving—
their works have failed in this world and the next;
those are the inhabitants of the Fire; therein
they shall dwell forever.
But the believers, and those who emigrate
and struggle in God's way—those have hopes of
God's compassion; and God is All-forgiving,
All-compassionate.

They will question thee concerning
wine, and arrow-shuffling. Say: "In both
is heinous sin, and uses for men,

but the sin in them is more heinous
than the usefulness."

They will question thee concerning
what they should expend. Say: "The abundance."
So God makes clear His signs to you; haply
you will reflect;
in this world, and the world to come.

They will question thee concerning
the orphans. Say: "To set their affairs
aright is good.
And if you intermix with them, they are
your brothers. God knows well
him who works corruption from him
who sets aright; and had He willed
He would have harassed you. Surely God is
All-mighty, All-wise."

Do not marry idolatresses, until
they believe; a believing slavegirl
is better than an idolatress, though
you may admire her. And do not marry
idolaters, until they believe. A believing
slave is better than an idolater, though
you may admire him.
Those call unto the Fire; and God calls unto
Paradise, and pardon, by His leave, and He
makes clear His signs to the people; haply
they will remember.

They will question thee concerning
the monthly course. Say: "It is hurt;
so go apart from women during
the monthly course, and do not approach them
till they are clean. When they have cleansed
themselves, then come unto them as God
has commanded you." Truly, God loves

those who repent, and He loves those
who cleanse themselves.
Your women are a tillage for you; so come
unto your tillage as you wish, and forward
for your souls; and fear God, and know that
you shall meet Him. Give thou good tidings
to the believers.

Do not make God a hindrance, through your oaths,
to being pious and godfearing, and putting
things right between men. Surely God is
All-hearing, All-knowing.
God will not take you to task for a slip
in your oaths; but He will take you to task
for what your hearts have earned; and God is
All-forgiving, All-clement. (2:216–225)

Such of your women as commit indecency,
call four of you to witness against them;
and if they witness, then detain them
in their houses until death takes them
or God appoints for them a way.
And when two of you commit indecency,
punish them both; but if they repent
and make amends, then suffer them to be;
God turns, and is All-compassionate.[5] (4:15–16)

O believers, draw not near to prayer
when you are drunken until you know
what you are saying, or defiled—unless
you are traversing a way—until you
have washed yourselves; but if you are
sick, or on a journey, or if any of you
comes from the privy, or you have touched
women, and you can find no water,
then have recourse to wholesome dust
and wipe your faces and your hands; God is
All-pardoning, All-forgiving. (4:43)

This is the recompense of those who fight
against God and His Messenger,[6] and hasten
about the earth, to do corruption there:
they shall be slaughtered, or crucified,
or their hands and feet shall alternately
be struck off, or they shall be banished
from the land. That is a degradation for them
in this world; and in the world to come awaits them
a mighty chastisement,
except for such as repent, before you
have power over them. So know you that
God is All-forgiving, All-compassionate.

O believers, fear God, and seek the means
to come to Him, and struggle in His way;
haply you will prosper. (6:33–35)

The fornicatress and the fornicator—
scourge each one of them a hundred stripes,
and in the matter of God's religion
let no tenderness for them seize you
if you believe in God and the Last Day;
and let a party of the believers
witness their chastisement.
The fornicator shall marry none but
a fornicatress or an idolatress,
and the fornicatress—none shall marry her
but a fornicator or an idolator;
that is forbidden to the believers.

And those who cast it up on women in
wedlock, and then bring not four witnesses,
scourge them with eighty stripes, and do not
accept any testimony of theirs ever; those—
they are the ungodly,
save such as repent thereafter and
make amends; surely God is All-forgiving,
All-compassionate.

And those who cast it up on their wives
having no witnesses except themselves,
the testimony of one of them shall be
to testify by God four times that he
is of the truthful.
and a fifth time, that the curse of
God shall be upon him, if he should
be of the liars.

It shall avert from her the chastisement
if she testify by God four times that he
is of the liars.
and a fifth time, that the wrath of
God shall be upon her, if he should
be of the truthful. (23:2–9)

And be thou not loud in thy prayer,
nor hushed therein,
but seek thou for a way between that.
And say:
"Praise belongs to God, who has not
taken to Him a son,
and who has not any associate in the
Kingdom,
nor any protector out of humbleness.
And magnify Him
With repeated magnificats. (17:110–111)

5. *He Rewards and Punishes*

When the sun shall be darkened,
when the stars shall be thrown down,
when the mountains shall be set moving,
when the pregnant camels shall be neglected,
when the savage beasts shall be mustered,
when the seas shall be set boiling,
when the souls shall be coupled,

when the buried infant shall be asked for what sin she was
  slain,
when the scrolls shall be unrolled,
when the heavens shall be stripped off,
when Hell shall be set blazing,
when Paradise shall be brought nigh,
then shall a soul know what it has produced.
  No! I swear by the slinkers,
  the runners, the sinkers,
  by the night swarming,
  by the dawn sighing,
truly this is the word of a noble Messenger
having power, with the Lord of the Throne secure,
  obeyed, moreover trusty. (81:1–21)

So, when the Trumpet is blown with a single blast
and the earth and the mountains are lifted up and
crushed with a single blow,
then, on that day, the Terror shall come to pass,
and heaven shall be split, for upon that day it
  shall be very frail,
and the angels shall stand upon its borders, and
upon that day eight shall carry above them the
  Throne of thy Lord.
On that day you shall be exposed, not one secret
  of yours concealed.
Then as for him who is given his book in his right hand,
he shall say, "Here, take and read my book! Certainly
I thought that I should encounter my reckoning." So he
  shall be in a pleasing life
  in a lofty Garden,
  its clusters nigh to gather.
"Eat and drink with wholesome appetite for that you did
  long ago, in the days gone by."
But as for him who is given his book in his left hand,
he shall say, "Would that I had not been given my book
and not known by reckoning! Would it had been the end!

My wealth has not availed me,
my authority is gone from me."
Take him, and fetter him, and then roast him in Hell,
then in a chain of seventy cubits' length insert him!
Behold, he never believed in God the All-mighty, and
he never urged the feeding of the needy; therefore he
today has not here one loyal friend, neither any food
saving foul pus, that none excepting the sinners eat.
(69:13–37)

When the Terror descends
(and none denies its descending)
abasing, exalting,
when the earth shall be rocked
and the mountains crumbled
and become a dust scattered,
and you shall be three bands—

Companions of the Right (O Companions of the Right!)
Companions of the Left (O Companions of the Left!)
and the Outstrippers: the Outstrippers
those are they brought nigh the Throne,
in the Gardens of Delight
(a throng of the ancients
and how few of the later folk)
upon close-wrought couches
reclining upon them, set face to face,
immortal youth going round about them
with goblets, and ewers, and a cup from a spring
(no brows throbbing, no intoxication)
and such fruits as they shall choose,
and such flesh of fowl as they desire,
and wide-eyed houris
as the likeness of hidden pearls,
a recompense for that they laboured.
Therein they shall hear no idle talk, no cause of sin,
only the saying "Peace, Peace!"

The Companions of the Right (O Companions of the Right!)
mid thornless lote-trees and serried acacias,
and spreading shade and outpoured waters,
  and fruits abounding
  unfailing, unforbidden,
  and upraised couches.
Perfectly We formed them, perfect,
and We made them spotless virgins,
chastely amorous, like of age
for the Companions of the Right.
A throng of the ancients
and a throng of the later folk.

The Companions of the Left (O Companions of the Left!)
  mid burning winds and boiling waters
  and the shadow of a smoking blaze
  neither cool, neither goodly;
  and before that they lived at ease,
  and persisted in the Great Sin,
  ever saying,
"What, when we are dead and become
dust and bones, shall we indeed
  be raised up?
What, and our fathers, the ancients?"

Say: "The ancients, and the later folk
shall be gathered to the appointed time
  of a known day.
Then you erring ones, you that cried lies,
you shall eat of a tree called Zakkoum,
and you shall fill therewith your bellies
and drink on top of that boiling water
lapping it down like thirsty camels."
This shall be their hospitality on the
  Day of Doom. (56:1–56)

By the loosed ones successively
storming tempestuously

by the scatters scattering
and the severally severing
and those hurling a reminder
excusing or warning,
Surely that which you are promised is about to fall!

When the stars shall be extinguished,
when heaven shall be split
when the mountains shall be scattered
and when the Messengers' time is set,
to what day shall they be delayed?
to the Day of Decision.
And what shall teach thee what is the Day of Decision?
Woe that day unto those who cry it lies!

Did We not destroy the ancients,
and then follow them with the later folk?
So We serve the sinners.
Woe that day unto those who cry it lies!

Did We not create you of a mean water,
that We laid within a sure lodging
till a known term decreed?[7]
We determined; excellent determiners are We.
Woe that day unto those who cry it lies!

Made We not the earth to be a housing
for the living and for the dead?
Set We not therein soaring mountains?
Sated you with sweetest water?
Woe that day unto those who cry it lies!

Depart to that you cried was lies!
Depart to a triple-massing shadow
unshading against the blazing flame
that shoots sparks like dry faggots,
sparks like to golden herds.
Woe that day unto those who cry it lies!

This is the day they shall not speak

neither be given leave, and excuse themselves.
Woe that day unto those who cry it lies!
"This is the Day of Decision; We have joined you with the
ancients;
if you have a trick, try you now to trick Me!
Woe that day unto those who cry it lies!

Truly the godfearing shall dwell amid shades and fountains,
and such fruits as their hearts desire:
"Eat and drink, with wholesome appetite, for
that you were working."
Even so do We recompense the good-doers.
Woe that day unto those who cry it lies!

"Eat and take your joy a little; you are sinners!"
Woe that day unto those who cry it lies!

When it is said to them, "Prostrate yourselves!" they prostrate
not.
Woe that day unto those who cry it lies!

In what discourse after this will they believe? (77:1–50)

CHAPTER TWO

THE *ḤADĪTH:* THE NEWS OF GOD'S MESSENGER

Next to the Qur'ān itself, the most important Islamic textual material is the *Ḥadīth:* the body of transmitted actions and sayings of the Prophet and his Companions.

Professor Wilfred C. Smith has made a most perceptive analogy: the Qur'ān is in Islam what Christ is in Christianity, and Muhammad stands in relation to it as the Twelve Apostles to the Logos. The *Ḥadīth*, the record of how the Revelation occurred, and the Acts of the Apostle, or Messenger, is to Islam then roughly what the New Testament is to Christianity.[1]

But here one must understand something which seems at first paradoxical; there are vast numbers of *ḥadīths* which are admitted by Muslim scholars to be spurious. Even among those accepted by the medieval scholars, there are many which the modernists would reject. No absolute canon of *Ḥadīth* has ever been established; certain compilers are recognized as more trustworthy than others, and some sects and schools accept *ḥadīths* not accepted by others. For example, the eponym of the Ḥanbalī law-school, Aḥmad ibn Ḥanbal, was a great collector of *Ḥadīth*, but his standards of criticism were not considered sufficiently rigorous, so his collection has never won full acceptance from the other law-schools.

This situation stems in part from the fact that each *ḥadīth* is a separate story handed down with the backing (*isnād*) of a chain (*sanad*) of narrators. To be fully sound the *ḥadīth* must include the name of each human link in the chain between the man who wrote it down and the Prophet.

One of the chief religious sciences of Islam rose to sift the stories thus transmitted and to investigate the veracity of each transmitter. To be sure, a man accepted as trustworthy by one school might not be accepted by another, and no way could be devised to keep men from manufacturing a "chain"—since all its links were dead men—along with the tradition they transmitted. The number of *ḥadīths* which could be demonstrated to be above suspicion would thus no doubt prove to be relatively small.

Nevertheless, the *Ḥadīth* conveys precious information: almost all the early history of Islam and many of the moral precepts of the Prophet. It is indeed precisely the preciousness of the material which led to its being counterfeited.

Moreover, traditions which are themselves false may have a certain historical and moral value for later generations, if they are accepted in the early collections; they reflect the religious opinions of the first generations of pious Muslim scholars, the "Consensus" which has been so vital in the formulation of law and doctrine. Thus they relay values which earlier generations of experts pronounced "Islamic," whether or not they relate a historical event. It follows then that not even *ḥadīths* of dubious authenticity may be rejected out of hand, much less the *Ḥadīth* as a whole, as some modernist extremists have wished to do.

It remains to be seen whether a new orthodox school of *Ḥadīth* criticism can rise in modern times. Certainly the first condition for it would be a general agreement by responsible people that this is desirable.

1. *Muhammad the Messenger*

The earliest biography of the Prophet is the great collection of *ḥadīths* compiled by Muhammad ibn Isḥāq of Medina (died *c.* A.H. 151/A.D. 768). While Ibn Isḥāq was accused in his own time of transmitting false *ḥadīths* by Mālik ibn Anas, his material is of the greatest importance. It is the earliest and presumably the most authentic biography of the Prophet, as well as the one most free of miraculous elements and pious fabrications. While he placed these materials together with a continuous narrative, it should be remembered that every individual *ḥadīth* has to be investigated on its own merits, and Ibn Isḥāq was well aware that some of his details were more historic than others.

His original work survived only in quotations from it by other authors, and in a deliberately altered recension and abridgment by Ibn Hishām of Baṣra (died *c.* A.H. 218/A.D. 833). However, it has been possible for modern scholars to re-establish much of the original text.

Beginnings of the Revelation: Muhammad's revelations began in the seventh century A.D. in the stony valley of Mecca, a well-watered stage on the ancient spice-and-incense road which connected South Arabia and the trade of the Indian Ocean with the civilizations of the Mediterranean world. It was a confused and lawless time. The ancient civilization of South Arabia had broken down, and its daughter-culture, Abyssinia, now Christianized from Egypt, had invaded South Arabia from across the Red Sea. In the North, the Christian Byzantine Empire was engaged in a centuries-old war with the Zoroastrian Persian Empire which was to bleed them both white. In the Arabian peninsula, dependent on the diminishing caravan trade between South and North, tribal wars, anarchy, economic decline and increasing camel-nomadism were the rule. Judaism, Manicheism and Christianity were penetrating slowly into the peninsula, and scattered communities of Jews and Christians could be found there, but most of the Arabians clung to the idols of their ancestors.

In these lean times, one tribe, the Quraysh, held Mecca and exercised a loose hegemony over the tribes of Western and Central Arabia. They controlled what was left of the trade of the incense road, as well as one of the chief cult-centers of North Arabia—a little temple called the Ka'ba, where all the gods were honored, but which was especially sacred to the Creator, Allah (El), who was seen as the father and king of the other gods.

In this tribe Muhammad was born (date uncertain, around A.D. 571) and early orphaned. His own clan, the Banū Hāshim, was of minor importance in the tribal oligarchy. As a poor young man he was employed by the high-minded widow of a rich merchant: Khadīja, a woman fifteen years older than he. Despite the difference in their ages she married him and bore him several children, including at least one son, al-Qāsim, who died in infancy. It was a happy marriage and Muhammad was comfortably established. He seems to have used a part of his new leisure to ponder religious questions and the state of his people, the Arabians.

Wahb b. Kaysan told me that 'Ubayd said to him: The Apostle would pray in seclusion on Mount Hirā' each year for a month to practice *taḥannuth* [religious exercises], as was the custom of the Quraysh in heathen days. When he completed the month and returned from his seclusion, first of all he would go to the Ka'ba and walk around it seven times, or as often as pleased God; then he would go to his house until in the year when God sent him, in the month of Ramadān, he set forth to Hirā' as was his wont, and his family with him.

When it was the night on which God honored him with his mission, and showed mercy on His servants thereby, Gabriel brought him the command of God. "He came to me," said the Apostle, "while I was asleep, with a piece of brocade whereon was writing, and said 'Recite!' and I said 'What shall I recite?' He pressed me with it so tightly that I thought it was death; then he let me go and said 'Recite!' I said, 'What shall I recite?' He pressed me with it again so that I thought it was death, then he let me go and said 'Recite!' I said 'But what shall I read?'—And this I said only to deliver myself from him lest he should do the same to me again, but he said:

'Recite: In the Name of thy Lord who created,
Created man from blood clotted,
Recite! Thy Lord is the most beneficent,
who taught by the Pen,
Taught that which they knew not unto men.'

So I recited it, and he departed from me. And I awoke from my sleep, and it was as though these words were written on my heart.

"Now none of God's creatures was more hateful to me than an (ecstatic) poet or a man possessed; I could not even bear to look at them. I thought, 'Woe is me—poet or possessed. Never shall Quraysh say that of me! I will go to the top of the mountain and throw myself down that I may kill myself and gain rest.' When I was midway on the mountain, I heard a voice from heaven saying, 'O Muhammad! Thou art the Apostle of God and I am Gabriel.' I raised my head towards heaven to see, and lo! Gabriel in the form of a man, with feet astride the horizon, saying, 'O Muhammad! Thou art the Apostle of God, and I am Gabriel.' I stood gazing at him, moving neither forward nor backward; then I began to turn my face away from him, but towards whatever region of the sky I looked, I saw him as before.

"I continued standing there, neither advancing nor turning back, until Khadīja sent her messengers in search of me, and they gained the high ground above Mecca and returned to her while I was standing in the same place; then he parted from me, and I from him, returning to my family. I went to Khadīja and sat by her thigh and drew close to her. She asked, 'Why Abū al-Qāsim (Father of al-Qāsim), where hast thou been? By Allah, I have sent my messengers in search of thee, and they reached the high ground above Mecca and returned.' I said to her, 'Woe is me—a poet, or a man possessed!' She said 'I take refuge in Allah from that, O Abū al-Qāsim! God would not treat you thus; He knows your truthfulness, your great trustworthiness, your fine character, and your kindness to your family. This cannot be, my dear [literally: son of my uncle]. Perhaps you have seen something.' 'Yes, I have,' I told her. Then I told her of what I had seen, and she said, 'Rejoice, O son of my uncle, and be of good heart! Verily by Him in whose hand is Khadīja's soul, I have hope that thou wilt be the prophet of this people.' " Then she rose and gathered her garments about her and set forth to her cousin Waraqa b. Naufal b. Asad b. 'Abd-al-'Uzza b. Qusayy, who had become a Christian and read the scriptures and learned from those who follow the Torah and the Gospel. And when she related to him what the Apostle of God told her he had seen and heard, Waraqa cried: "Holy! Holy! Verily, by Him in whose hand is Waraqa's soul, if thou hast spoken to me the truth, O Khadīja, there hath come unto him the greatest *Nāmūs*,[2] who came to Moses, and lo, he will be the prophet of this people. Bid him to be of good heart." So Khadīja returned to the Apostle of God and told him what Waraqa had said, and that calmed his anxiety somewhat.

And when the Apostle of God . . . returned to Mecca . . . Waraqa met him and said, "Son of my brother, tell me what thou hast seen and heard." The Apostle told him, and Waraqa said, "Surely by Him in whose hand is Waraqa's soul, thou art the prophet of these people. There has come to thee the greatest *Nāmūs*, who came to Moses. Thou wilt be called a liar, and they will use thee despitefully and cast thee out and fight against thee. Should I live to see that day, I will help God in such wise as He knoweth." Then he lowered his head and kissed Muhammad's forehead; and the Apostle went to his own house, encouraged by Waraqa's words, and with his anxiety relieved.[3]

The First Converts: Khadīja . . . was the first to believe in God and His Apostle, and the truth of the message. By her, God lightened the burden of the Prophet. He never met with contradiction and charges of falsehood, which saddened him, but God comforted him by her when he went home. She strengthened him, lightened his burden, proclaimed his truth, and belittled men's opposition. May God Almighty have mercy on her![4]

'Ali son of the Prophet's uncle Abū Ṭālib was the first male to believe in the Apostle of God, to pray with him, and to believe in his divine message, when he was a boy of ten. God favored him, in that he had been brought up in the care of the Prophet before Islam began.—A traditionist mentions that when the time of prayer began the Apostle used to go out to the glens of Mecca accompanied by 'Ali, who went unbeknown to his father . . . there they would pray the ritual prayers. One day Abū Ṭālib came upon them while they were praying, and said to the Apostle, "O nephew, what is this religion I see you practising?" He replied, "O uncle, this is the religion of God, His angels, His Apostles, and the religion of our father Abraham. God has sent me as a messenger to mankind, and you, my uncle . . . are the most worthy to respond and help me." His uncle replied, "I cannot give up the religion which my fathers followed, but by God you shall never meet with any harm so long as I live." . . . He said to 'Ali, "My son, what is this religion of yours?" He answered, "I believe in God and in His Messenger, and I declare what he brought is true, and pray with him." They allege that Abū Ṭālib said: "He would not call you to do anything but what is good, so cleave to him."

Zayd, the freedman of the Prophet, was the first male to accept Islam after 'Ali.

Then Abū Bakr b. Abī Quḥāfa . . . became a Muslim. He showed his faith openly and called others to God and His Apostle. He was a man whose society was desired, well liked, and of easy manners . . . a merchant of high character and kindliness. People used to come to him to discuss many matters . . . because of his wide knowledge, his experience of commerce, and his sociable nature. He began to call to God and to Islam all whom he trusted.[5]

There soon grew up around Muhammad a party within the tribe on whom the leaders of the Quraysh looked with disfavor and alarm; while not particularly devoted to their gods as such, they distrusted any sign of social or political innovation. As long as the Prophet's clan protected him, he could not be harmed, but his followers in the other clans were more vulnerable. Muhammad therefore sent some of them to Abyssinia, where they were protected by the Negus. It is conceivable that at this time the Prophet was contemplating some sort of alliance with Abyssinia.[6] The following story about this is almost certainly not historical in all particulars, but it is a very early apologia for Islam.

Muhammad b. Muslim al-Zuhrī, from Abū Bakr b. 'Abd al-Rahman b. al. Harīth b. Hishām al-Makhzūmī, from Umm Salama bint Abī Umayya the wife of the Apostle said: "When we reached Abyssinia the Negus gave us a kind reception. We safely practised our religion and worshipped God and suffered no wrong in word or deed. When the Quraysh got to know that, they decided to send two determined men to the Negus and give him presents of the choicest wares of Mecca. . . . They were to give their presents to the Negus and ask him to give up the men, before he spoke to them. . . . [But the Negus] summoned the Apostle's companions, and . . . when they came into the royal presence, they found the king had summoned his bishops with their sacred books exposed around them. He asked them what was the religion for which they had forsaken their people, without entering his religion or any other.

"Ja'far b. Abī Ṭālib answered, 'O King, we were an uncivilized people, worshipping idols, eating carrion, committing abominations, breaking natural ties, ill-treating guests, and our strong devouring our weak. Thus we were until God sent us an apostle whose lineage, truth, trustworthiness, and clemency we know. He summoned us to acknowledge God's unity and to worship him and renounce the stones and images which we and our fathers formerly worshipped. He commanded us to speak the truth, to be faithful to our engagements, mindful of the ties of kinship and kindly hospitality, and to refrain from crimes and bloodshed. He forbade us to commit abominations and to speak lies, or to devour the property of orphans or vilify chaste women. He commanded us to worship God alone and not to associate anything with Him. . . . We followed him in what he brought from God, and we worshipped God alone. . . . We treated as forbidden what he forbade, and as lawful what he declared lawful. Thereupon our people attacked us, treated us harshly . . . to try to make us go back to the worship of idols instead of the worship of God, and to regard as lawful the evil deeds we once committed. . . . When they treated us unjustly and came between us and our religion, we came to your country, having chosen you above all others. Here we have been happy in your protection, and we hope we shall not be treated unjustly while we are with you, O King.'

"The Negus asked if they had with them anything that had come from God. When Ja'far said that he had, the Negus commanded him to read it to him, so he read a passage from Sūra 19 ['Mary']. The Negus wept until his beard was wet, and the bishops wept until their scrolls were wet, when they heard what he read. Then the Negus said, 'Of a truth, this and what Jesus brought have come from the same niche. You two may go, for by God, I will never give them up to you, and they shall not be betrayed.' "[7]

One of the most beloved themes connected with the Prophet is the story of his night journey (*isrā'*), his ascension (*mi'rāj*) and his vision of the Afterworld. Art, poesy and pious imagination have lavished attention on the story. It is now generally admitted that not only the general plan but many small details of Dante's *Divine Comedy* were borrowed from the later fancifully developed treatments of this Islamic theme.[8] Ibn Isḥāq presents the story in one of its earliest forms as he pieced it together. The main elements are all present—the journey to Jerusalem, the ascent to the heavens and the vision of the afterlife.

The following account reached me from 'Abdallah b. Mas'ūd and Abū Sa'īd al-Khudrī, and 'A'isha the Prophet's wife, and Mu'awiyah b. Abī Sufyān, and al-Ḥasan al-Basrī, and Ibn Shihāb al-Zuhrī and Qatāda and other traditionists, and Umm Hāni' daughter of Abū Ṭālib. It is pieced together in the story that follows, each one contributing something of what he was told about what happened when he was taken on the night journey.

Al-Ḥasan said that the Apostle said: "While I was sleeping in the Ḥijr, Gabriel came and stirred me with his feet . . . he brought me out of the door . . . and there was a white animal, half mule, half donkey, with wings at its sides with which it propelled its feet. . . ."

Qatāda said that he was told the Apostle said: "When I came to mount him he shied. Gabriel placed his hand on its mane and said, 'Are you not ashamed, O Burāq, to behave this way? By God, none more honourable before God than Muhammad has ever ridden you before.' The animal was so ashamed that he broke out in a sweat and stood still so that I could mount him."

In his story al-Ḥasan said: "The Apostle and Gabriel went their way until they arrived at the temple in Jerusalem. There he found Abraham, Moses, and Jesus among a company of the Prophets. The Apostle acted as their leader in prayer. Then he was brought two vessels, one containing wine and the other milk. The Apostle took the milk and drank it, leaving the wine.

Gabriel said: 'You have been rightly guided, and so will your people be, Muhammad. Wine is forbidden you.' "

One of Abū Bakr's family told me that 'A'isha, the Prophet's wife, used to say, "The Apostle's body remained where it was but God removed his spirit by night. . . ."

I have heard that the Apostle used to say, "My eyes sleep while my heart is awake." Only God knows how the revelation came and what he saw. But whether he was asleep or awake, it was all true and actually happened.

One of whom I have no reason to doubt told me on the authority of Abū Sa'īd al-Khudrī; I heard the Apostle say, "After the completion of my business in Jerusalem a ladder was brought to me finer than any I have ever seen. It was that to which the dying man looks when death approaches. My companion mounted it with me until we came to one of the gates of heaven called the Gate of the Watchers. An angel called Ismā'īl was in charge of it, and under his command were twelve thousand angels, each having twelve thousand under his command."

A traditionist who had got it from one who had heard it from the Apostle told me that the latter said, "All the angels who met me when I entered the lowest heaven smiled in welcome and wished me well except one, who said the same things but did not smile or show the joyful expression of the others. When I asked Gabriel the reason he told me that if he had ever smiled before or would smile hereafter he would have smiled at me, but he does not smile because he is Mālik, the Keeper of Hell. I said to Gabriel, who holds the position with God which He has described to you, 'obeyed there, trustworthy.' [Sūra 74:34] 'Will you not order him to show me Hell?' And he said 'Certainly! O Mālik, show Muhammad Hell.' Thereupon he removed its covering and the flames blazed high into the air until I thought they would consume everything. So I asked Gabriel to order him to send them back to their place, and he did. . . ."

In his tradition Abū Sa'īd al-Khudrī said that the Apostle said: "When I entered the lowest heaven I saw a man sitting there with the spirits of men passing before him. To one he would speak well and rejoice in him saying 'A good spirit from a good body' and of another he would say 'Faugh!' and frown. . . . . Gabriel told me this was our father Adam, reviewing the spirits of his offspring; the spirit of a believer excited his pleasure, and the spirit of a disbeliever excited his disgust.

"Then I saw men with lips like camels; in their hands were pieces of fire like stones which they used to thrust into their mouths and they would come out of their posteriors. I was told that these were those who sinfully devoured the wealth of orphans.

"Then I saw men like those of the family of Pharaoh with such bellies as I have never seen; there were passing over them as it were camels maddened by thirst when they were cast into Hell, treading them down, and they were unable to move out of the way. These were the usurers.

"Then I saw men with good fat meat before them side by side with lean stinking meat, eating the latter and leaving the former. These are those who forsake the women which God has permitted them, and go after those He has forbidden.

"Then I saw women hanging by their breasts. These were those who had fathered bastards on their husbands. . . .

"Then I was taken up to the second heaven and there were the two maternal cousins, Jesus Son of Mary and John son of Zakariah. Then to the third heaven and there was a man whose face was as the moon at the full. This was my brother Joseph son of Jacob. Then to the seventh heaven and there was a man sitting on a throne at the gate of the Immortal Mansion (*al-bayt al-maʿmūr*). Every day seventy thousand angels went in not to come back until the resurrection day. Never have I seen a man more like myself. This was my father Abraham. Then he took me into Paradise and there I saw a damsel with dark red lips and I asked her to whom she belonged, for she pleased me much when I saw her, and she told me 'Zayd ibn Ḥāritha.'" The Apostle gave [his adopted son] Zayd the good news about her.[9]

Opposition of the Quraysh: Khadīja and Abū Ṭālib died in the same year, and with Khadīja's death troubles followed fast on each other's heels, for she had been a faithful support to him in Islam, and he used to tell her of his troubles. With the death of Abū Ṭālib he lost a strength and stay in his personal life and a defense and protection against the tribe. Abū Ṭālib died some three years before he migrated to Medina, and it was then that Quraysh began to treat him in an offensive way which they would not have dared to follow in his uncle's lifetime. A young lout actually threw dust on his head.

Hishām on the death of his father 'Urwa told me that when this happened the Apostle went into his house with the dust still on his head and one of his daughters got up to wash it off, weeping as she did so. "Don't weep, my little girl," he said, "for God will protect your father." Meanwhile he was saying, "The Quraysh never treated me thus while Abū Ṭālib was alive. . . ."[10]

2. *The Founding of the Community*

The new leader of the Banū Hāshim, Muhammad's uncle Abū Lahab, was allied by marriage with the leaders of the Meccan oligarchy. Since Muhammad could no longer rely on the protection of his clan, his life and his mission were in danger. It was becoming clear that the chaotic nature of Arabian society demanded that his preaching take a political form, in order to be effective. He therefore began to look for a new base for his movement, with another tribe. He found it with the people of Medina (*Yathrib*), a sizable oasis to the North.

The Hijra (A.D. *622*)*:* When God wished to display His religion openly and to glorify His prophet and fulfill His promise to him . . . while he was offering himself to the Arab tribes (at the fairs) as was his wont, he met at al-'Aqaba a number of the Khazraj (of Medina), whom God intended to benefit.

'Asim b. 'Umar b. Qatāda told me on the authority of some of the shaykhs of his tribe that when the Apostle met them he learned by inquiry that they were of the Khazraj and allies of the Jews of Medina. He invited them to sit with him and expounded Islam and recited the Qur'ān to them. Now God had prepared the way for Islam in that they lived side by side with the Jews who were people of the scriptures and knowledge, while they themselves were polytheists and idolators. They had often raided them, and whenever bad feeling arose the Jews would say to them, "A prophet will be sent soon! His day is at hand. We shall follow him and kill you by his aid as 'Ad and Iram perished." So when they heard the Apostle's message they said one to another: "This is the very prophet of whom the Jews warned us. Don't let them get to him before us!" Thereupon they accepted his teaching and became Muslims, saying: "We have left our people, for no tribe is so divided by hatred and rancor as they. Perhaps God will unite them through you. So let us go and invite them to this religion of yours; and if God unites them in it, then no man will be mightier than you!" Thus saying they returned to Medina as believers. . . .[11]

The Apostle had not been given permission to fight or allowed to shed blood . . . he had simply been ordered to call men to God, endure insult, and forgive the ignorant. The Quraysh persecuted his followers, seducing some from their religion, and exiling others from their country. They had to choose whether to give up their religion, be maltreated at home, or to flee, some to Abyssinia, others to Medina.

When Quraysh became insolent toward God and rejected His gracious purpose, accused His prophet of lying, and ill-treated and exiled those who served Him and proclaimed His unity, believed in His prophet, and held fast to His religion, He gave permission to his Apostle to fight and to protect himself against those who wronged them and treated them badly. . . .

When God had given permission to fight, and this clan of the Anṣār had pledged their support to him in Islam, the Apostle commanded his companions . . . who were with him in Mecca to emigrate to Medina. . . . So they went out in companies and the Apostle stayed in Mecca waiting for his Lord's permission to leave Mecca and migrate to Medina. . . .

Except for Abū Bakr and 'Ali, none of his supporters were left but those under restraint and those who had been forced to apostacise. . . .

When the Quraysh saw that the Apostle had a party and companions not of their tribe and outside their territory, and that his companions had migrated to join them, and knew that they had settled in a new home and had gained protectors, they feared that the Apostle might join them, since they knew that he had decided to fight them. So they assembled in their council chambers, the house of Qusayy b. Kilāb where all their important business was conducted, to take counsel what they should do in regard to the Apostle, for now they feared him. . . .

Thereupon Abū Jahl said that he had a plan which had not been suggested hitherto, namely that each clan should provide a young, powerful, well-born warrior . . . then each of these should strike a blow at him and kill him. Thus they would be relieved of him, and responsibility for his blood would lie on all of the clans. His clan could not fight them all and would have to accept the blood money, to which they would all contribute. . . .[12]

Among the verses of the Qur'ān which God sent down about that day and what they had agreed on are: "And when the unbelievers plot to shut thee up or to kill thee or to drive thee out they plot, but God plots also, and God is the best of plotters." (Sūra 8:30)

Now Abū Bakr was a man of means and . . . he bought two camels and kept them tied up in his house supplying them with fodder in preparation for departure. . . .

When the Apostle decided to go he came to Abū Bakr and the two of them left by a window in the back of the latter's house and made for a cave on Thaur, a mountain below Mecca. Having entered, Abū Bakr ordered his son 'Abdallah . . . to come to them by night with the day's news. He ordered 'Amir b. Fuhayra, his freedman, to feed his flock by day and to bring to them in the evening in the cave. Asmā' his daughter used to come by night with food to sustain them. . . .

When three days had passed, and men's interest waned, the man they had hired came with their camels and one of his own. Asmā' came too with a bag of provisions, but finding she had forgotten a rope, she undid her girdle and used it to tie the bag to the saddle. Thus she got the name "She of the girdle." . . .

They rode off, and Abū Bakr carried his freedman 'Amir behind him to act as a servant on the journey. . . . (In Medina, each of the clans) came to him and asked him to enjoy their wealth and protection, but he said, "Let the camel go her way," for she was under God's orders. . . . Finally she came to the home of the Banū Mālik b. al-Najjār where she knelt at (what later became the door of his mosque) which was used at that time as a drying floor for dates and belonged to two orphans of that clan. When it knelt, the Prophet did not alight, and it rose and went a short distance, then . . . returned to the place where it had knelt at first and knelt there again. . . .

The Apostle alighted . . . when he asked to whom the date-store belonged, Mu'adh b. 'Afrā told him the owners were orphans in his care . . . and he could take it for a mosque and he would pay the young men for it.

The Apostle ordered that a mosque (and lodgings for his family) be built, and he joined in the work to encourage the Muhājirīn and the Anṣār. . . . (Emigrants and Medinans.)[13]

The Muslim community was thus established. Significantly, it is this year—the *Hijra* and the founding of the community of the Believers—rather than the first revelation or the birth of the Prophet from which the Islamic calendar is dated.

When the Prophet was firmly established in Medina and his brethren the emigrants were gathered to him and the affairs of the helpers arranged, Islam became firmly established. Prayer was instituted, the alms-tax and fasting were prescribed, legal punishments were fixed, the forbidden and the permitted prescribed, and Islam took up its abode with them. . . .

The people gathered to him at the appointed times of prayer. . . . At first the Prophet thought of using a trumpet like that of the Jews who used it to summon to prayer. Afterwards he disliked the idea and ordered a clapper to be made . . . to be beaten when the Muslims should pray.

Meanwhile 'Abdallah b. Zayd b. Tha'laba b. 'Abdu Rabbihi brother of Banū al-Hārith heard a voice in a dream, and came to the Apostle saying: "A phantom visited me in the night. There passed by me a man wearing two green garments carrying a clapper in his hand, and I asked him to sell it to me. When he asked me what I wanted it for I told him it was to summon people to prayer, whereupon he offered to show me a better way; it was to say thrice:

> '*Allāhu Akbar!* [God is most great] *Allāhu Akbar!*
> I bear witness that there is no god but God!
> I bear witness that Muhammad is the Apostle of God!
> Come to prayer! Come to prayer!
> Come to salvation![14] Come to salvation!
> *Allāhu Akbar! Allāhu Akbar!*
> There is no god but God!' "

When the Apostle was told of this he said that it was a true vision if God so willed it, and that he should go with Bilāl and communicate it to him so he might call to prayer thus, for Bilāl had the most penetrating voice. When Bilāl acted as the first muezzin 'Umar . . . came to the Apostle dragging his cloak on the ground and saying that he had seen precisely the same vision. The Apostle said, "God be praised for that!"

I was told this tradition . . . on the authority of Muhammad b. 'Abdallah b. Zayd b. Tha'laba himself.

Muhammad b. Ja'far b. Zubayr told me on the authority of 'Urwa b. Zubayr of a woman of the Banū al-Najjār who said: "My house was the highest of those round the mosque, and

Bilāl used to give the call from the top of it every day. He would sit on the housetop waiting for the dawn; when he saw it, he would stretch out his arms and say, 'Oh God, I praise Thee and ask Thy help for Quraysh, that they may accept Thy religion.' I never knew him to omit those words for a single night."[15]

While Muhammad had hoped that the Jews of Medina, as monotheists with a scripture, would recognize his prophetic claims, most of them opposed him with ridicule and rebellion. In this they were joined by the "Hypocrites" (*munāfiqīn*), those Medinans who had accepted him insincerely. In the ensuing struggles, most of the Jews were killed or banished. The direction of prayer for the Muslims was changed by revelation from Jerusalem to Mecca, and the Arabian character of Islam as the spiritual heir of Abraham, the monotheist ancestor of the Semites, was stressed in the revelations which continued to come.

Muhammad also began to lead his followers in raids on the caravans of the Quraysh of Mecca. By a skillful combination of military, economic and political pressure, he was able to secure the capitulation of the Quraysh in A.H. 8/A.D. 630, and in the end his native city came to his side as a willing partner.

The *Ka'ba* was cleansed of its idols, and rededicated as the center of the Islamic world, the temple of Abraham and Ishmael.

Seeing this victory over the chief tribe of Arabia, most of the tribes sent deputations to Medina to submit to his authority. They were ordered to pay a tax (the *zakāt*) to Medina, and if they did not choose to accept Islam, to hinder in no way those of their members who became Muslims. Agents were sent to them from Medina to teach them the Qur'ān and the rites of religion, and to collect the taxes.

Muhammad continued to live a simple and patriarchal existence at Medina. He could view his work with satisfaction. Everywhere the pagan cults were dying. His religion and his authority were unchallenged. The quarreling tribes had been united in one nation, the moral tone of the peninsula was unquestionably higher, and in Medina at least, where he ruled as beloved patriarch, judge, lawgiver, commander in chief and intercessor with God, his community was well established. The mission was accomplished—with a completeness of success given to few religious leaders.

The Death of the Prophet: 'A'isha, the Prophet's wife, the daughter of Abū Bakr, said: "The Apostle returned from (prayers for the dead in) the cemetery to find me suffering from a severe headache, and I was saying, 'O, my head!' He said, 'Nay, 'A'isha, O *my* head!' Then he said, 'Would it distress you if you should die before me so I might wrap you in your shroud and pray over you and bury you?' I said, 'Methinks I see you returning therefrom to my house and spending a bridal night in it with one of your wives!' He smiled at that, and then his pain overtook him. . . . He called his wives and asked their permission to be nursed in my house, and they agreed. . . ."

'A'isha used to hear the Apostle say, "God never takes a prophet to Himself without giving him the choice." "The last word I heard the Apostle saying was, 'Nay, rather the Exalted Companion of paradise.' I said (to myself), 'Then by God, he is not choosing us!' And I knew it was as he used to tell us, that a prophet does not die without being given the choice. . . .

"The Apostle died in my bosom during my turn: I wronged none in regard to him. It was due to my ignorance and extreme youth that the Apostle died in my arms. Then I laid his head on a pillow, and got up beating my breast and slapping my face."

Sa'īd b. al-Musayyib told me on the authority of Abū Hurayra: When the Apostle was dead 'Umar got up and said, "Some of the disaffected will allege that the Apostle is dead, but by God he is not dead: he has gone to his Lord as Moses went and was hidden from his people for forty days, returning to them after it was said that he was dead. By God, the Apostle will return as Moses returned, and will cut off the hands and feet of those who allege that he is dead!"

When Abū Bakr heard this . . . he paid no attention but went into 'A'isha's house to the Apostle who was lying covered by a mantle of Yamanī cloth. He uncovered his face and kissed him, saying, "Dearer than my father and my mother! You have tasted the death which God had decreed; a second death will never overtake you." Then he replaced the mantle and went out. 'Umar was still speaking, and he said, "Gently, 'Umar, be quiet." But 'Umar went on talking. When Abū Bakr saw he would not be silent he went forward to the people, who came to him and left 'Umar. Giving thanks and praise to God, he said: "O men, if anyone worships Muhammad, Muhammad is dead. If anyone worships God, God is alive, immortal!" Then he recited this verse: "Muhammad is nothing but an Apostle. Apostles have passed away before him. Can it be that if he were to die or be killed you would turn back on your heels? He who turns back does no harm to God, but God will reward the grateful." (Sūra 3:38)

'Umar said, "By God, when I heard Abū Bakr recite these words, I was dumbfounded so that my legs would not bear me and I fell to the ground, knowing that the Apostle was indeed dead."[12]

The Prophet's death in 632 was the first great crisis of the Muslim community. Neither the Qur'ān nor Muhammad had made any provision for a successor; indeed, he is quoted as saying, "Prophets have no heirs." Although he had contracted several marriages after Khadīja's death, his wives had borne him no children. His son Ibrahīm (Abraham) by his Egyptian concubine, Mary the Copt, had died in infancy.

His closest relative was his cousin and son-in-law 'Ali, who as the husband of Khadīja's daughter Fāṭima was father of Muhammad's grandchildren, Ḥasan and Ḥusayn. However, even the claims of a chieftain's sons to succeed him were not conclusive in Arabian society; still less the claim of a son-in-law. Also, 'Ali was a young man in a patriarchal culture.

By traditional standards, the head of the Prophet's clan, his uncle 'Abbās, would have had a strong claim, but 'Abbās was a late convert and hence under a certain cloud.

As tribesmen of the Prophet, with a traditional hegemony in the *Hijāz*, the Quraysh felt they must not be dominated by another people. As his helpers, and the fighters of his battles, the people of his capital Medina felt they had the right to rule themselves.

The leader was dead, and his *charisma* had not been transferred. Many felt that the old tribal patterns should emerge again, and each tribe go its separate ways. . . . Years later, his friend, tribesman and early convert, 'Umar ibn-al-Khaṭṭāb, made a solemn public statement on the events of the night of Muhammad's death.

'Umar sat in the pulpit, and when the muezzins were silent he praised God as was fitting and said: "I am about to say to you today something which God has willed that I should say, and I do not know whether perhaps it is my last utterance. . . .

"I have heard that someone said, 'If 'Umar were dead, I would hail so-and-so as ruler.' Let not a man deceive himself by saying that the acceptance of Abū Bakr was an unpremeditated affair which was ratified. Admittedly, it *was* that, but God averted the evil of it. There is none among you to whom people would devote themselves as they did to Abū Bakr. What happened was that when God took away His apostle, the Anṣār [Muslims of Medina] opposed us and gathered with their chiefs in the hall of the Banū-Sā'ida; and 'Ali and Zubayr and their companions withdrew from us (they had gathered at the deathbed) while the Muhājirīn gathered around Abū Bakr. (In the Prophet's mosque.)

"I told Abū Bakr that we should go to our brothers the Anṣār, so we went off to go to them, when two honest fellows met us and told us of the conclusion the people [the Anṣār] had come to. . . . I said, 'By God, we will go to them, and we found them in the hall of the Banū Sā'ida. In the middle of them was a man wrapped up. In answer to my inquiries they said that he was Sa'd b. 'Ubāda and that he was ill. When we sat down their speaker pronounced the *shahāda* and praised God as was fitting, and then continued: 'We are God's Helpers and the squadron of Islam. You, O Muhājirīn, are a family of ours and a company of your people have come to settle here.' And lo, they were trying to cut us off from our origin and wrest authority from us.

"When he had finished, I wanted to speak, for I had prepared a speech in my mind which pleased me much. I wanted to produce it before Abū Bakr and I was trying to soften a certain asperity of his, but Abū Bakr said, 'Gently, 'Umar!' I did not like to anger him, and so he spoke. He was a man with more knowledge and dignity than I, and by God he did not omit a single word which I had thought of, and he uttered it in his inimitable way better than I could have done.

"He said: 'All the good that you have said about yourselves is deserved. But the Arabs will recognise authority only in this clan of Quraysh, they being the best of the Arabs in blood and country. I offer you one of these two men: accept which you please.' Thus saying he took hold of my hand and that of Abū 'Ubayda b. al-Jarrāḥ who was sitting between us. Nothing he said displeased me more than that. By God, I would rather have come forward and have had my head struck off—if that were no sin—than rule over a people of whom Abū Bakr was one!

"One of the Anṣār said: 'I am the rubbing-post and the fruitful propped-up palm [*i.e.* a man to whom all come to solve their problems]. Let us have one ruler and you another, O Quraysh.'

Altercation waxed hotter and voices were raised until when a complete breach was to be feared I said, 'Stretch out your hand, Abū Bakr.' He did so and I paid him homage; the Muhājirīn followed and then the Anṣār. In doing so, we jumped on Sa'd b. 'Ubāda [the man whom the Anṣār had been electing] and someone said that we had killed him. I said, 'God killed him!' "

Al-Zuhri told me on the authority of Anas b. Mālik: On the morrow of Abū Bakr's acceptance in the hall, he sat in the pulpit and 'Umar got up and spoke before him, and after praising God as was meet he said: "Oh men, yesterday I said something ['Umar had denied the death of the Prophet], which I do not find in God's Book, nor was it something the Apostle entrusted to me, but I thought that the Apostle would order our affairs until he was the last of us alive. God has left His Book with you, that by which He guided His apostle, and if you hold fast to that, God will guide you as He guided him. God has placed your affairs in the hands of the best one among you, the companion of the Apostle, 'The second of the two when they were in the cave (Sūra 9:40) so arise and swear fealty to him." Thereupon the people swore fealty to Abū Bakr as a body after the pledge in the hall.[17]

In sudden crisis, a decision of world-shaking significance had been reached. The Muslim community was to have one ruler, as Successor of the Prophet (*Khalīfa:* Caliph). Had each tribe elected its own leaders, the unity Muhammad had imposed on the quarrelsome Arabs would soon have been dissipated. Had the Muslims decided to be governed by a council of the leading Companions, Islamic government would have developed along oligarchic or republican lines; instead, it has historically tended to be characterized by one-man rule. It was then necessary to enforce the decision of Medina on the other tribes of the peninsula, who felt there was no reason to follow Abū

Bakr. The majority of them refused to send the *zakāt* to Medina or obey, and some tribes turned to new prophets who claimed to have inherited the authority of Muhammad. It took two years of bitter warfare to re-establish the authority of Medina.

But it was a sulky obedience. To reunite the spirit of the community, Abū Bakr and ʻUmar, who succeeded him as Caliph, sent the people on foreign campaigns against the weakened Byzantine and Persian empires. The results surpassed the Caliphs' highest hopes; Persia, the Fertile Crescent and Egypt were conquered for Islam. The incredulous and grateful people of Muhammad gave thanks to God, as the followers of Moses had once before when Joshua led the Hebrew tribes from the deserts into southern Syria.

3. *Muhammad as Founder and Legislator*

Muhammad is often referred to by the Muslim philosophers as "The Lawgiver," since from his governing of the early community and the example of his life the Islamic Law has been systematized. The Law is usually seen as of Divine origin, but mediated by the Prophet. In the important task of establishing God's community on earth, there could be no error, and by continually referring to the prophetic period, the Muslim community hopes to be preserved from error. In a sense, then, the Prophet's *sunna* is revelation, and it is embodied in the *Ḥadīth*.

Historically speaking, Muhammad was the exponent of a more civilized existence in a land dominated by the wild and violent norms of the Beduins. Even the life of the towns of Arabia was deeply affected by their setting in the sea of nomadism, and changing this barbaric world was no easy task.

The cultural situation of Arabia in the seventh century was not too dissimilar to that described in the Book of Judges, and one is struck by the essential similarity of Muhammad to the prophets of the Old Testament—there is his tenderness for his people, his personal mildness where his own affairs were concerned and his relentless zeal where he considered that the affairs of God were concerned.

However, the *ḥadīth* literature is so rich that one may, while never feeling that he has fully understood this extraordinary man, add vivid details to the general prophetic type; his daily life is depicted for us, and there are the flashes of kindly irony, and his joy in the simple pleasures of life.

The typical form of a fully sound *ḥadīth* is as follows:

Al-Bukhārī writes: " 'Abdallah ibn al-Aswad told me: 'Al-Fadl ibn al-'Atā' told us: 'Isma'īl ibn Umayya told us on the authority of Yaḥya ibn 'Abdallah ibn Ṣayfī that he heard Abū Ma'bad, the freedman of Ibn 'Abbās, say, 'I heard Ibn 'Abbās say: 'When the Prophet, the blessings of God be upon him, and peace, sent Mu'adh to the Yemen, he said to him: 'You will come upon some of the People of the Book, so the first thing you will call on them to do is to profess the Oneness of God. When they have learned that, inform them that God has prescribed for the five ritual prayers a day. When they have made the ritual prayers, inform them that God has imposed *zakāt* on their possessions, to be taken from the rich and given to the poor. When they have accepted all this, then take the tax from them, but leave them their most precious possessions.' " ' " ' "[18]

The following *ḥadīths* are taken from the "sound" collections of Bukhārī and Muslim, and I have suppressed all but the first and last links of the *isnāds*.

Bukhārī . . . from 'Abdallah: "I said, 'Messenger of God, what is the greatest sin?' 'It is to make an idol for God, who created you.' 'Then what?' 'To kill your own child from motives of economy.' [*lit.*, fearing lest he eat with you.] 'And then what?' 'To commit adultery with your neighbor's wife.' "[19]

Bukhārī . . . from 'A'isha: "The Prophet did something and thus permitted it for others, but some people still abstained from it. And that came to the Prophet, and he went into the pulpit, and praised God. Then he said, 'What ails those people who refrain from a thing I have done? For by God, I know God better than they do, and I am more fearful of offending him.' "[20]

Bukhārī . . . from Abū Sa'īd al-Khudrī: "The Prophet was more shy than a virgin in her green years. When he saw a thing he disliked, we knew it from his face."[21]

Bukhārī . . . from Abū Salama from Jābir: "A man who had become a Muslim came to the Prophet, God's benediction and peace be on him, and confessed to fornication. The Prophet turned away from him. This happened until the man had confessed four times. Then the Prophet said to him, 'Are you insane?' 'No,' he said. 'Are you married?' He replied 'Yes,' and the Prophet ordered him to be stoned at the Muṣalla [mosque outside Medina]. When the stones struck him, he ran away, but he was caught and stoned until he was dead. Then the Prophet—the blessing of God and peace be upon him—spoke well of him and prayed over him."[22]

Bukhārī . . . from Ibn 'Umar: "They brought the Prophet, on whom be God's benediction and peace, a Jew and a Jewess who had committed fornication. He said to them: 'What do you find in your book?' They said: 'Our rabbis blacken the face of the guilty and expose them to public ridicule.' 'Abdallah ibn Salām (who had been a Jew) said, 'Messenger of God, tell the Jews to bring the Torah.' They brought it, but a Jew put his hand over the verse which prescribes stoning and began to read what came before it and after it. Ibn Salām said to him 'Raise your hand,' and there was the verse about stoning beneath his hand. The Messenger of God gave the order, and they were stoned." Ibn 'Umar added: "They were stoned on the level ground and I saw the man leaning over the woman to shield her from the stones."[23]

Bukhārī . . . from Anas ibn Mālik, servant of the Prophet: "A group of people from the tribe of 'Ukl came to the Prophet and accepted Islam. Then they became ill in Medina, and he ordered them to go to the camel-herd of the public purse and drink the urine and the milk (as medicine). They did, and were cured. Then they renounced their religion, killed the herdsmen and stole the camels. He sent trackers after them, and they were captured. And he cut off their hands and their feet and burnt out their eyes and did not cauterize their wounds, so that they died."[24]

Bukhārī . . . from Ibn 'Abbās: "The Prophet cursed men who act like women and women who act like men, and said, 'Drive them from your houses.' He expelled such people, and 'Umar did it as well."[25]

Bukhārī . . . from Sa'd ibn Abī Waqqāṣ: "The Messenger of God refused to let 'Uthmān ibn Maẓ'ūn make a vow of chastity. Had he allowed him, we would all have been castrated."[26]

Bukhārī . . . from 'A'isha: "A Beduin came to the Prophet and said 'Do you kiss children? We never do.' And the Prophet said, 'What shall I do to give back to you the mercy God has taken from your heart?' "[27]

Bukhārī . . . from Abū Hurayra: "A Beduin came to the Messenger of God and said, 'Messenger of God, my wife has given birth to a black male-child.' 'Have you camels?' the Prophet asked. 'Yes,' said the Beduin. 'Are they ever ash-colored?' 'Yes,' said the Beduin. 'And how is that?' he asked. 'Something in the blood changed them.' 'Then perhaps something in the blood has changed your son,' said the Prophet."[28]

Bukhārī . . . from Sahl ibn Sa'd: "A woman came to the Messenger of God, and said, 'Messenger of God, I have come to offer you my person.' The Messenger of God gazed upon her and looked her up and down. Then he lowered his head. And when the woman saw that he had made no decision about her, she sat down. One of the Prophet's Companions rose and said, 'Messenger of God, if you have no need of her, marry her to me.' He asked, 'Do you have anything (to give her as marriage portion)?' 'No, by God, Messenger of God.' 'Then go to your people and see if you can find something.' The man went and returned, and said, 'No, by God, I found nothing, Messenger of God.' He said, 'Look; even for a ring made of iron.' He went and came back and said, 'No, by God, Messenger of God, not even a ring made of iron, but here is my waist-wrapper.' Sahl added, 'It was not large enough as that he could have given her the half of it.' The Messenger of God asked, 'What would she do with your waist-wrapper? If you wear it, she will get nothing out of it, and if she wears it you will get nothing out of it.' The man sat down for a long time, and then he rose to go. The Messenger of God saw him leaving and ordered him to be called back. When he came, he said, 'How much of the Qur'ān do you know?' He replied, 'I know sūra so and so, and such a one, and such a one.' He said, 'Could you read them on the surface of your heart?' 'Yes,' said the man. 'Go then. I give her to you for what you have of the Qur'ān.' "[29]

4. *Muhammad as Model and Guide*

The Prophet is not only the founder and legislator of the community: he is the model for Muslims. It is accepted as axiomatic that every act he made after the beginning of the Revelation was preserved by God from error; had it not been so, then the Revelation itself would be cast into doubt, a thing God could never have permitted. Therefore, Muhammad's slightest act was rightly guided, and of moral value. For traditional Muslims, everything the Prophet did is a part of his *sunna:* his treatment of children, the way he broke his fast, how he cleaned his teeth and wore his beard, are all worthy of study and emulation.

Bukhārī . . . from Abū Hurayra: "The Messenger of God said: 'While a man was walking on the road, his thirst grew strong and he found a well and descended into it and drank and was leaving, when he saw a dog hanging out its tongue and licking the ground from thirst, and the man said, 'This dog's thirst is like the thirst I had,' and he went into the well again, filled his shoe with water, and held it between his teeth (while he climbed out), and gave the dog to drink. And God approved of his act, and pardoned his sins.' They said, 'What, Messenger of God, shall we be rewarded for what we do for animals?' He replied, 'Yes. There is a reward on every living creature.' "[30]

Bukhārī . . . from 'A'isha: "A man asked permission to speak to the Prophet, and when the Prophet saw him he said, 'Unhappy the brother of his clan! Unhappy the son of his clan! (What a bad fellow!)' Then when the man sat down the Prophet looked cheerfully on him and spoke kindly to him. When the man went away, 'A'isha said, 'Messenger of God, when you saw him you said this and that, then to his face you were cheerful and kindly!' And the Messenger of God said, 'Why, 'A'isha, when have you ever seen me act grossly with people? Verily, the worst place on the resurrection day in the sight of God will be that of the man whom people avoided fearing his mischief.' "[31]

Bukhārī . . . from 'Abdallah ibn 'Umar: "The Messenger of God said, 'When any man says to his brother 'Thou infidel!' one of the two deserves the name.' "[32]

Bukhāri . . . from Ibn 'Abbās: "A woman came to the Prophet and said, 'My mother vowed to go on the pilgrimage, and died before fulfilling it. Should I make the pilgrimage in her place?' He said, 'Yes, do it. If your mother had had a debt, would you have paid it?' She said, 'Yes.' 'Then pay what she owes, for God is more worthy than anyone that we should keep our promises to Him.' "[33]

Bukhārī ... from Anas ibn Mālik: "Three persons came to the houses of the Prophet's wives to ask about his religious practice, and when they told them, it was as if they belittled it. And they said, 'In what do we differ from the Prophet? Yet God has pardoned all his past and future faults.' One of them said, 'As for me, I shall pray all night long.' Another said, 'I shall fast every day continuously.' The third said, 'I shall draw apart from women and never marry.' Then the Messenger of God went to them and said: 'Are you those who said thus and so? But I dread God more than you and revere him more, yet I fast and break the fast; I pray and I sleep too, and I marry women. Whosoever turns from my practice [*sunna*] is none of mine.' "[34]

Bukhārī ... from Abū Sa'īd al-Khudrī: "We took some women captives, and in coition practised withdrawal [*kunnā na'zilu*] so as not to have offspring from them. We asked the Messenger of God about this and he said, 'Is that what you did?' Then he said three times: 'There is not a soul who is to be born for the day of resurrection, but that it will be born.' "[35] [This *ḥadīth* is used today to overcome objections to birth control.]

Bukhārī ... from 'Abdallah ibn Ja'far ibn Abī Ṭālib: "I saw the Messenger of God eating fresh dates with cucumbers."[36]

Bukhārī ... from Abū Hurayra: "The Prophet said, 'The time draws near, and the good works grow less, and avarice appears, and the *ḥarj* increases.' They said, 'What is the *ḥarj?*' And he said, 'It is murder, murder!' "[37]

Bukhārī ... from Anas ibn Mālik: "I served the Prophet for ten years, and never did he say 'Uff!' (disgustedly) either for what I had done or left undone."[38]

Bukhārī ... from Usāma ibn Zayd: "One of the Prophet's daughters sent him this message while we were with him. 'My son is at the point of death.' We said, 'There is no god but God!' and he sent her as follows: 'Peace be upon you. What God takes is His, and what He gives is His. Everything is determined by

Him, therefore take this into account and be patient.' Then she sent adjuring him to come, so the Prophet went, and we went with him. And the child was placed on the Prophet's lap, who was trembling, while his eyes flowed tears. Then Sa'd said to him, 'What is this, Messenger of God?' He said, 'It is compassion, which God places as He will in the hearts of His servants. God has no mercy on those who do not have mercy.' "[39]

Muslim . . . from Abū Dharr: "Some of the Companions of the Prophet said to him, 'Messenger of God, the rich have borne away the rewards. They pray as we do, fast as we do, and besides they make alms with the surplus of their wealth!' He answered, 'And how has God not given you wherewithal to make alms? To say 'Glory to God' is an alms; to say 'God is most great!' is an alms, and similarly, 'Praise be to God. There is no god but God!' Whenever you bid to the good, it is an alms, when you reject the disapproved, it is an alms. Each time you perform the conjugal act, it is an alms.' They said, 'What? We can satisfy our fleshly appetites and gain a reward?' He answered, 'Is not the one who satisfies his appetites illicitly guilty of a sin? Just so, one who satisfies them lawfully gains a reward.' "[40]

Bukhārī . . . from Anas: "The Prophet said: 'No one has tasted the sweetness of faith who does not love his fellowman, not loving him for anything but God's sake, or would not find being thrown into a fire preferable to infidelity after God had delivered him from that, and to whom God and His prophet are not dearer than all other things.' "[41]

5. *The Preservation of the Prophetic Practice* (Sunna)

We have indicated that the *Ḥadīth* transmits the *sunna*, the tradition or practice of the Prophet, and even if a *ḥadīth* is not in itself true, it may still transmit *sunna;* it may illustrate what the Prophet would approve of, or what he might have said had he been asked.

The preservation of the *sunna* has been Islam's way of

maintaining its historical continuity, its link with the Apostolic period. One of the important ways this has been done is by the study and criticism of the *Ḥadīth*.

The following essay is by the fourteenth-century savant and historian 'Abd al-Rahmān Ibn Khaldūn (died A.H. 808/A.D. 1406), a Spanish Arab of Tunis, who was a professor of *Ḥadīth* and jurisprudence as well as a historian, statesman and diplomat. It serves to illustrate the categories within which the religious scholars have operated, and the way in which they have conceived their task.

The sciences concerned with Prophetic traditions (*ḥadīth*) are numerous and varied. One of them concerns abrogating. The permission to abrogate previous statements and the occurrence of abrogation have been established. . . . God said: "Whenever We abrogate a verse or consign it to oblivion, We bring one that is better, or as good." (Sūra 2:100)

Two traditions may be mutually exclusive, and it may be difficult to reconcile them. . . . If in such a case it is known that one is earlier than the other, it is definite that the later abrogates (it).

This is one of the most important and difficult of the sciences of tradition. Al-Zuhrī said: "It has been a baffling and impossible task for the jurists to distinguish traditions of the Messenger of God abrogating others from those that were abrogated by them."

Another of the sciences of tradition is the knowledge of the norms that leading *Ḥadīth*-scholars have invented in order to know the chains of transmitters, the (individual) transmitters, their names, how the transmission took place. . . . (The student may verify the tradition) by scrutinizing the chains of transmitters. For that purpose one may use such knowledge of the probity, accuracy, thoroughness and lack of . . . negligence as the most reliable Muslims describe a transmitter as possessing. . . .

The highest grade of transmitted material is called "sound" (*ṣaḥīḥ*) by the scholars. Next comes "good" (*ḥasan*). The lowest (acceptable) grade is "weak" (*ḍa'īf*). The classification includes also "skipping the first transmitter's name" (*mursal*), "omitting one link" (*munqaṭiʿ*), "omitting two links" (*muʿḍal*), "affected by some infirmity" (*muʿallal*), "singular" (*shādhdh*), "unusual" (*gharīb*) and "singular and suspect" (*munkar*). In some cases there is a difference of opinion as to whether (traditions so described) should be rejected. In other cases there is general agreement that (they should be rejected). The same is the case with (traditions with) sound chains. In some cases, there is general agreement as to their acceptability and soundness, whereas in other cases, there is difference of opinion. *Ḥadīth* scholars differ greatly in their explanations of these terms.

Then there follows the discussion of terms applying to the texts of the traditions. A text may be "unusual" (*gharīb*), "ambiguous" (*mushkil*), "affected by misspelling or misreading," "containing homonyms" (*muftariq*) or "containing homographs." . . .

The purpose of the discipline is a noble one. It is concerned with the knowledge of how to preserve the traditions (*sunna*) . . . until it is definite which are to be accepted and which are to be rejected.

The Companions of the Prophet and the men of the second generation who transmitted the Sunna were well known in the cities of Islam. There were transmitters in the Ḥijāz, in al-Baṣra and al-Kūfa, and then in Syria and Egypt. They were famous in their time. The transmitters of the Ḥijāz had fewer links in their chains of transmitters (than others) and were sounder because they were reluctant to accept (as reliable transmitters) those who were obscure and whose conditions were not known.

At the beginning, knowledge of the religious Law was entirely based on (oral) tradition. It involved no speculation, no use of opinion, and no intricate reasoning. . . . Mālik wrote the *Muwaṭṭa'* according to Ḥijāzī tradition, in which he laid down the principal laws on the basis of sound, generally agreed upon (material). He arranged the work according to juridical categories.

There was Muhammad ibn Ismā'īl al-Bukhārī, the leading *Ḥadīth* scholar of his time. In his *Musnad al-Ṣaḥīḥ* . . . he published the orthodox traditions according to subject. He combined all the different ways of the Ḥijāzīs, Iraqīs and Syrians, accepting the material on which they were all agreed but excluding material concerning which there were differences of opinion. . . . His work thus comprised 7,200 traditions of which 3,000 are repeated. In each chapter, he kept separate the rescensions with the different chains of interpreters belonging to them.

Then came the *imām* Muslim b. al-Hajjāj al-Qushayrī. He composed his *Musnad al-Ṣaḥīḥ* in which he followed al-Bukhārī in that he transmitted the material that was generally agreed upon. . . .

Scholars have corrected the two (authors), noting the cases of the sound traditions not included in their works.

Abū Dawūd al-Sijistānī, Abū'Isa al-Tirmidhī, and Abū 'Abd al-Rahmān al-Nasā'ī wrote works that included more than merely "sound" traditions. Their intent was to include all traditions that fulfilled amply the conditions making them actionable traditions . . . to serve as a guide to orthodox practice.

These are the collections of traditions that are used as reference works in Islam. They are the chief orthodox works on traditions. [Ibn Khaldūn does not mention the *Sunan* of Ibn Mājā (died A.H. 271/A.D. 886), usually considered the sixth orthodox work.—ED.] Other collections have been added to these five. At this time traditions are no longer published nor are (the publications of) traditions of former scholars corrected. Common experience attests that these numerous religious men, close to each other in time, were too capable and too firmly possessed of independent judgment to have neglected or omitted any tradition, so it is impossible that some later scholar might discover one. At this time one is concerned with correcting the principal written works and fixing the accuracy of their transmission. . . .

Al-Bukhārī's Ṣaḥīḥ occupies the chief place among them.[42]

CHAPTER THREE

THE LAW: *FIQH, SHARĪ'A*

The most characteristic activity of Islamic scholarship has not been, as in other religions, theology, but the study and explication of the Law. The concept of a divine law is of course a very ancient one in the Semitic Orient; in Islam the concept of the Law follows naturally enough from the Qur'ān, where God appears as commanding and forbidding, rewarding and punishing. In addition, there is the *Ḥadīth*, and the belief, present from the earliest times, that rules of right behavior may be found in the example of the Prophet and the practice of the early Community at Medina. We may add that the early Arab-Muslim Empire found itself in need of a legal system for the exigencies of political power and did not have any coherent earlier legal system of its own at its disposal, as the early Christians did in the legal system of the Roman Empire. Islam is submission to the will of God; it follows therefore that the will of God, already partly made explicit in the Qur'ān, is knowable and that its study is a matter of primary concern for Muslims.

Early Islam made no distinction between law and religion. It is significant that the word for the legal system of Islam—the *Sharī'a*—or "Way"—was relatively late in making an appearance, and the somewhat earlier word, *fiqh*, as "understanding," was used at first equally for the study of law and theology, though it has come to have an almost exclusively legal connotation. God speaks and commands, man submits and obeys. This obedience is not simply a passive or servile acceptance, however; Muslims conceive of their religion as a community which says "Yes" to God and His world, and the joyful performance of the Law, in most areas of the Islamic world, is looked on as a positive religious value. It is true that important segments of the Community have registered from early times a protest against the activities of the lawyers because they felt that the spirit was in danger of being lost in the legalistic debates of the jurisprudents; one must submit oneself to God, the mystics argued, not to the *Sharī'a*. The lawyers could reply, however, that God is made known by His Word, and right conduct by the *sunna;* the *Sharī'a* is only the explication of the Sacred Law contained in both; moreover, it is necessary for the right ordinance of the Community.

In later times, the *Sharī'a* is seen by Muslims primarily as an all-embracing legal system, which should ideally govern all phases of Islamic life—though for reasons of public welfare the legists grant the Muslim rulers the right of suspending the application of certain portions of the public law and substituting secular law; this has especially been true for the laws of punishment. Still, the *Sharī'a* is not thereby abolished or revoked—one does not revoke Divine Law—it is merely not enforced, because for temporal reasons it may not be feasible at that time and place to do so.

The collecting of the *Ḥadīth* and the codification of the Law formed the chief activity of the Muslim scholars of the first four centuries. Of the various law-schools, four main tendencies have survived and absorbed the other schools in Sunnī (Traditional) Islam, the orthodoxy of the Muslim majority, or better, their orthopraxy[1] (as one orientalist has penetratingly observed): for Muslims, consonant with their emphasis on the Law, have been more concerned with what men do than with what they believe, and very slow to reject any group of Muslims for wrong doctrine, unless that doctrine led the group to actively exclude itself, by its deeds, from the Community.

Every Sunnī must follow one school (*madhhab*) of the four accepted schools—Ḥanafī, Mālikī, Shafi'ī or Ḥanbalī. Its precepts dictate how he performs religious duties and how he interprets the Law. Though he may properly feel that his own school is in some sense "better"—and there have been occasions of religious and political tensions between one school and another—the official position is that all four are right and acceptable.

While there is no priesthood or clergy in Islam, properly speaking, there is a class which has played a clerical role in Islamic society, and which has acquired social and religious prestige identical in kind to that exercised by the priests of other religions. This is the *'ulamā'* (the "learned") and the *fuqahā'* ("lawyers"), the scholars and custodians of the Law. It is they who have traditionally decided what is an "official position."

Perhaps a word is in order about the legal texts which follow. All of them are the work of medieval *'ulamā'*, who were revered because their work was held to indeed explicate the Divine Law in some way. But while authoritative, they are not held to have been infallible, and they frequently differed among themselves. Exactly what bearing their endeavors should have on the life of Muslims today is one of the more pressing and hotly debated issues of modern Islam. How much of their work is to be incorporated in the legislation of modern Muslim states is a matter of earnest questioning among the responsible classes of Muslims, while it still forms an important part of the studies of the *'ulamā.'*

1. *'Ibādāt*

The first section of the *fiqh* books is always concerned with the laws governing man's conduct toward God: the necessary acts of worship or obedience demanded of a Muslim, such as prayer, fasting, almsgiving and pilgrimage, which together with the profession of faith, the *shahāda*, make up the so-called "five pillars" of Islam. Highly important is the question of ritual purity, since without it, the prayers of the worshiper are rendered invalid, and he may not touch the Qur'ān. The following sections on ritual purity are taken from the *Kitāb al-'Umda* of the Syrian Ḥanbalī legist Ibn Qudāma (born A.H. 541/A.D. 1146, died A.H. 620/A.D. 1223).

Aḥmad ibn Ḥanbal of Baghdad, whom the Ḥanbalīs claim for their founder, spearheaded the fundamentalist opposition to the early rationalist school, the *Mu'tazila*, in Islam, whose rationalism led them to the unacceptable assertion that the Qur'ān had been created.

The Ḥanbalī school has since been characterized by a fundamentalist rejection of any statement which cannot be firmly based on the Qur'ān and *Ḥadīth*, has tended to preserve its suspicion of the use of reason in religious matters, and is usually considered the strictest and most uncompromising of the legal schools. Today it is chiefly found in the Arabian Peninsula, where it is the official school of Sa'udi Arabia. The Ḥanbalī doctors, almost alone, still recommend the full punishments of the Law (*e.g.*, cutting off the hands of thieves).

Ritual Purity: Water: Water was created pure; it purifies the breach of ritual purity (*ḥadath*), and impure matter (*najāsa*). It is impossible to purify oneself with any other liquid.

Water to the quantity of two large jars (*qulla*) and running water becomes impure only after an alteration of color, taste, or odor. Aside from this any water mixed with impure matter becomes impure.

Two large jars represent about 108 Damascus *raṭls* of water. (About 266 liters.)

When one has doubts about the purity of water or some other liquid, or as to whether impure matter is present, he should take steps to find out with certainty (before using it).

When one is not certain which part of a garment or other object has been rendered impure, he must wash the garment or object in such a manner as to be certain he has dispelled the impurity.

A true believer who cannot tell whether the water in question is pure or impure and who has access to no other water must perform his ablution with dust or sand (*tayammum*); he may not use water about which there is a doubt. . . .

Vessels: It is forbidden to use vessels of gold or silver for ablutions or any other thing. . . . The same is true of plated articles, unless it be a silver plating of low value.

It is permissible to use all other vessels, provided they are pure. It is also permitted to use the utensils of the People of the Book; garments of the People of the Book are also pure, insofar as they are not known to be otherwise. [Not all lawyers agree on this.]

The wool or hair of an animal which has not been ritually slaughtered is pure; its skin and bones are impure.

Any animal which has died without ritual slaughter is impure, except: (1) Man. (2) Animals which live constantly in water. The Prophet has said: "Sea water is pure, and the bodies of creatures which live in it are permissible food." (3) Animals who do not have blood, providing they are not generated in filth.

The Lesser Ablutions (Wuḍū'): *Wuḍū'*, like all other ritual acts, is only made valid when accompanied by intent (*nīya*). The Prophet said: "Acts are only worth the intention which accompanies them. To every man according to his intentions."

The believer must first say "In the name of God!" He then washes his hands three times; three times he rinses out his mouth and snuffs water back into the nostrils, pouring water into his hand for both these acts.

He then washes his face, from the hairline to the neck, the chin, and the openings of the nostrils. He combs out his beard with wet fingers if it is thick, and washes it if it is sparse. He then washes his hands up to and including the wrists, three times.

He should then proceed to the rubbing of his head, including the ears; this rubbing he does with both hands, going from the forehead to the nape of the neck, and back.

He then washes three times his feet, including the ankles, taking care to pass his fingers between the toes.

Finally he raises his face toward heaven and says: "I witness that there is no god but God, the Unique, who has no partner. I witness that Muhammad is His servant and His messenger."

... It is *sunna* (praiseworthy but not necessary) to repeat each washing three times; but it is blameworthy to repeat the washing more than three times and to waste water.

It is *sunna* to cleanse the teeth with a *siwāk* (chewed stick), when the taste alters, when one rises, or when one prepares for prayer. The Prophet said: "If I did not fear to overburden my community, I should order the believers to cleanse their teeth before each prayer." It is recommended to clean the teeth at any time except when the sun is setting in the month of fasting.

The Causes Which Annul the Ablution: These are seven:

1. Anything which comes out of the two natural orifices (urethra, anus).
2. Anything which comes out of the other body openings if it has a repugnant aspect.

3. Loss of consciousness, except in a light sleep, whether one is standing or seated.
4. Touching the male organ.
5. Touching a woman, if it is accompanied by desire.
6. Apostacy.
7. Eating camel's flesh. [Most lawyers do not include this.]

The Prophet said, when asked if one should make ablutions after eating camel's meat: "Yes, make them." When asked if one should also perform ablution after eating mutton, he said: "If you want to, do it; if not, you may dispense with it." . . .

The Greater Ablution (Ghuṣl): Things which oblige one to make the greater ablution are:

1. Any seminal emission.
2. Contact with sexual organs.

The greater ablution involves, as a strict duty, the intention and the washing of the entire body; this washing should include rinsing of the mouth and the nostrils.

It is *sunna* to say: "In the name of God!" and to rub the body with the hands. . . .

It is not obligatory in the greater ablution to cut off the body hair, if one washes the parts with plenty of water.

One may accomplish the lesser and the greater ablution, providing one formulates the intention of doing so. . . .

Ablution with Dust or Sand (Tayammum): The *tayammum* consists of placing the hands once on the soil, rubbing the face with the hands, and rubbing the hands together . . . it is permissible to touch the soil more than once. Four conditions are necessary for validly performing the *tayammum:*

1. The impossibility of using water . . .
2. The time. One may not perform it except in the limits of the time assigned for one obligatory prayer . . . (for the next prayer, it must be repeated).
3. The intention.

4. The soil. One must not make the *tayammum* except with pure soil containing dust.

Menstruation: The monthly courses of women involve ten prohibitions: (1 and 2) Performance of prayer and the obligation to perform it; (3 and 4) Fasting and Circumambulation of Holy Places (*ṭawāf*); (5) Reading the Qur'ān; (6) Touching a copy of the Qur'ān; (7) Remaining in a mosque; (8) Sexual contacts; (9) Formal repudiation of a wife; (10) Being counted in a period of voluntary continence.[2]

Ritual Prayer (Ṣalāt): Ubāda b. al-Ṣāmit reports: "I heard the Prophet say: 'There are five prayers which God has prescribed for His servants in the space of a day and a night. He who observes the prayers has the promise of God that He will cause him to enter Paradise. He who does not perform them has no promise from God: If God wills, He will punish him, and if He wills, He will pardon him.' "

The five prayers are obligatory for every Muslim who has reached puberty and has the use of reason, except women who are in their courses or recovering from childbirth.

If a Muslim denies the necessity of prayer by ignorance, one should instruct him; if he does it wilfully, he should be treated as an infidel (*kāfir*).

It is only permissible to perform the prayers in the assigned times, unless one has pronounced the intention of saying them all at once, or has not fulfilled the conditions (of preparation).

When a Muslim abstains from saying his prayers from negligence, one should ask him three times to repent; if he repents, all is well; if he refuses it is lawful to put him to death.[3]

Times: The time of the noon-prayer (*ẓuhr*) falls from the time when the sun begins to decline until the shadow of an object is equal in length to the object itself.

The time of the prayer of the afternoon (*'ashr*), which is the central prayer (*al-wusṭā*), falls from the end of the time of the noon-prayer until the time when the sun turns yellow; this is when the "delay by choice" ends and the "delay of necessity" begins (when it is not lawful to pray until the next time of prayer).

The time of the evening-prayer (*maghrib*) falls from the setting of the sun until the red has disappeared from the sky.

The time of the night-prayer (*'ishā'*) falls from that time until mid-night. Then begins the "delay of necessity" which persists until the true dawn.

The time of the dawn-prayer falls from the true dawn until the sun has risen.[4]

[It is characteristic of the type of differences between the law-schools that the exact times of prayer vary from school to school.]

The Performance of the Ṣalāt: The following instructions for performing the ritual prayers are taken from the *Risāla* of Ibn Abi Zayd al-Qayrawānī (born in Nafza, Spain A.H. 310/A.D. 922, died A.H. 386/A.D. 996, in Qayrawān, Tunisia). He is one of the leading doctors of the Mālikī school, the old school of Medina, which prevailed in North Africa including Upper Egypt, where it is still the chief school, and in Muslim Spain. From North Africa it spread to Sub-Saharan Africa and the Sudan. The "founder" of the Mālikī school, Mālik b. Anas, died A.H. 179/A.D. 795. Historically the school has been distinguished by rigid traditionalism and *taqlīd* (uncritical acceptance of authority).

The consecrating act (*iḥrām*) in prayer is that you should say: "*Allahu Akbar* (God is most great!)." No other word is permissible. You should raise your hands as high as your shoulders or less, and then recite from the Qur'ān. If you are in the morning-prayer, recite the opening *sūra* of the Qur'ān. Do not begin with the formula "In the name of God, the Merciful, the Compassionate," either in this *sūra* or the one which you recite after it. When you have said "not of those who go astray," say "Amen" whether you are alone or praying behind a leader (*imām*), in a low voice. The *imām* should not say it loudly (like the rest of the prayer) but also in a low voice, though there are differences of opinion about this.

Then recite a *sūra* from the last part of the Qur'ān (in which the shorter *sūras* are found); if it is longer than that, well and good, but the recitation should not exceed the space of time allotted for that prayer, and recite it in an audible voice.

When this *sūra* is finished, repeat "God is most great!" while leaning forward to begin the inclination (*rukū'*). Place your hands upon your knees, and keep your back straight, not arching it, neither lifting up your head nor ducking it. Keep your arms free of your body. Be sure to preserve sincere humility in both the inclination and the prostration which follows. Do not pray while making the inclination: if you wish, say "Praise unto my Lord, the Great! Glorified be He!" For that, there is no fixed time, nor for the length of the inclination.

Then raise your head, saying: "God hears those who praise Him." Then say: "My God, Our Lord, to Thee be praise!" if you are alone. An *imām* does not repeat these formulas. Those who pray behind an *imām* also do not say "God hears those who praise Him," but do say "My God, Our Lord, to Thee be praise!"

You should then stand erect serenely and quietly. Then begin the prostration, not sitting back on the heels but going directly into a prostration. Say "God is most great!" while leaning forward in the prostration, and touch your forehead and nose to the ground, placing your palms spread flat on the ground, pointing toward the *qibla* (the direction of Mecca), placing them near the ears, or somewhat to the rear of them. All of this is prescribed generally, not strictly. Do not spread the forearms on the ground, or clasp the upper arms to your sides, but hold them slightly away. Your feet should be perpendicular to the ground in the prostration, with the ends of the big toes touching it.

You may, in your prostration, say "Glory unto Thee, my Lord! I have wronged myself and done evil. Forgive me!" or something similar. You may utter a private prayer in the prostration, if you wish, and there is no set time for this, but at the least your members should remain still in a fixed position.

Then you should raise your head, saying "God is most great!" and sit back, folding back the left foot in the time between the two prostrations, and putting the right foot vertical to the ground with the bottoms of your toes touching the ground. Lift your hands from the earth and place them on your knees, and then make a second prostration as you did the first. Then rise from the ground as you are, supporting yourself on both hands, not returning to the sitting position before rising, but directly, as I have mentioned. While rising, say "God is most great!"

Then recite a part of the Qur'ān as you did at first, or a little less, doing it just as you did before, but add the invocation (*qunūt*) after the inclination or if you prefer before performing it, after the end of your recitation. The invocation is as follows: "O God! I ask Thy aid and pardon. We believe truly in Thee, we put our trust in Thee, we submit humbly to Thee, we confide in Thee; and we forsake those who repudiate Thee. O God! Thee only we serve, to Thee we pray and prostrate ourselves, to Thee we strive. We put our hope in Thy mercy, and fear Thy grave chastisements. Surely Thy chastisement shall attain those who repudiate Thee."

Then make the prostration and sit back as has been described before. If you sit back after the two prostrations, place the right foot vertical to the soil with the bottom of your toes touching the ground, and place the left foot flat letting your posterior come in contact with the ground. Do not sit on your left foot, and if you wish let the right foot incline from its vertical position until the side of the big toe touches the ground; this permits of latitude.

After this, you recite the *tashahhud*, as follows: "Unto God be all salutations, all things good, all things pleasing, all benedictions. Peace be upon thee, O Prophet, and the mercy of God and His blessings! Peace be upon us all, and all righteous servants of God. I witness that there is no god but God, the Unique, without partner. I witness that Muhammad is His servant and messenger." If after this you utter the final salutation, it is fitting and permissible, or you may add other formulas....

Then say "Peace be upon thee" one time only, looking straight ahead, toward the *qibla*, and turning the head slightly to the right. It is thus that an *imām* or man alone does; as for one praying behind an *imām*, he utters the salutation once, turning slightly to the right at the same time; he utters it again in response to the salutation of the man on his left. If there is no-one there, he does not say anything to his left.

While reciting the *tashahhud* he also puts his hands in his lap and closes the fingers of the right hand, pointing with his index finger the side of which faces his face. Opinions differ as to whether it should move. It is held that the believer with this gesture indicates his belief that God is One God; those who move it explain it as subduing Satan. As for myself, I believe one must explain it as a way of warning oneself in this way—if God so wills—of the things which in the matter of prayer could importune (the attention) and distract it. The left hand should be left open, on the right thigh, and one should not move it or point with it....

It is advisable to make two inclinations at the dawn, before the dawn-prayer which follows the dawn. At each of these inclinations, one should recite the opening chapter (*fātiḥa*) of the Qur'ān, in a low voice.

The recitation at the noon-prayer should be as long as that at the dawn-prayer or a little shorter, and nothing should be recited loudly. One should recite the *fātiḥa* in both the first and second inclination, as well as one other *sūra*, in a low voice. In the two last inclinations of the noon-prayer, he should recite the *fātiḥa* alone, and in a low voice....

After this, one should perform supererogatory prayers. It is recommended to add four inclinations, saying the final salutation after each group of two. The same supererogatory prayers are recommended before afternoon-prayers.

At the afternoon-prayer one does what we have prescribed for the noon-prayer. . . .

For the evening-prayer, he should recite audibly in the first two inclinations, and recite the *fattiḥa* with each inclination as well as one of the shorter *sūras*. In the third he should recite the *fattiḥa* only, and the *tashahhud* and the salutation . . . it is reprovable to sleep before the evening-prayer or to converse after it, except for good reason. . . .

"Reciting softly" in the ritual prayer is moving the tongue to form the words in the recitation. As for "reciting loudly," it is for one to hear himself and be heard by a man near him, if he is not acting as an *imām*. A woman should speak more softly than a man.[5]

[Friday is the Muslim day of Congregational Prayer, though it does not have to be kept as a day of rest. The noon-prayers are recited by the congregation, and a *khuṭba* or public address given.]

Funeral Rites: This section is taken from one of the earliest extant law-books, the *Muwaṭṭa'*, compiled by Mālik ibn Anas (died A.H. 179/A.D. 795), whom the Mālikīs regard as the founder of their school. The *Muwaṭṭa'* has been so admired that al-Shāfi'ī once remarked that it ranked second in value only to the Qur'ān. Mālik was known to his contemporaries more as a collector of *Ḥadīth* than as a legist; and this early law-book is simply a great collection of *ḥadīths* approved by Mālik and arranged for use under the headings of various aspects of the Law. Mālik did not so much write the *Muwaṭṭa'* as teach it, and some fifteen early recensions, made from the lecture notes of his students, are known to have survived. He is thus always quoted as the transmitter of each *ḥadīth*.

Washing the Dead: It was told me by Yaḥya on Mālik's authority from Ja'far ibn Muhammad from his father, that the Messenger of God—God's benediction and peace be on him—was in his shirt when he was washed.

It was told me by Mālik, from Ayyūb ibn Tamīma al-Sakhtiyānī from Muhammad ibn Sīrīn, on the authority of Umm 'Aṭīya of the Anṣār. She said: "The Messenger of God —God's benediction and peace be upon him!—came in where we women were, when his daughter passed away, and said: 'Be certain to wash her three times, or five or even more than that if it seems proper to you, with water and lote-tree leaves. At the last, use camphor or something camphor-scented. Then, when you are finished, call me.'" She added, "And when we were finished, we called him and he gave us a wrapper of his, and said: 'Wrap her in this'—that is, with his waist-wrapper.'"

It was told me by Mālik from 'Abdallah ibn Abī Bakr that Asmā'bint 'Umīs washed Abū Bakr al-Ṣiddīq when he died. Then she went out and asked those who were present from the Muhājirīn, and said, "I am fasting, and this is a very cold day. Must I wash him completely?" They answered, "No."

It was told me by Mālik that he heard the people of authority say: "If a woman dies, and there is no woman present to wash her, or any man from her near kinsmen who should do it, or her husband who would be next in line, the *tayammum* should be performed for her. Her face and hands should be lightly rubbed with dust" (rather than uncovering the body).

Mālik also said, "When a man dies and there is no-one present except a woman, she should also perform the *tayammum* for him."

Mālik said, "Washing the dead is not prescribed us so as to consist of an exact procedure, but they should (only) be washed and purified."

Shrouding the Dead: It was told me by Mālik from Hishām ibn 'Urwa, from his father, from 'A'isha wife of the Prophet, God's benediction and peace be on him, that the Messenger of God was shrouded in three white Yamanī garments, with no shirt or turban.

It was told me by Mālik, that Yaḥya ibn Sa'īd said: "It has reached me that Abū Bakr al-Siddīq said to 'A'isha when he was ill: 'In how many shrouds was wrapped the Messenger of God—God's blessing and peace be on him?' She answered, 'In three white garments of Yamanī stuff.' Then Abū Bakr said, 'Take this garment'—indicating a robe of his which had been stained by musk or saffron—'and wash it. Then use it as my shroud, along with two other white garments.' 'A'isha asked, 'What about this one here instead?' And Abū Bakr said, 'No, the living have more need of new garments than the dead, and this is only for corpse-ichor.' "

Funeral Processions: It was told me by Yaḥya on Mālik's authority, from Ibn Shihāb, that the Messenger of God— God's benediction and peace be upon him—and Abū Bakr and 'Umar used to walk before the bier, as well as the other early Caliphs and 'Abdallah ibn 'Umar.

It was told me on Mālik's authority from Ibn Shihāb that he said, "Walking behind the bier is a transgression (*khaṭā'*) against the *sunna.*"

On Saying "God is Most Great" over the Dead: Yaḥya told me on Mālik's authority from Ibn Shihāb from Sa'īd ibn Musayyib from Abū Hurayra that the Messenger of God—God's benediction and peace be on him—announced the death of the Negus of Abyssinia to the people of Medina, on the day the Negus died, and went out of the town with them to the mosque of the *Muṣalla,* and stood them in the ranks of prayer. Then he cried "God is most great!" four times.

It was told me by Mālik from Ibn Shihāb from Abū Umāma ibn Sahl ibn Ḥunayf, that a poor woman of Medina fell ill, and the Messenger of God was told about it, for (the benediction of God and peace be upon him!) he used to visit the poor people and ask about them. So he said, "If she should die, be sure to call me."

The burial took place at night [Washing and burial customarily follow promptly at death.—Ed.], so they disliked to awaken the Messenger of God, God's blessing and peace be on him. When he awakened next morning he was told about her, and said, "Did I not order you to call me for her?" They answered, "Messenger of God! We hated to get you out at night, and to waken you."

Then the Messenger of God went out with the people and put them in ranks at her grave, and cried four times, "God is most great!"

Funeral Prayers: Yaḥya told me on Mālik's authority, from Sa'īd ibn Abī Sa'īd al-Maqbūrī from his father, that he once asked Abū Hurayra (Companion of the Prophet), "How do you pray at a funeral?" Abū Hurayra said, "I shall tell you, in God's name, exactly. First there is the procession with the family following the bier, then when it is placed on the ground, I say 'God is most great,' and praise Him and bless His prophet. Then I say, 'Lord, it is Thy servant, and the son of Thy servant, the child of Thy Community. He used to testify that there is no god but Thee, and that Muhammad is Thy servant and Thy messenger, and Thou knowest him best of all. O God, if he did well, then increase him in good deeds, and if he did wrong, then let his offense pass without punishment. O God! Deprive us not of his reward, and try us not after his death.' "

Funeral Prayers in the Mosque: Yaḥya told me on Mālik's authority from Abū Nadr, the freeman of 'Umar ibn 'Ubaydallah, from 'A'isha the wife of the Prophet, God's benediction and peace be on him. She ordered that the people pass at her house with the bier of Sa'd ibn Abī Waqqāṣ (her house was inside the walls of the Prophet's mosque) so she might pray for him. People found fault with her for this. Then 'A'isha said, "How hasty people are! It was nowhere but in this mosque that the Prophet, God's blessing and peace be on him, prayed over Suhayl ibn Bayḍā'."

Burial of the Dead: It was told me by Yaḥya on Mālik's authority that the Prophet, God's benediction and peace be upon him, died on a Monday and was buried on Tuesday, and the people prayed over him one by one; not one of them prayed behind an *imām*. Some said, "He should be buried under his pulpit," and others said, "Bury him at the cemetery of al-Baqī'." Then Abū Bakr came forward and said, "I once heard him say, 'There is no prophet at all who is not buried at the place where he died.' " So they dug his grave in ('A'isha's room). And when they were washing him, they wished to remove his shirt, when they heard a voice say, "Do not remove his shirt!" So they did not, but washed him with it on.

It was told me by Mālik from Hishām ibn 'Urwa that his father said, "There were two men in Medina (who dug graves); one of them used to (put a niche in the grave for the body) and the other did not. So they said, "Whoever comes first shall perform his office." And the man who (made niches at the bottom of the grave) came first, so he dug a niche for the Messenger of God—God's blessing and peace be on him!"[6] [Virtually all Muslim graves have this recess at the sides.]

Zakāt: These regulations for the payment of the obligatory religious tax of *zakāt* are taken from the *Kitāb al-Tanbīh* of Abū Ishāq Ibrahīm ibn 'Alī al-Shīrāzī al-Fīrūzābādī, a Persian doctor of the Shāfi'ī school (died A.H. 476/A.D. 1083).

The Shāfi'ī school traces its founding to Abū 'Abdallah Muhammad ibn Idrīs al-Shāfi'ī, a Meccan of the Quraysh, who taught in Egypt in Fusṭāt (now part of Cairo). He died there A.H. 204/A.D. 920. He represents a medial position between the use of reason and personal interpretation found in the Iraqī school of his day, and the rigid traditionalism preferred by the Medinan school of Mālik.

The school has produced many distinguished legists and theologians, and became especially important in promoting the official neo-orthodoxy of the fifth A.H./eleventh A.D. century Saljūq restoration. It is found today chiefly in Lower Egypt, parts of South Arabia and Central Asia, and it spread from the Red Sea area across the Indian Ocean to Malaya and Indonesia, where it is the only law-school of any importance.

Clearly much of this section is chiefly of antiquarian interest: few Muslims today have occasion to figure the *zakāt* they owe on camels. In the early Islamic state, the *zakāt* was the only tax paid by Muslims, was used for community purposes and together with the taxes levied on non-Muslims made up the revenue of the state. While a few of the ultra-orthodox still regard these taxes and land tax as the only taxes a Muslim government can legally levy, *zakāt* is usually treated today as an obligation to spend money for charitable purposes and is hardly distinguished from almsgiving.

Who is affected: The obligation only applies to a free Muslim who has complete ownership of the property on which it is due. Therefore a contractual freedman (whose slavery has not been officially and legally terminated) does not owe *zakāt*, nor an infidel who has always been so. As to whether he owes it if he was a Muslim and apostacized, there are three opinions:

1. He must pay it.
2. He must not.
3. He must only pay it if he returns to Islam.

Zakāt is due only for animals, agricultural products, precious metals, objects intended for sale, the product of mines and treasure trove. . . .

The *zakāt* on animals is due only for camels, cattle, sheep and goats. If one possesses the minimum number on which the *zakāt is* due and has been the owner for the term of a full year, it is obligatory to pay, according to the soundest opinion; according to another it is not, if one is unable.

The increase of the flock born during the year is considered with the rest of the flock even though this increase may not have been possessed for a full year. . . .

The taxable minimum of camels is five; on each group of five a goat is due; for a herd of twenty-five camels a she-camel between one and two years' age is due; for thirty-six, one two-year-old female....

The taxable minimum of cattle is thirty head, on these a one-year-old calf is due; for forty, a two-year-old heifer.

The taxable minimum of sheep and goats is forty head; on these one goat is due; on 121 two goats; on 201 three goats, and after that another goat for every additional fifty....

Agricultural Products: This *zakāt* is only obligatory on cereals eaten for food and cultivated by men, such as wheat, barley, millet, sorghum, rice and the like; then it applies to legumes such as lentils, chickpeas, vetches, beans and peas. Fruits are not subject, except for dates and grapes, to which al-Shāfi'i used to add olives, turmeric, and saffron. The payment does not become due . . . except when the grain or fruit of the owner has begun . . . to show the marks of maturity.

The taxable minimum for each sort, when the grain has been threshed and the fruit dried, is five camel-packs, for 1600 Baghdad *raṭls*, but for rice and *'alas*, a grain which is left in the husk, the minimum is ten camel-packs....

Precious Metal: Whoever has a taxable minimum of gold or silver for a full year and is otherwise subject to the *zakāt*, must pay *zakāt* on this. The minimum for gold is 20 *mithqals* [a mithqal is 1½ drachms] and *zakāt* for gold is half a *mithqal* for every twenty *mithqals*. For silver the minimum is 100 drachms and one pays five drachms. For every like quantity the *zakāt* is the same. Any adornment one may have for lawful use is exempted, according to one of two opinions, but if it is for an unlawful or reprovable use or in order for evading the tax, one must pay *zakāt* for it....

Zakāt of Fast-Breaking: This is obligatory for every free Muslim who has something to spare apart from his own provisions and those of his dependents, which will allow him to pay this *fitra.*

Whoever owes it, owes it for all his dependents who are Muslims, if he can afford it. . . .

This alms at breaking the fast is due at the end of Ramadān . . . before the prayers of the Feast of Fast-breaking. It is lawful to make it all during Ramadān, but not to delay until the day after the Feast. If one does that, he has committed a fault which he must expiate.

It is necessary to give one measure of the quantity of the Prophet, on whom be God's benediction and peace; that is 5 Baghdad *raṭls,* composed of foods which are subject to the *zakāt;* such as dates, raisins, wheat, barley and similar things. . . .

On Payment: Whoever has the obligation to pay *zakāt* and is able to, may not lawfully delay; if he does, he commits a fault for which he must answer. Whoever refuses to pay it and denies its obligatory character has apostacized, and the amount may be taken from him and he may be put to death. Whoever refuses to pay it from motives of avarice shall have the amount taken from him and be given a sentence at the discretion of the judge; it is the same for one who behaves fraudulently. . . .

It is reprehensible to transport the *zakāt* out of the region where it was paid. If this is done, there are two opinions:

1. It shall be considered permissible.
2. It shall not. . . .

If the *zakāt* is paid on wealth found in a desert, the money shall be distributed among the poor of the nearest inhabited areas.

Distribution: The *zakāt* must be distributed among the following eight classes:

1. The collectors, who must be free, versed in the law, and trustworthy. They should not be of the (clan of the Prophet, because they are already entitled to funds). They may receive up to an eighth (for their trouble).
2. The poor: those who cannot pay for their needs. They are given what is needful to help them, such as tools or capital for a business.

3. The needy: those who are unable entirely to support themselves; they are given a supplement. . . .
4. Those whose hearts it is necessary to conciliate. These are of two categories:

   a. Infidels, of two sorts: those whose conversion is hoped for, and those from whom some evil is feared; to these last, part of the 25th of the booty of war.
   b. Muslims; also of two sorts: important people of whom it is hoped they will convert their followers, and tribes whose faith, it is hoped, will improve. The Prophet (on whom be God's blessing and peace), gave such tribes a share; in later times opinions are three:

      1. One should give them nothing.
      2. One should give them part of the *zakāt*.
      3. One should give them from the 25th (of the spoils of war, set aside for such purposes). . . .

5. Slaves, who are under legal contract to pay a certain amount for their freedom. They may be given what they are bound to pay, if they have no means to get it, but not more than that. . . .
6. Debtors. . . .
7. Those who fight in "The Way of God," that is, who are not entitled to an allotment, because they are volunteers, not written in the regular army registers. They are given a sum calculated to outfit them (for the *jihād*).
8. Travellers, if their travel is for lawful purposes (such as seeking religious knowledge or going on a pilgrimage).

Zakāt may not be distributed to an infidel, or to a member of the Prophet's clan (who is entitled to a regular allotment).[7]

Fasting: These regulations are taken from perhaps the leading Shāfi'ī legal work, the *Minhāj al-Ṭālibīn* of the Syrian Muḥyī al-Dīn al-Nawawī (died A.H. 676/A.D.

1277). It has tended to replace the earlier work of al-Shīrāzī, and other doctors of the school.

Obligation to Fast: The Fast of Ramadān becomes obligatory when thirty days of the preceding month, *Sha'bān*, are past, or with the seeing of the new moon of Ramadān. This seeing is established with the testimony of one trustworthy witness, or as some say, two. If one witness is accepted, it is a condition that he must have the quality of veracity, and thus be neither a slave nor a woman. If we should fast because of such testimony and did not see the moon after thirty days, we might still end the fast even if the sky was cloudy....

Thus if fast is not yet obligatory in one area and a traveller comes to a locality where the moon has been seen, the most proper thing is for him to conform with the inhabitants in fasting. One who travels to an area where the new moon of the Feast has been seen should feast with its people, and afterwards make up the day of fast he has lost thus.

Intention is a condition of the fast; the intention should be formulated each night . . . the full formulation in Ramadān is: "to fast tomorrow to acquit my duty towards God of fasting Ramadān this year."

The Conditions: To fast, one must rigorously avoid coition, vomiting . . . or introducing any substance to the "interior of the body." Some make it a condition that there be in the body power to absorb the food or the medicine thus introduced. It does not matter if "the interior" is inside the head, or the belly, or the intestines or the bladder; all can break the fast with the introduction of a substance by snuffing or eating or injection, or through incision in the belly or the head, or the like.

According to the soundest opinion, putting drops in the nose or the urethra breaks the fast.

It is necessary for such an introduction to be by an open passage. Thus there is no harm in oil's entering the pores by absorption, or when *koḥl* (eye cosmetic) is used, and its taste is afterward perceived in the throat.

The introduction must be intended, so that if a fly or gnat or dust of the road or flour-dust entered by accident, the fast would not be broken. It also would not be broken if one swallowed saliva carelessly.

But the fast *is* broken if saliva leaves the mouth and one brings it back into the mouth, or if one moistens a thread in one's mouth and then puts it back in one's mouth still moist, or if one swallows saliva in which a foreign substance or something unclean is mixed.

If one swallows the saliva in his mouth he does not break fast, but if he swallows water from the mouth or nose remaining after the ablutions, if it is in any quantity, he does. If food remaining between his teeth is dislodged by saliva, it does not break the fast. . . .

If one eats something truly forgetting (that he is fasting) he has not broken the fast, unless he repeats this, according to the best opinions. I too say that he has not broken the fast, and God is most knowing.

Coition is like eating, according to our school (if committed during the time of fast and one has truly forgotten that he is fasting, it does not break the fast). But any seminal emission (otherwise) breaks the fast. . . . [The time of fasting is from that time of the night when a white thread can be distinguished from a black one—*e.g.* the false dawn—until the sun has fully set below the horizon in the evening.—ED.]

A traveller or sick person who has legally broken the fast must fast the number of days he has missed when he is able. This is true also for menstruating women, for those who broke the fast without a valid excuse, for those who did not formulate the intention before fasting, for one who was unconscious the entire day, for an apostate but not for the period of infidelity before one was converted to Islam.

A pregnant or nursing woman must fast for lost days when she is able, but if she did not fast for reasons of her own health, she need not pay expiation; while if she broke the fast fearing for the child, she does pay expiation (*fidya*) as well. . . .

The expiation is a day's food given to the poor and needy, of the same sort given in alms at the Feast of Fast-breaking. . . .
One owes an atonement (*kaffāra*) for breaking the fast of Ramadān by coition. . . . The atonement consists of freeing a slave. If one cannot do that, he must fast sixty days, or if he cannot do that, give sixty days' provisions to the poor. If he is unable to do all this, the obligation remains, and he must still do it if ever he is able. . . . It is not possible for a poor person to pay his atonement to his own family.[8]

Pilgrimage (*Ḥajj*): No religious rite has done more to unite the Muslims than the pilgrimage, where each year at the same time thousands of pilgrims meet and act together in complete equality; here the fraternalism of Islam is guaranteed and compellingly demonstrated. The pilgrims are incidentally able to exchange ideas and experiences; in the medieval period this made for remarkably rapid dissemination of books, which were carried home by the pilgrims.

The following regulations are taken from the *Risāla* of Ibn Abī Zayd al-Qayrawānī.

Obligation: Pilgrimage to the inviolate House of God which is in Bekka [*i.e.* Mecca] is a religious duty to every one who is able to make his way there, if he is a free mature Muslim, once in his life. "Able" signifies a practical way of access and sufficient means, as well as the physical ability to arrive, whether riding or walking, in health of body.

It is ordained that one take the ritual state of *iḥrām* (consecration for pilgrimage) at the proper post on the routes. The post (*mīqāt*) of the People of Syria, Egypt, and North Africa is al-Juḥfa. If they pass by Medina, it is better for them to use the post of its people, which is Dhū-al-Ḥulaya. The post of the people of Iraq is Dhāt 'Irq, that of the Yaman's people is Yalamlam, and that of the people of Najd, or Central Arabia, is Qarn. Whoever is passing to Mecca from Medina is obliged to take the *iḥrām* at Dhū-al-Ḥulaya, unless he should return from there to his proper post.

A pilgrim, or a man who is only making the visitation of the holy places (*'umra*) should take the *iḥrām* after either one of the obligatory prayers or a supererogatory prayer, after which he says, "I am here, Lord, I am here. I am here; no partner hast Thou. I am here. Thine is the praise; Thine is the grace; Thine is the kingdom." Then he formulates his intention in his own words, to make the pilgrimage or the visitation.

It is ordered that one perform the greater ablution before taking the *iḥrām*, and that one remove all sewn garments. [The pilgrim's garb is two seamless white garments; a waist-wrapper, from navel to knee, and a shawl covering the left shoulder, and tied under the right. Sandals but not shoes may be worn.—Ed.] One is recommended to perform the greater ablution on entering Mecca, and to continue using the formula "I am here" after his prayers, on each elevation along the road, and when encountering fellow pilgrims. Great insistency in this is not incumbent on him.

When he has entered Mecca, he abstains from the formula until he has performed the circumambulation and the course. Then he continues to use it until sunset on the Day of 'Arafat and his hasting to the Oratory in 'Arafat.

It is recommended to enter Mecca by Kadā', the way above Mecca, and when leaving to leave by Kudā, though if one does neither it is no sin.

Mālik says that on entering Mecca, one should enter the Inviolate Mosque, and it is best to enter from the Gate of the Banū Shayba. Then one touches the Black Stone at the corner of the Ka'ba with his lips, if he is able; if not, he puts his hand on it and then lays his hand on his lips, without kissing it. He then circumambulates the Holy House—keeping it on his left—seven times, of which three are quick, and four walking. He touches the corner of the Ka'ba each time he passes it, in the way we have described, and says "God is most great!"

He should not touch the Southern corner with his lips but with his hand and then lay it on his lips without kissing. When he has finished the circumambulation he says a prayer of two prostrations at the "Stance of Abraham" (between Ka'ba and Gate of Banū Shayba) and then touches the Black Stone, if he can reach it. He goes out afterward to Mount Ṣafā and stands on it while he makes an invocation. He then goes to Mount Marwa, taking a brisk pace in the bottom of the valley. When he comes to Marwa, he stands on it, makes his invocation, and hastens to Ṣafā. He does this seven times, making in all four stops on Ṣafā and four on Marwa.

On the 8th of the month of Pilgrimage he goes out to Minā, and there prays the prayers of Midday, Afternoon, Sunset, Night and Dawn. He then goes to Mount 'Arafāt, not ceasing to cry "I am here, Oh Lord!" until the sun sets and until he has arrived at the oratory of Mount 'Arafāt. Before going there he must put himself in a state of ritual purity, and pray the noon-prayer and the afternoon-prayer at one time under the direction of the *imām* of the pilgrims.

He then goes with the *imām* to 'Arafāt and they halt there until sunset. He then rushes with the throng and the *imām* to al-Muzdalifa, and prays there the sunset-prayer, the night-prayer, and the dawn-prayer. They then make the "Station" of the place called Mash 'ar al-Ḥaram. Then when the sun is near rising, he hastens to Minā, driving his mount on (if he is mounted), in the Valley of Muḥassir. When he has arrived at Minā, he throws seven small stones at the first *jamra* (stone heap), that called al-'Aqaba and with each stone he cries "God is most great." [This is an ancient Semitic cursing ceremony, regarded as recalling the stoning of Satan by Abraham.—Ed.] He then sacrifices, if he has led his victim with him. (Sheep, goat, or camel. The meat must be given to the poor or left untouched.) Then he shaves his head and goes to the House (of God: the Ka'ba) with the throng and performs seven circumambulations and the inclinations. He then stays at Minā for three days, and when the sun sets each day he throws at the *jamra* near Minā with seven pebbles, and cries "God is most great!" with each stone. He throws also at each of the other two *jamras* in the same fashion, calling "God is most great!" with each stone, and stations himself for invocations after throwing at the first and second *jamras*, but not at the *jamra* of al-'Aqaba. When he has thrown for the third day, which is the Fourth Day from the Sacrifice, he may leave for Mecca; his pilgrimage is completed. If he desires, he may compress the rites of Minā into two days, and leave. When he leaves Mecca, he makes the Circumambulation of Farewell, and performs inclinations.

The Visitation (*'umra*) is made as we have described up until the hasting between Ṣafā and Marwa. Then he may shave his head, and the Visitation is finished.

Shaving the head is best, in Pilgrimage and Visitation, but merely cropping it close is permitted. *Sunna* for a woman is cropping.[9]

2. *The Regulation of Personal Status*

The *fiqh* books, after dealing with *'ibādāt*—the Law of Man's Relations with God—usually pass to *mu'āmalāt*, or the laws governing human relations. Of these the most universally observed by Muslims are those of personal status—marriage, divorce, fosterage, etc. They are involved, and will only be suggested here. These sections are taken from the *Hidāya* of Burhān al-Dīn al-Marghinānī, of Farghāna in Central Asia (died A.H. 593/A.D. 1197), one of the authoritative works of this school. The Ḥanafī school claims as its founder Abū Ḥanīfa (died A.H. 150/A.D. 767), the systematizer of the old school of Kūfa in Iraq. His pupils, Abū Yūsuf the chief justice of Harūn al-Rashīd, and al-Shaybānī, had perhaps more to do with founding the school that bears his name. Since it developed in Baghdad in close association with the early

ʿAbbāsīs, the Ḥanafī school was always concerned with questions of a practical as well as of a theoretical nature; it is characterized by its reasoned approach and logical consistency and a certain wideness of view which has recommended it to Muslim rulers. It was the chief law-school of the Ottoman and Mughal empires, and today is found chiefly in Turkey, Syria, Central Asia, Afghanistan, India and Pakistan.

Nikāḥ or Marriage: Nikāḥ in its primitive sense means carnal conjunction. . . . In the language of the Law it implies a particular contract used for the purpose of legalizing generation.

Marriage is contracted—that is to say, is effected and legally confirmed—by means of declaration and consent. . . . Where both the parties are Muslims it cannot be contracted but in the presence of two male witnesses or of one man and two women, who are sane, adult, and Muslim . . . evidence is an essential condition of marriage . . . against Mālik, who maintains that in marriage general knowledge is a condition and not positive evidence. It is necessary that the witnesses be free, the evidence of slaves being in no wise valid. . . . If a Muslim marries a woman of the People of the Book in the presence of two men of her kind it is lawful, according to Abū Yūsuf and Abū Ḥanīfa. Muhammad and Zufar hold it is not legal, because their testimony . . . amounts to evidence and the evidence of unbelievers regarding Muslims is illegal . . . the argument of the two elders in reply to this objection is that evidence is necessary . . . merely in order to establish the husband's right of cohabitation, which is in this case the object. . . .

It is not lawful for a man to marry his foster-mother or his foster-sister, the Almighty having commanded "Marry not your mothers who have suckled you or your sisters by fosterage," and the Prophet also declared "Everything is prohibited by reason of fosterage which is so by reason of kindred."

It is not lawful to marry and cohabit with two women being sisters, neither is it lawful for a man to cohabit with two sisters in virtue of a right of possession (as being his slaves) because the Almighty has declared that such cohabitation with sisters is unlawful.

A master may not marry his own slavewoman (except he set her free) or a mistress her bondsman, for marriage was instituted with a view that the fruit might belong equally to the father and the mother, and marriage and servitude are contradictory to each other. . . .

Marriage with Women of the Book is legal. . . . It is unlawful to marry a Zoroastrian woman or a polytheist (until she becomes a Muslim), . . .

It is lawful for a Muslim who is free to marry a female slave, whether a Muslim or Woman of the Book (if she is not his own); his seed is born then in bondage. . . . It is unlawful for a man already married to a free woman to marry a slave; the Prophet (said): "Do not marry a slave after a free woman." Shāfiʿī says the marriage of a slave after a free woman is lawful to a man who is a slave, and Mālik likewise maintains it is lawful, providing it is with the free woman's consent. The above *ḥadīth* however is an answer to both as it is general and unconditional.

Moreover the legal marriage is a blessing to men and women equally, but the enjoyment of it is by bondage restricted to one half, inasmuch as slaves can have only two wives whereas free men may legally have four. . . .

A temporary marriage, where a man marries a woman (for a contract of) ten days (for instance), is null. . . .[10]

A woman who is adult and of sound mind may be married by virtue of her own consent although the contract may not have been made or acceded to by her guardians, and this whether she be a virgin or otherwise. (Though) Abū Yūsuf says her marriage cannot be contracted except through her guardian. Mālik and Shāfiʿī assert that a woman can by no means contract herself whether with or without the consent of her guardians (it is they who must do the contracting) nor is she competent to act as a matrimonial agent for anyone . . . if the performance of this contract were in any respect committed to women its end might be defeated (they argue), women being of weak reason and open to flattery and deceit. . . . But an adult virgin may not be forced into marriage against her will.[11]

The marriage of a boy or girl under age by the authority of their paternal kindred is lawful, the Prophet having declared "Marriage is committed to the paternal kindred. . . ."[12]

Marriage without a dower [*mahr:* given to the bride by the groom] is valid . . . but this is contrary to the teaching of Mālik. . . . If a man marry a woman without specifying any dower . . . she is thereby entitled to the (minimum legal dower) *mahr mathl* . . . it shall not consist of less than ten *dirhams* [silver coins]. . . .[13]

If a man have two or more wives, all free women (he must cohabit equally with them) because the Prophet has said "The man who has two wives and who inclines particularly to one of them shall on the day of judgement be paralyzed on one side," and it is recorded by 'A'isha that he made such equal partition of cohabitation among his wives, saying, "O God, I thus make equal partition as to that which is in my power; do not therefore bring me to account for that which is not in my power," (by which he means the affections, these not being optional). . . .[14]

Divorce: The most laudable divorce is where the husband repudiates his wife by a single formula with her term of ritual purity (not during the menstrual period) and leaves her (untouched) to the observance of the *'idda* (period of waiting to ascertain she is not with child). This is held to be most laudable for two reasons: (1) The Companions of the Prophet held this to be a more excellent method. . . . (2) In pursuing this method the husband leaves it within his power to recover his wife without shame by reversing the divorce during her *'idda* (it is final only after three pronouncements); the method is moreover least injurious to the woman, as she remains (married to her husband until after the expiration of the *'idda*). . . . Express divorce is where a husband delivers the sentence in direct and unequivocal terms, as "I have divorced you," or "you are divorced." (To be final, the divorce must be pronounced three times.) This effects a reversible divorce such as leaves it in his power to take her back before the expiration of the *'idda*.[15]

3. *The Ordinance of the Community*

The religious-political disturbances of the first Islamic century all centered on the vital question of who should be the *Khalīfa*, the Prophet's Caliph or successor, or as he is often called, the *Imām*, the "leader" of Muslim religious life. The two terms are used interchangeably, with a few exceptions.

A very important view is that expressed by the Shāfi'ī legist al-Māwardī (died A.H. 450/A.D. 1058). The Caliph is seen as the sole legitimate Muslim authority, and all other authority is legitimatized by delegation of power from him.

In his book on the rules governing the exercise of power al-Māwardī is moved more by theoretical than by practical considerations. The 'Abbāsī Caliph in his days, from being the ruler of a world-wide Muslim empire, had become little more than the prisoner of a Shī'ī Persian family of military dictators, the Buwayhīs, and there were rival Caliphs in Cairo (the Fāṭimīs) and Cordoba (the Spanish Umawīs). Still, al-Māwardī saw his Caliph as the fountainhead of all validly exercised power in Muslim lands.

The *Imāmate* is placed on earth to succeed the Prophet in the duties of defending the Religion and of governing the world (*al-dunyā*). To invest with authority that person in the Community who performs these duties is a religious obligation, according to the Concensus of (*Sunnī*) *'Ulama'*, even though al-Aṣamm (the Mu'tazilī) stands alone against them, and opinions differ as to whether this duty is necessitated by Reason or by Law. One party has held that it is necessitated by Reason, since it pertains to intelligent beings to submit themselves to a leader who will keep them from wronging one another, and will judge between them in their contentions and disputes, so that if there were no supremacy there would be anarchy and men would be a confused rabble. Al-Afwa al-Awdī, the pre-Islamic Arabian poet, has this to say:

> Ill for men is chaos, with no chiefs their own,
> And no chiefs there are, when the ignorant lord it.

According to another party, it is necessitated rather by the Law, which goes beyond Reason: so that Reason would not demand it if the service of God did not demand otherwise, for Reason only demands of intelligent men that they forbid themselves to commit wrongs against each other or cut relations with one another and that they act in accordance with justice, in equality and friendly conduct; to follow their own reason and not the reason of another. However, the Law has come to give jurisdiction to its delegate in the Religion. For God, the Mighty and Glorious, has said: "Oh ye who believe, obey God and obey the Messenger, and those set in authority (*Ūli al-Amr*), among you" (4:58), so that it is a religious obligation for us to obey the ones set in authority among us, and these are the Imāms reigning over us.

Hishām ibn 'Urwa relates on the authority of Abū Ṣālih from Abū Hurayra that the Messenger of God, the benediction of God and peace be upon him, said: "Other rulers will govern you after me. The pious will govern you with his piety, and the libertine with his immorality. Listen to them both, and obey them in everything that conforms with the truth. If they do well, it is to their credit and yours, but if they do evil, it will be to your credit and their discredit." . . .

As for those persons fitted for the Imāmate, the conditions relating to them are seven.

1. Justice, in all its characteristics.

2. Knowledge requisite for independent judgments (*ijtihād*) about revealed and legal matters.
3. Soundness of the senses in hearing, sight, and speech, in a degree to accord with their normal functioning.
4. Soundness of the members from any defect which would prevent freedom of movement and agility.
5. Judgment conducive to the governing of subjects and administering matters of general welfare.
6. Courage and bravery, for protecting Muslim territory and waging the Holy War (*jihād*) against the enemy.
7. Pedigree: he must be of the tribe of Quraysh, since there has come down an explicit statement on this and the concensus has agreed. There is no need to take account of Ḍirār ibn 'Amr, who stood alone when he declared all men eligible. The Prophet said, "The Quraysh have precedence, so do not go before them," and there is no pretext for any disagreement, given this clear statement delivered to us, and no word that one can raise against it.[16]

With time, the Caliphal government at Baghdad was destroyed by the Mongol invasions (1258). Descendants of the 'Abbāsīs were honored with the title and a pension by the Mamlūk Sulṭāns of Cairo (until 1517), as living symbols of Muslim unity in a defunct empire. It was in this context that the great scholar and historian Ibn Khaldūn lived and wrote (born A.H. 732/A.D. 1332, died A.H. 808/A.D. 1406). While his masterpiece, the "Introduction" (*Muqaddima*) to his "History" is not a *fiqh* book, Ibn Khaldūn was a prominent Mālikī professor and judge. His view is a legal one, and has been widely accepted in later times. In effect, he is saying that every ruler who rules Islamically is, in a sense, the successor or Caliph of the Prophet.

The Meaning of the Caliphate: Political laws consider only worldly interests. "They know the outward life of this world" (Qur'ān 30:7). On the other hand, the intention the Lawgiver has concerning mankind is their welfare in the other world. Therefore, it is necessary, as required by the religious law, to cause the mass to act in accordance with the religious laws in all their affairs touching both this world and the other world. The authority to do so was possessed by representatives of the religious law, the prophets. (Later on, it was possessed) by those who took their place, the caliphs.

This makes it clear what the caliphate means. Natural royal authority means to cause the masses to act as required by purpose and desire. Political (royal authority) means to cause the masses to act as required by intellectual (rational) insight into the means of furthering their worldly interests and avoiding anything that is harmful (in that respect). The caliphate means to cause the masses to act as required by religious insight into their interests in the other world as well as in this world. (The worldly interests) have bearing upon (the interests in the other world), since according to the Lawgiver (Muhammad), all worldly conditions are to be considered in their relation to their value for the other world. Thus (the caliphate) in reality substitutes for the Lawgiver (Muhammad), in as much as it serves, like him, to protect the religion and to exercise (political) leadership of the world. This should be understood and be kept in mind in the following discussion. . . .

The institution is called "the caliphate" or "the imāmate." The person in charge is called "the caliph" or "the imām."

In later times he has (also) been called "the sultan," when there were numerous (claimants to the position) or when, in view of the distances (separating different regions) and in disregard of the conditions governing the institution, people were forced to render the oath of allegiance to anybody who seized power.[17]

4. *The Bidding Unto Good* (al-amr bi al-ma'rūf)

The Law orders men to do good and reject what is reprehensible, and it is also obligatory for Muslims to enjoin right behavior on their fellows and deter them from wrong action. This aspect of Islamic ethics (the *ḥisba*) explains a degree of being one's brother's keeper in Islamic civilization that would probably have been regarded as officious in other societies. The following regulations are chosen almost at random.

Of Dhabḥ or ritual slaughter of animals for food: All animals killed for food except fish and locusts must be slain by *dhabḥ*, but when slain by *dhabḥ* they are lawful, as by means of *dhabḥ* the unclean blood is separated from the clean flesh, whence it is that all animals not eatable (such as rats, dogs, and cats) are rendered clean by *dhabḥ* (for medicine, though not for food), except hogs and men. . . .

It is one of the laws of *dhabḥ* that the person who performs it be either a Muslim or a Person of the Book. The *dhabḥ* of a Person of the Book is therefore lawful, (even) though he should not be a subject of a Muslim state, providing however that he has done it in the name of God, for in the Qur'ān we find these words: "The victuals of the People of the Book are lawful for you."

The *dhabḥ* is lawful provided the slayer be acquainted with the form of *tasmīya* or invocation of the name of God, and the method of cutting the veins of the animal, and it signifies not whether the person be a man or a woman, an infant or an idiot, a circumcised person or uncircumcised.

An animal slain by a Zoroastrian is unlawful, because the Prophet has said: "Ye may deal with them as well as with People of the Book, but ye must not marry their women or eat of animals slain by them," and also because a Zoroastrian is a polytheist and does not acknowledge the unity of God.

The *dhabḥ* of an idolator is unlawful, because he does not believe in the prophets. . . .

If the slayer wilfully omit the invocation "in the name of God," the animal is carrion and must not be eaten. If however he omit the invocation through forgetfulness, it is lawful. Al-Shāfi'ī is of the opinion that it is lawful in either case; Mālik, on the contrary, maintains that it is unlawful in both, and Muslims and People of the Book are the same with respect to omission of the invocation. . . . The opinion of al-Shāfi'ī in this particular, is opposite to that of all our sages. . . .[18]

Sacrifice: It is the duty of every free Muslim (male) arrived at the age of maturity to offer a sacrifice on the *'Id al-Qurbān* (tenth of the month of Pilgrimage) if he possesses the requisite amount and is not a traveller . . . in the opinion of al-Shāfi'ī sacrifice is not an indispensable duty but only laudable. . . .

The sacrifice established for one person is a goat and that for seven a cow or camel. . . .

It is lawful for a person who offers a sacrifice either to eat the flesh or to bestow it on whomever he pleases whether rich or poor, and he may also lay it up in store. It is most advisable that the third part of the flesh of a sacrifice be bestowed in charity.[19]

Cultivation of Waste Lands: Whosoever cultivates waste lands with the permission of the Imām obtains a property in them; whereas if a person cultivates them without such permission he does not in that case become a proprietor, according to Abū Ḥanīfa. The two disciples (of Abū Ḥanīfa) maintain that in this case also the cultivator becomes proprietor, because of a saying of the Prophet, "Whoever cultivates waste lands does thereby acquire the property of them."[20]

The Muḥtasib: Growing out of the *ḥisba* is the office of the *muḥtasib*, who in premodern times, though scarcely anywhere today, was custodian of public morals and inspector of markets. The following excerpts are taken from a manual of instruction for *muḥtasibs* written by the Egyptian Shāfi'ī lawyer Ibn al-Ukhūwa (died A.H. 729/A.D. 1329).

Market Regulations: The *muḥtasib* must order (transporters of goods) if they stay long in one place to unload the pack animals, for if the animals stand with loads, it will hurt them, and that is cruelty. The Messenger of God has forbidden cruelty to animals. The *muḥtasib* should order the people of the market to keep it clean of filth which collects in it and will hurt the people . . . and he should allow no one to spy on his neighbors from the roofs or through windows, or men to sit in the paths of women needlessly; whoever does something of this sort must be corrected by the *muḥtasib*. . . .[21]

Money Changers: Earning a living by changing money is a great danger to the religion of him who practices it; indeed there is no preserving his religion for him, except after knowledge of the Law so as to avoid falling into forbidden practices. It is incumbent on the *muḥtasib* to search out their market and to spy on them, and if he finds one of them practising usury or doing something illegal in his money-changing, to punish him. . . .[22]

Barber-Surgeons: . . . They must carry with them tools for circumcision, razor and scissors, for circumcision is a religious obligation for men and for women according to the generality of men of learning. Abū Ḥanīfa says it is confirmed *sunna,* but not obligatory. . . . Our guide is what is related of the Prophet—the blessing of God and peace be on him—when he said to a man who had become a Muslim, "Get rid of the long hair of paganism, and be circumcised," and because also cutting off a part of the body is a part of God's right on us . . . like the cutting off the hand of a thief. If this is established, then circumcision for a man consists of cutting off the foreskin, and for a woman in (clitoral excision: practiced chiefly by Shāfi'ī school). So it is obligatory for men and women to do this for themselves and their children, and if they neglect it, the Imām may force them to do it for it is right and necessary. . . .[23]

Ship-Men: Owners of ships and boats shall be prevented from loading their vessels above the usual load, for fear of sinking. For the same reason the *muḥtasib* must forbid them to sail during windstorms. If they carry women on the same boat with men there must be a partition set between (men and women).

Sellers of Earthenware and Pottery: The sellers of earthenware jars, pots and vessels shall not overlay any that are pierced or cracked with gypsum made into a paste with fat and white of egg and sell them as if they were sound. If vessels of such description are found with one of them, they shall be disciplined so as to deter others like them. . . .[24]

Punishments: Know that the first order of the *ḥisba* is prohibition, the second admonition and the third deterring and restraining. Deterring is for the future, punishment for the past, and restraining for the present and current. It is not for one of the subjects [common people] to do anything more than restrain. . . . What goes beyond stopping illegal acts . . . pertains to the authorities.

Admonition is useless from one who does not admonish himself, and we say that one who knows his words will not be accepted, because the people know of his delinquency, should not undertake the *ḥisba* by admonishing, since there is no good in his admonishment. How shall one who is not himself honest make others honest? . . .

The second stage is putting the fear of God (in the culprit) and threatening him with physical punishment until he is deterred from what he is doing. . . .

The third is reviling him and upbraiding him with rough words, though not (libellously) but with words that do not count as moral excess, such as "Libertine!" "Stupid!" "Ignorant! Will you not fear God?" "Loose of morals!" and that sort of thing, for if he is a libertine he is stupid—if he were not, why would he offend God? . . .[25]

5. *The Rejecting of the Reprehensible* (al-nahī 'an al-munkar)

Among things reprehensible there are degrees: *ḥarām*, which means positively tabu, and *makrūh*, or disapproved.

Prohibited Liquors: [It should be noted that al-Marghinānī, a Hanafī, is taking a particularly liberal view as to what constitutes forbidden beverages, since he indicates that drinks made from honey or grain may legally be considered as falling outside the prohibition on wine. Most lawyers do not agree with him.]

The first of these is *khamr* (wine) meaning, according to Abū Ḥanīfa, the juice of the grape fermented. . . . Others maintain that *khamr* is applicable to whatever is of an inebriating quality, because it is mentioned in the traditions that "Whatever inebriates is *khamr*," and in another tradition "Khamr is produced from two trees, namely the vine and the date-palm. . . ."

Khamr is in itself unlawful whether it be used . . . even in so small a quantity as not to be sufficient to intoxicate; yet the same law does not apply to other things of an inebriating quality, for a little of them, if not sufficient to intoxicate, is not forbidden. Al-Shāfi'ī, indeed, is of the opinion that these are likewise unlawful in any quantity.

Khamr is filth in an extreme degree, in the same manner as urine; for the illegality of it is indisputably proven.

Whosoever maintains *khamr* to be lawful is an infidel (and exposed to the penalty for apostacy), for he rejects incontestable proof.

It cannot constitute property with a Muslim, and if it is destroyed or usurped by any person there is no responsibility. The sale of it is moreover unlawful (for a Muslim, but not for People of the Book). . . . Whoever drinks *khamr* incurs punishment, although he be not intoxicated, for it is said in the traditions, "Let him who drinks *khamr* be whipped, and if he drinks it again, let him be again in the same manner punished." The whole of the Companions are agreed upon this point, and the number of stripes prescribed is eighty. . . .

If a person boil *khamr* until two-thirds of it evaporate, it is not thereby rendered lawful. If, however, a person drink of it after such a process he is not liable to punishment unless he is intoxicated. . . .

Liquor produced by means of honey, wheat, barley, or millet

is lawful, according to Abū Ḥanīfa and Abū Yūsuf, although it be not boiled, provided it not be drunk in a wanton manner. The argument they adduce is the saying of the Prophet, "*Khamr* is the product of these two trees" (meaning the vine and the date-palm). . . . It has likewise been disputed whether a person who gets drunk with any of these liquors is to be punished. Some have said he is not; the learned in the Law, however, have determined otherwise.[26]

Disapproved Things: It is disapproved to distinguish the sentences of the Qur'ān with marks or insert in it the points or short vowels. Nevertheless the learned . . . have said it is proper when done for the use of a non-Arab.

There is no impropriety in a polytheist entering the Inviolate Mosque (at Mecca). Shāfi'ī holds it to be disapproved, and Mālik has said it is improper for such to enter any mosque. The argument of Shāfi'ī . . . is that God says: "Those who associate anyone with God are impure, and must not be permitted to enter the Inviolate Mosque." Another argument (used by Mālik) is that an unbeliever is never free from impurity as he does not perform ablution in such a manner as to work a purification, and an impure man is not allowed to enter (any) mosque. . . . The argument of our (Ḥanafī) doctors on this point is drawn from a tradition that the Prophet lodged several of the tribe of Thaqīf who were unbelievers in his own mosque. As the impurity of an unbeliever lies in his unbelief, he does not thereby defile a mosque.

. . . It is disapproved for a Muslim to keep eunuchs in his service, as the employment of them is a motive with men to reduce others to a like state, a practice which is proscribed in the Law.

. . . There is no impropriety in visiting a Jew or Christian in their illness . . . the Law does not prohibit us from thus consoling them.

. . . It is disapproved to say in a prayer, "I beseech thee, Oh God, by the right of (any person or prophet)," because none of His creatures is possessed of any right with respect to the Creator.

. . . It is disapproved to play at chess, dice, or any other game, for if anything be staked it is gambling, which is expressly prohibited in the Qur'ān; or if on the other hand nothing is hazarded, it is useless and vain. . . . Several of the learned, however, deem the game of chess to be allowed as having a tendency to quicken the understanding. . . .

There is no impropriety in selling the juice of dates or grapes to a person whom the seller may know intends making wine of it, for the evil does not exist in the juice but in the liquor after it has been essentially changed. The case is different with respect to selling arms at a time of tumult, since in that instance the evil is established and exists in the original thing, arms being the instruments of sedition and rebellion.[27]

6. *The Universality of The Law*

Until the nineteenth century A.D. the general tendency of the *'ulamā'* was to expand the practical application of the Law—already in theory eternal and universal—so as to give religious value to every act and aspect of life.

One means of doing this was the legal interpretations of the *muftīs*, the jurisconsults. While the *qāḍī*, or judge, heard cases and administered law, the *muftī* gave his expert opinion only when it was formally requested about some point of law not fully covered by the *fiqh* books. Thus new situations could be met within the framework of the Law. The answer of the *muftī* constituted a *fatwa*, a legal opinion which formed legal precedent and helped determine the practical application of the Law.

The following *fatwas* were given by Ebū Su'ūd (Abū Sa'ūd), the famous *muftī* of Sulayman "The Magnificent" (Ottoman Emperor, A.D. 1520-1566), who was Shaykh-al-

Islam, or Grand Muftī of the empire, from A.D. 1545 to 1574.

In themselves historically interesting, they illustrate the point that within the traditional confines of the Law there is a considerable area for freedom of interpretation. When the ruler could rely on co-operative *'ulamā'*—and due to his control of posts, professorships and fellowships, this was usually possible, after the neo-orthodox Saljūq restoration—this freedom of interpretation could be invoked on behalf of the ruler's interests.

The "People of the Book"—Christians, Jews, Samaritans, Mandaeans, etc.—were permitted to apply their own legal systems in Muslim states, but certain aspects of the Muslim law applied to them as well, especially when they offended against Muslim morality.

In giving his *fatwas*, Ebū Su'ūd is guided by the Ḥanafī School, the official school of the Ottoman Empire.

1. *Question:* When in several Muslim villages there is not a single mosque, and the inhabitants do not perform the congregational prayers, must the authorities force them to build a mosque and punish those who neglect to pray there?
Answer: Yes. In A.H. 940 [A.D. 1533] express edicts were issued for the attention of the local rulers of the Well-protected [Ottoman] Empire, that they compel the inhabitants of such villages to construct mosques and establish regular prayers. They shall proceed accordingly. Ebū Su'ūd wrote as follows, God have mercy on him: "The Call to Prayer is one of the distinguishing characteristics of Islam, so that if the people of a city, town, or village refuse, the Imām should force them, and if they do not do it, he should take up arms against them. And if the people of a town neglect the Call to Prayer, the performance of prayer, and the congregational prayers, he must fight them, for these are earmarks and outward signs of religion."[28]

2. *Question:* One of the conditions of marriage is the *walī* (the

legally empowered representative of the bride), who is a necessary condition for the valid performance of matrimony for minors, mentally-ill women, and slave-women. There is disagreement in the case of a mature free woman of sound mind, as to whether she may independently contract marriage. Abū Sulaymān (the disciple of the Ḥanafī doctor Muhammad al-Shaybānī) reports Shaybānī as holding her marriage null and void. Abū Hafs (also his student), reports him as saying it is permissible if she has no representative, but if she does it depends on his consent; if he permits it takes place; if he refuses the marriage is void, regardless of whether the husband is her equal or not. Is the decision a judge may make on this conflicting evidence effective?
Answer: In the year A.H. 951 [A.D. 1544] the *qāḍīs* were enjoined to accept no marriage contract without the permission of the bride's *walī;* Ebū Su'ud wrote this.

3. *Question:* In the *Muḥīt* (law-book) it says: "A Ḥanafī may reckon by Shāfi'ī law as regards eating hyena-flesh and purposely neglecting to say 'In the name of God!' and a Shāfi'ī may reckon by Ḥanafī law as regards drinking *muthallath* [wine boiled to a third of the original volume: not punishable for Ḥanafīs], and marriage without a *walī.*" Now if the judge says "In this matter the precedents and opinions differ, so I shall follow the other doctrine here; it is permissible to regard her marriage as legal," is his verdict legally valid?
Answer: Since it is illegal, it is certainly not valid. The authority of the *qāḍī* stems from the permission and authority of the holder of caliphal power. Also, the *qāḍīs* have been enjoined to make use of the soundest opinion, so that the option of basing themselves on this legal disagreement is taken from them, especially since the general corruption of our era is obvious (and very few can correctly interpret the Law).

The original of the Imperial Decree is preserved in the Law courts of Istanbul, Pera, and Scutari, forbidding such practices. The corruptness of such practices is clearer than day; if they are followed, the families of certain people will come to ruin![29]

4. *Question:* If the Jew Bakr says to the Christian Bishr, "Your Prophet Jesus (God's blessing be upon him!) was (God forbid!) an illegitimate child," what must be done with the accursed one according to the Law?
Answer: The unbelievers who publicly abuse the prophets (God's blessing be upon them all) shall be put to death; Ebū Su'ūd wrote this.[30]

5. *Question:* If Zayd says "The book *Fuṣūṣ al-Ḥikam* of the *Ṣūfī* Shaykh Ibn al-'Arabī is outside the sublime *Sharī'a* and was composed to misguide people; whoever studies it is a heretic (*mulḥid*)," what should be done with him according to the Law?
Answer: It is well known that this book contains expressions impossible to reconcile correctly with the *Sharī'a;* the false superstition with which certain ignoramuses who are unaware of the procedures of the sublime *Sharī'a* have attempted to reconcile them deserve neither confidence nor respect. There is no doubt that the correct statements found in his book are his own, but as for those which it is impossible to reconcile with the *Sharī'a,* the shaykh's fame as well as his verifiable testimony in his other works testify that they are erroneously ascribed to him. It is well known that a certain Jew interpolated them so as to lead people into error. [This is a fable designed to avoid condemnation of a brother Muslim.]

It is necessary for Muslims to be on guard against them, and an Imperial Prohibition has been issued to that effect. In any case, avoidance is necessary.[31]

CHAPTER FOUR

ṢŪFISM: THE INTERIOR RELIGION OF THE COMMUNITY

Despite the claims of the Law, another aspect of Islam has been almost equally important for the rank and file of the faithful—this is Ṣūfism: mysticism, as it is usually translated.

The Ṣūfīs are those Muslims who have most sought for direct personal experience of the Divine. While some of them have been legalists of the most fundamentalist stamp, their emphasis on direct religious experience has more often led the Ṣūfīs into tension with the legalists, and their attitude toward the Law has ranged from patronizing irony to outright hostility.

The discredit brought upon Ṣūfīsm by its more extravagant adherents has led in most areas of the modern Muslim world to the disrepute and neglect of mysticism, and at times, even to its persecution. It is quite possible that this aspect of Islam is doomed today. But one may doubt it. Proteuslike, Ṣūfism has assumed many forms and guises in the past, and as long as there are lovers of God among the Muslims, there will be those who will respond to the moving testimony of the Ṣūfī saints.

The Ṣūfīs have been the great missionaries of Islam. Their interpretation of what Muhammad brought has proved the most winning to members of alien religious traditions, in India, Anatolia, Africa and Indonesia; and even in those parts of the world longest Muslim, the Ṣūfīs made themselves responsible for the spiritual care of the masses. One eminent scholar even maintains, "It is thanks to its mysticism that Islam is an international and universal religion."[1]

1. *The Ascetics*

The first century of Islam found the Muslims in possession of a great empire, in newly conquered Persia, Mesopotamia, Syria, Egypt and North Africa. The conquered People of the Book were allowed to retain their old religions, with the payment of tribute money, and the conquering Arabs dwelt apart in new garrison-cities, supported by the taxation money and the booty from their continuing campaigns. They surrounded themselves with captive concubines and slaves, and lived on a scale of luxury unknown to their ancestors. There was a strong temptation to regard themselves as a Chosen People, and while some of the conquered adopted Islam, the lack of equality accorded them by the Arabs was a source of constant discontent.

The more pious members of the Community saw this situation with distaste and dismay. They looked back nostalgically to the simplicity of Medina, and felt that the best part of Islam was in danger of being disregarded or wholly lost. As a form of social protest, they clothed themselves in rough wool (*ṣūf*) and held themselves aloof from the *dunyā*, the "lower" material life. They studied the sayings of Muhammad and the lives of the prophets, and they laid the foundations of the Law and the religious sciences of Islam. Many of them found that the ascetic practices of the Syriac Christian monks were congenial to their religious attitudes.

This religious ferment within Islam was particularly strong in the new camp town of Baṣra in Iraq, and no single figure is more typical of it than al-Ḥasan al-Baṣrī (died A.H. 110/A.D. 728), a religious scholar universally revered by later generations. The Ṣūfīs regard him as one of their leading early lights, and he is claimed as well by the lawyers and theologians.

Al-Ḥasan said: "The good things have departed; only the reprehensible remains, and whoever is left among the Muslims is afflicted."

. . . Al-Ḥasan said: "This Believer wakens grieving and goes to bed grieving, and nothing else encompasses him, for he is between two fearful things: between sin which has so passed that he knows not what God will do to him, and between his allotted term which so remains that he knows not what mortal thing may strike him."

. . . Al-Ḥasan said: "The Believer wakens grieving and goes to bed grieving, overturned by his certainty of grief, and there suffices for him the sufficiency of a woman tried by misfortunes: a handful of dates and a drink of water."

. . . Al-Ḥasan preached to his companions, saying: "The lower world is a house whose inmates labor for loss, and only abstention from it makes one happy in it. He who befriends it in desire and love for it will be rendered wretched by it, and his portion with God will be laid waste. It will deliver him to punishments from God for which there is no patience and no enduring. Its worth is small and its pleasure little, and its passing is written upon it. God is the administrator of its legacy, and its people will change for mansions which long ages shall not decay or alter; and the life there shall not pass away so that they die, and however long their halt there grows, they shall not move on. Then beware this dwelling place, for there is no power and no might save in God, and remember the future life. Son of Adam, cut away your anxiety about the lower world."[2]

A brief period of hope appeared when a pious member of the ruling Umawī dynasty came to the Caliphal throne in the new capital of Damascus. This was 'Umar ibn 'Abd-al-'Azīz (ruled A.D. 717–720), whose ascetic friends hailed him as the restorer of true Islam. He fought corruption and chose as his example the righteous first Caliphs, Abū Bakr and 'Umar. He preached conversion to the conquered peoples and offered them equality within the fold, so that they embraced Islam in great numbers. A part of al-Ḥasan's correspondence with him has been preserved.

Beware of this world (*dunyā*) with all wariness; for it is like to a snake, smooth to the touch, but its venom is deadly. . . . The more it pleases thee, the more do thou be wary of it, for the man of this world, whenever he feels secure in any pleasure thereof, the world drives him over into some unpleasantness, and whenever he attains any part of it and squats him down in it, the world turns him upside down. And again beware of this world, for its hopes are lies, its expectations false; its easefulness is all harshness, muddied its limpidity. . . . Even had the Almighty not pronounced upon the world at all or coined for it any similitude . . . yet would the world itself have awakened the slumberer and roused the heedless; how much more then, seeing that God has Himself sent us a warning against it! . . . For this world has neither worth nor weight with God, so slight it is. . . . It was offered to our Prophet, with all its keys and treasures . . . but he refused to accept it, and nothing prevented him from accepting it—for there is naught that can lessen him in God's sight—but he disdained to love what his Creator hated, and to exalt what his Sovereign had debased. As for Muhammad, he bound a stone upon his belly when he was hungry; and as for Moses . . . it is said of him in the stories that God revealed to him, "Moses, when thou seest poverty approaching, say, 'Welcome to the badge of the righteous!' And when thou seest wealth approaching, say, 'Lo! a sin whose punishment has been put on aforetime.' " If thou shouldst wish, thou mightest name as a third the Lord of the Spirit and the Word [Jesus], for in his affair there is a marvel; he used to say, "My daily bread is hunger, my badge is fear, my raiment is wool, my mount is my foot, my lantern at night is the moon, and my fire by day is the sun, and my fruit and fragrant herbs are such things as the earth brings forth for the wild beasts and the cattle. All the night I have nothing, yet there is none richer than I!"[3]

The Ṣūfī name remained long after the woolen habit (*ṣūf*) passed into disuse. Asceticism traveled with the Arabs to the frontiers of their empire, and took root also in Khurasan, the old eastern march provinces of Persia, where Zoroastrianism and Nestorian Christianity met with Central Asian Buddhism. One of the great Khurasanī ascetics was Ibrāhīm ibn Adham, an Arab,[4] whom the legend makes the son of one of the native princes of Balkh. The story of his conversion to asceticism recalls that of Gautama Buddha.

My father was one of the princes of Khurasan, and I was a youth, and rode to the chase. I went out one day on a horse of mine, with my dog along, and raised a hare or fox. While I was chasing it, I heard the voice of an unseen speaker say, "Oh Ibrāhīm, for this wast thou created? Is it this thou wast commanded to do?" I felt dread, and stopped—then I began again, and urged my horse on. Three times it happened, like that. Then I heard the voice—from the horn of my saddle, by God!—saying, "It was not for this thou wast created! It is not this thou wast commanded to perform!" I dismounted then, and came across one of my father's shepherds, and took from him his woolen tunic and put it on. I gave him my mare and all I had with me in exchange, and turned my steps toward Mecca.[5]

He wandered as far as Syria and became a hermit near

the Dead Sea. He is quoted as saying that he learned true knowledge of God (*ma'rifa:* gnosis) from a solitary Syrian monk.[6] As the beggar-prince, he is very popular in Ṣūfī poetry and literature.

A certain man was constantly bewailing his condition and complaining of his poverty. Ibrāhīm ibn Adham said to him: "My son, perhaps you paid but little for your poverty?" "You are talking nonsense," said the man, "you should be ashamed of yourself. Does anyone buy poverty?" Ibrāhīm replied: "For my part, I chose it of my own free will: nay, more; I bought it at the price of this world's sovereignty, and I would buy one instant of this poverty again with a hundred worlds, for every moment it becomes worth yet more to me. . . . Without any doubt, I know the value of poverty, while you remain in ignorance of it. I give thanks for it, while you are ungrateful."[7]

Ibrāhīm is said to have prayed: "O God, Thou knowest that Paradise weighs not with me so much as the wing of a gnat. If Thou befriendest me by Thy recollection, and sustainest me with Thy love, and makest it easy for me to obey Thee, then give Thou Thy Paradise to whomsoever Thou wilt."[8]

Ḥātim al-Aṣamm of Khurasan (died A.H. 237/A.D. 851) was asked, "On what do you base your trust in God?" He replied: "On four principles. I learned that no one can eat my daily bread except me, and quieted myself with this knowledge. I learned that no one performs my acts except me, so I am busy with them; I learned that Death will come suddenly, and so I run to meet him, and I learned that I am never hidden from the eye of God wherever I may be, so I behave modestly before Him."[9]

One of the greatest ascetics of Baṣra was the holy woman Rābi'a al-'Adawīya, a former slave of non-Arab origin who had been trained as a flute player before she turned to the contemplative life. With her, we find fully developed mystical doctrine: the ardent longing of the soul for God, who reveals Himself to those who love Him. She lived until A.H. 185/A.D. 801.

The Ṣūfīs of Baṣra urged Rābi'a to choose a husband from among them, rather than continue to live unmarried. She replied, "Willingly," and asked which of them was most religious. They replied that it was Ḥasan. So she said to him that if he could give her the answer to four questions, she would become his wife.

"What will the Judge of the world say when I die? That I have come forth from the world a Muslim, or an unbeliever?"

Ḥasan answered, "This is among the hidden things known only to God Most High."

Then she said, "When I am put in the grave and Munkar and Nakīr [the angels who question the dead] question me, shall I be able to answer them (satisfactorily) or not?" He replied, "This is also hidden."

"When people are assembled at the Resurrection and the books are distributed, shall I be given mine in my right hand or my left?" . . . "This also is among the hidden things."

Finally she asked, "When mankind is summoned (at the Judgment), some to Paradise and some to Hell, in which group shall I be?" He answered, "This too is hidden, and none knows what is hidden save God—His is the glory and the majesty."

Then she said to him, "Since this is so, and I have these four questions with which to concern myself, how should I need a husband, with whom to be occupied?"[10] [She remained unmarried.]

Rābi'a said, "I saw the Prophet in a dream, and he said to me, 'O Rābi'a, dost thou love me?' I said, 'O Prophet of God, who is there who does not love thee? But my love to God has so possessed me that no place remains for loving or hating any save Him.' "[11]

Rābi'a said, "It is a bad servant who serves God from fear and terror or from the desire of a reward—but there are many of these." They asked her, "Why do you worship God: have you no desire for Paradise?" She replied, "The Neighbor first, and then the House. Is it not enough for me that I am given leave to worship Him? Even if Heaven and Hell were not, does it not behoove us to obey Him? He is worthy of worship without any intermediary (motive)."[12]

It is related that Rābiʿa prayed once, "Oh my God, wilt Thou burn in Hell a heart which loves Thee?" and an unseen voice answered her, "We shall not do thus. Do not think of Us an evil thought!"[13]

It is related of her that at night she would go up to her roof and pray thus:

"Oh my Lord, the stars are shining and the eyes of men are closed, and kings have shut their doors, and every lover is alone with his beloved, and here am I alone with Thee."[14]

The Umawī dynasty was swept away by the ʿAbbāsī revolution (A.H. 132/A.D. 750) and a new capital of the Islamic World Empire rose at Baghdad. One of the figures who bridges the school of Baṣra with that of Baghdad is Ḥārith ibn Aṣad al-Muḥāsibī (died A.H. 234/A.D. 857). For him, asceticism seems only valuable because it purges the soul for its companionship with God.

God has appointed self-mortification for the seekers, for the training of the soul. Men are ignorant of the high station of that one who is preoccupied with his Lord, who is seen to be thinking little of this world, who is humble, fearful, sorrowful, weeping, showing a meek spirit, keeping far from the children of this world, suffering oppression and not seeking revenge, despoiled, yet not seeking requital. He is dishevelled, dusty, shabby, thinking little of what he wears, wounded, alone, a stranger—but if the ignorant were to look upon the heart of that seeker, and see how God has fulfilled in him what He promised of His favor and what He gives him in exchange for that which he renounced of the vain glory of this world and its pleasure, he would desire to be in that one's place, and would realize that it is he, the seeker after God, who is truly rich, and fair to look upon, who tastes delight, who is joyous and happy, for he has attained his desire and has secured that which he sought from his Lord. Let him who wishes to be near to God abandon all that alienates him from God.[15]

Al-Junayd, his pupil, said, "I used often to say to al-Muḥāsibī, 'My solitude has become my consolation, and will you drag me forth to the desert, to the sight of men and the public highways?' And he would say, 'How often will you say "my consolation"; "my solitude"? If half of mankind were to draw near me, I should find no consolation in them, and if the other half stayed far away from me, I should not feel lonely because of their distance from me.' "[16]

2. *The Ecstatics*

In so far as they believe in the *via purgativa*, the purgation of the soul by asceticism, all the Ṣūfīs have been ascetics. But it was early discovered that the mystic underwent emotional transports in which he attained to a heightened awareness of God. These states were in effect a condition of private, personal revelation—the illuminative life. The Ṣūfīs had begun among the Ahl al-Ḥadīth, the early pietists to whom the legalists and religious scholars also trace their origins. But with the third and fourth Islamic centuries, there began a fateful separation. Ṣūfīs of heightened sensitivity fell into ecstatic trances, or were so preoccupied with the contemplation of the Divine Perfection that they felt they had even lost awareness of their own selfhood, and were conscious only of the existence of God. Here their experience, to judge by their accounts, was the "unitive state" attested to by mystics of many religions—

the stage of religious experience where *atman* becomes *brahman*, where the soul feels that it is merged with ultimate reality.

For some Ṣūfīs, the intoxication of the illuminative stage itself became the object of ardent seeking. It was found that the coming of this religious state could be assisted with chanting of the Qur'ān, or music, or the recitation of poetry in which God is addressed as the Eternal Beloved. Al-Muḥāsibī's disciple, Junayd of Baghdad (died A.H. 298/A.D. 910), while he insisted that the goal of the mystic must be God Himself, and not the titillation of the emotions in self-induced ecstacy, nevertheless attests to ecstatic experiences of a high order, as in these verses where he describes his sense of union and separation with God.

> Now I have known, O Lord,
> What lies within my heart;
> In secret, from the world apart
> My tongue hath talked with my Adored.
>
> So in a manner we
> United are, and one;
> Yet otherwise disunion
> Is our estate eternally.
>
> Though from my gaze profound
> Deep awe hath hid Thy Face,
> In wondrous and ecstatic Grace
> I feel Thee touch my inmost ground.[17]

Junayd was also one of the first Ṣūfīs to develop a mystical system, a theosophy. Original, sincere and penetrating, he is one of the great "sober" Ṣūfīs of the conservative type, whose doctrines have proved least offensive to the '*ulamā*'.

The journey from this world to the next [*i.e.* to give up worldly things for spiritual things] is easy for the believer: the journey from the creatures [*i.e.* separation from them and from dependence on them] to the Creator is hard: the journey from the self to God is very hard: and to be able to abide in God is still harder.

Ṣūfism means that God makes you to die to yourself and makes you alive in Him. It is to purify the heart from the recurrence of creaturely temptations, to say farewell to all the natural inclinations, to subdue the qualities which belong to human nature, to keep far from the claims of the senses, to adhere to spiritual qualities, to ascend by means of Divine knowledge, to be occupied with that which is eternally the best, to give wise counsel to all people, faithfully to observe the truth, and to follow the Prophet in respect of the religious law.[18]

Love means that the attributes of the lover are changed into those of the Beloved. Now he lives in accordance with the saying of God: "When I love him, I will be his eye by which he sees and his hearing by which he hears and his hand by which he reaches out."[19]

The characteristic play between the imagery of divine and earthly love, divine and earthly intoxication, begins early in Ṣūfism.

It is told that Abū al-Ḥusayn al-Nūrī came once to Junayd and said, "It has reached me that you talk about everything, so talk about anything you like, and I shall discuss it with you."

Junayd said, "What shall I talk about?" And he said, "About love." Then Junayd said, "I shall tell you an allegory. Once a group of my companions and I were in a walled orchard, and the one who was to come bringing with him some things we needed was detained, so we began to climb the wall, when we became aware of a blind man who had with him a beautiful youth, and the blind man was saying to him, 'You have ordered me to do thus and so, and I have done it. And you have forbidden me such and such, and I have abandoned it, nor do I oppose you in anything you desire; so what more do you wish of me?'

"The youth said, 'I want you to die.' Then the blind man said, 'Why, then, here I die,' and he lay down and covered his face and closed his eyes. I said to my companions, 'This blind man has tried everything—he even makes it appear that he is dead! But death in reality will hardly be possible for him.' Then we climbed down and went out to where he lay and moved him, and lo! He was dead."

Then Nūrī rose and went his way.[20]

Abū Muḥammad al-Jarīrī said: "We once met at Abū Ja'far al-Ḥaffār's, near the Damascus Gate in Baghdad—Junayd and Abū Ṣāliḥ al-Malāmatī and Abū al-'Abbās ibn Masrūq were with us. There was a cantor (*qawwāl*) present, and when the chant began, Abū Ṣāliḥ rose and went into an ecstacy until his knees buckled, whereupon he fell down. Then Ibn Masrūq rose and went into an ecstacy, and then walked off barefoot [compare Exodus 3:5] so Junayd and I remained. I said to him, "Sir, do you feel nothing similar to what happened to them?" He replied, "Thou shalt see the mountains, that thou supposest fixed, passing by like clouds" (Sūra 27:88). Then he said to me, "And you—do you feel nothing at the *samā'*?" I replied, "Oh yes—sometimes I am present with someone I respect and honor, so I control myself, but when I am alone, I release the ecstacy upon my inmost heart, and become ecstatic."[21]

The crisis threatening between the Ṣūfīs and the legalists came with the death of the popular ecstatic Ḥusayn ibn Manṣūr al-Ḥallāj, in A.H. 309/A.D. 922. A younger contemporary of Junayd, and probably his student, Ḥallāj was charged with blasphemy. He chose Jesus as his model among the prophets and (perhaps on the basis of his acquaintance with the Christian scriptures) claimed, "I am the Truth (*Ana al-Ḥaqq*)" (cf. John 14:6). Since *al-Ḥaqq,* the Truth, is one of the names of God, he was accused of claiming divinity. This accusation was apparently supported by his doctrine of the "*unitive life,*" according to which God manifests Himself on earth in His saints, and in the supreme mystical experience permits them a temporary union with Him.[22] These teachings scandalized the conventional, but he refused to recant. He was publicly scourged and crucified, and a wave of persecution of the Ṣūfīs of Baghdad ensued. His image among the later Ṣūfīs is that of a holy martyr, whose only fault was that he could not conceal the secret of existence. In so far as the historical figure is perceptible through the cloud of polemic and legend, he appears as a tragic and misunderstood lover of God, in whom private insight conflicted with the Law. His poems and sayings appear to exonerate him of the charge of self-divinization or pantheism.

> Betwixt me and Thee there lingers an "it is I" that
> torments me.
> Ah, of Thy grace, take this "I" from between us!
>
> I am He whom I love, and He whom I love is I,
> We are two spirits dwelling in one body.
> If thou seest me, thou seest Him,
> And if thou seest Him, thou seest us both.[23]

Ibrāhīm ibn Fātik, his servant, said: "When al-Hallāj was brought to be crucified and saw the cross and the nails . . . he prayed a prayer of two inclinations, and I was standing near him. He recited in the first the Opening of the Qur'ān and the verse 'And we shall try you with something of fear and of hunger.' (Sūra 21:35). In the second he recited the Opening and the verse beginning 'Every soul shall taste of death' (Sūra 29:57). When he was finished he said some words I do not remember, but of what I remember was: '. . . Oh my God, who art revealed in every place and who art not in any place, I beseech Thee by the truth of Thy Divine word which declares that I am, and by the truth of my weak human word which declares that Thou art, sustain me in gratitude for this Thy grace, that Thou didst hide from others what Thou didst reveal to me of the glory of Thy countenance, and didst forbid to them what thou didst permit to me: the sight of things hidden by Thy mystery.

" 'And these Thy servants, who are gathered together to slay me in zeal for Thy religion, seeking Thy favor, forgive them. For if Thou hadst revealed to them that which Thou hast revealed to me, they would not have done that which they have done; hadst Thou withheld from me what Thou hast withheld from them, I should never have been tried with this tribulation. To Thee be praise in all Thou doest; to Thee be praise in whatsoever Thou willest.'

"Then he was silent. The Headsman stepped up and dealt him a smashing blow which broke his nose, and the blood ran onto his white robe. The mystic al-Shiblī, who was in the crowd, cried aloud and rent his garment, and Abū Ḥusayn al-Wasiṭī fell fainting, and so did other famous Ṣūfīs who were there, so that a riot nearly broke out. Then the executioners did their work."[24]

3. *The Antinomians*

Many of the Ṣūfīs who had been sympathetic to Ḥallāj seem to have moved to Khurasan and Transoxania, where the semiautonomous Samānī dynasty had a milder policy toward mystics. Ṣūfīs were chiefly responsible for the conversion of the Central Asiatic Turks to Islam. Characteristic of Khurasanī Ṣūfism was its antinomian tendency—its hostility toward the *'ulamā'*, whom it accused of the "murder of God's lovers"; its separation of faith from works and its hospitality to theosophical ideas common among the extremist Shī'a, or otherwise rejected by orthoprax Muslims. One of the great Khurasanis was Abū Sa'īd ibn Abī Khayr[25] (died A.H. 440/A.D. 1049). We find him living as the abbot of a large urban Ṣūfī monastery, waited on like a sultan by his disciples, accepting with complacency the veneration of the crowds and the reputation of being a miracle worker. He was also apparently willing to hold the doctrine of human divinization attributed to al-Ḥallāj, in a more extravagant interpretation which might have distressed the earlier mystic. He encouraged his Ṣūfīs to dance and feast, and worship God with joyful hearts. Among Persian poets he is perhaps the first to introduce that dexterous juggling with the mundane and the sublime—God and the wine cups—which gives later Persian poetry such extraordinary charm. Some of his *rubā'iyāt*, or quatrains, have proved sufficiently impertinent to be wrongly included among those of 'Umar Khayyām. Of the many *rubā'iyāt* attributed to Abū Sa'īd, the most are perhaps spurious, but they are part of the image of the man. Some of his sayings, like the ones quoted here, reflect ideals thoroughly Islamic, but the same man regarded the Law as bondage, and referred to the *Ka'ba* as "a stone house."[26]

If men wish to draw near to God, they must seek Him in the hearts of men. They should speak well of all men, whether present or absent, and if they themselves seek to be a light to guide others, then like the sun, they must show the same face to all. To bring joy to a single heart is better than to build many shrines for worship, and to enslave one soul by kindness is worth more than the setting free of a thousand slaves.

The (true saint) sits in the midst of his fellow-men, and rises up and eats and sleeps and buys and sells and gives and takes in the bazaars among other people, and marries and has social intercourse with other folk, and never for an instant forgets God.[27]

Quatrains

Thy sinful servant I—Thy mercy, where now?
In my heart darkness lies—Thy comfort, where now?
Obedience can buy Thy Paradise—why, then
A Merchant Thou—Thy goodness, where now?[28]

Long did we rest ere yet the arch of the sphere over the void was flung,
Long ere the azure vaults of the courts of heaven appeared.
In eternal non-being we slept secure and on us was stamped
The seal of Thy love, before we had known what it was to be.[29]

I said to Him: "For whom dost Thy Beauty thus unfold?"
He answered me: "For myself, as I am I was of old.
For lover am I and love and I alone the Beloved,
Mirror and Beauty am I: Me in myself behold."[30]

Till every madrasa and minaret beneath the sun
Lies desolate, the Qalandar's work will not be done.
Not one true Muslim will appear,
Till True Belief and Infidelity are one.[31]

Thy Path, wherein we walk, in every step, is fair.
Meeting with Thee, whatever way we go, is fair.
Whatever eye doth look upon Thy Face, finds Beauty there.
Thy Praise, whatever tongue doth give it Thee, is fair.[32]

Some Ṣūfīs, like the Qalandars named above, Islamic beatniks, violated all the norms of Islamic society. With the passing of time and the social decline of the eighteenth and nineteenth centuries, almost every pervert entered a

Ṣūfī order, and almost every madman was accounted a saint. This was partly because Islam lacks ecclesiastic machinery for defining dogma or casting out heretics; in any case, these abuses have little to do with the intrinsic value of the religious ideas of the Ṣūfīs.

From believing that men may become God, one has not too far to go to believe that everything is God. Pantheistic mysticism has been a constant temptation for the Ṣūfīs, and no one more systematized it than the Spanish Muslim Ṣūfī theosopher Muḥyī al-Dīn ibn al-'Arabī (died A.H. 638/A.D. 1240). He is a complete monist: not only is there no god but God, there is nothing but God, and the world is His outward aspect. His prolific writings swarm with strange expressions and striking images, and had an extraordinary influence on later generations of Muslims; his poetry and imagery left their imprint on Dante and on the Spanish Catholic mystics (*e.g.* Ramon Lull and St. John of the Cross) although they are quite innocent of his pantheism. His doctrines probably influenced the Spanish-Jewish pantheist, Spinoza. But his Ṣūfism was basically antinomian: if everything is somehow God, then evil is only an illusion. This undercuts all Law or religious ethic, and it is not surprising that the *'ulamā'* resisted it stoutly, or that Ṣūfism where most affected by these doctrines tended to lose all moral earnestness and become a speculative system of metaphysics. The following quotation is from the section on Adam, from his famous work *Fuṣūṣ al-Ḥikam:* (Bezels of Wisdom).

When God desired to see the essences of His most beautiful names, whose number is immeasurable—or, if you like, when He desired to see His own essence in one universal Being, who, being endowed with existence would reveal all the Divine Order, so that He might behold His mystery in it (for the vision of oneself is not as when one beholds oneself in another as in a mirror, for then he is self-manifest in a form resulting from the place which he beholds, which is the mirror)—and when he had created the entire world as a fully-formed body without a soul so that it was like an unpolished mirror, and since it is a rule of the Divine Activity to prepare no locus which does not receive a Divine spirit—as explained by His infusing a soul in Adam, which is no less than the actualizing of potentiality possessed by that locus to receive some of the outpouring of the manifesting of the Everlasting, who ever was and ever shall be. . . . Adam became the polish of that mirror, and the spirit of that body.

The Angels became faculties of that form of the world which the Ṣūfīs call "The Cosmic Man" [each man is a microcosm, and the macrocosm is a Man], so that they are to it like the physical and spiritual faculties of the human organism. Each of these faculties is veiled from the others, by its own nature, and can conceive of nothing finer than itself, so that it is its property to hold that it is entitled, in itself, to the high place it has with God. For this is a matter which reflective reason cannot grasp; understanding can come here only by the Divine unveiling. Only by this unveiling can one know the origin of the forms of the World which receive their spirits. This being God named man (*insān*), and viceregent (*khalīfa*) of God . . . he is to God as the pupil of the eye (*insān al-'ayn*); through him God sees His creation and has mercy on it. Thus man is both created accident and eternal principle, being created and immortal, the Word which defines and which comprehends. Through him, all things came to be; he is the bezel-stone of the signet ring, on which is inscribed the sign with which the King seals his treasures. Thus he is the King's viceroy, who bears His seal and safeguards His treasure, and the world shall not cease to be safeguarded so long as the Perfect Man (*insān kāmil*) remains in it. . . .[33]

1. O doves that haunt the *arāk* and *bān* trees, have pity!
   Do not double my woes by your lamentation!

2. Have pity! Do not reveal, by wailing and weeping, my hidden desires and my secret sorrows!

3. I respond to her, at eve and morn, with the plaintive cry of a longing man and the moan of an impassioned lover.

4. The spirits faced one another in the thicket of *ghaḍā* trees and bent their branches towards me, and it (the bending) annihilated me;

5. And they brought me divers sorts of tormenting desire and passion and untried affliction.

6. Who will give me sure promise of Jam' and al-Muḥaṣṣab of Minā? Who of Dhāt al-Athl? Who of Na'mān?

7. They encompass my heart moment after moment, for the sake of love and anguish, and kiss my pillars,

8. Even as the best of mankind [Muhammad] encompassed the Ka'ba, which the evidence of Reason proclaims to be imperfect,

9. And kissed stones therein, although he was a Nāṭiq [prophet]. And what is the rank of the Temple in comparison with the dignity of Man?

10. How often did they vow and swear that they would not change, but one dyed with henna does not keep oaths.

11. And one of the most wonderful things is a veiled gazelle, who points with red finger-tip and winks with eyelids,

12. A gazelle whose pasture is between the breast-bones and the bowels. O marvel! a garden amidst fires!

13. My heart has become capable of every form: it is a pasture of gazelles and a convent for Christian monks,

14. And a temple for idols and the pilgrim's Ka'ba and the tables of the Tora and the book of the Koran.

15. I follow the religion of Love: whatever way Love's camels take, that is my religion and my faith.[34]

God is: there is no existence save His existence. To this the Prophet pointed when he said, "Revile not the world, for the world is God's"—It is related that . . . God said to Moses, "O my servant, I was sick, and thou didst not visit me: I asked help of thee and thou didst not give it to me," and other similar expressions. This means that the existence of the beggar and the sick is His existence. . . .

Just as he who dies the death of the body loses all his attributes, both those worthy of praise and those worthy of condemnation, so in the spiritual death all attributes, both those worthy of praise and those to be condemned, come to an end, and in all the man's states what is Divine comes to take the place of what was mortal. . . . He who knows himself sees his whole existence to be the Divine existence, but does not realize that any change has taken place in his own nature or qualities. For when you know yourself, your "I" ness vanishes and you know that you and God are One and the Same.[35]

4. *The Poets*

Eastern Iran had been hospitable to Ṣūfism, and with the development of Persian vernacular literature from the eleventh century onward, Ṣūfī poets made an immortal contribution to Islamic literature. This was particularly true wherever Persian became the literary language—chiefly those areas where Arabic was not (Persia, Turkey, India, Central Asia), and with the devastation of the Eastern Islamic world by the Mongol invasions of the thirteenth century and the career of Tīmūr (Tamerlane) in the fourteenth this tendency became stronger; Ṣūfism succeeded in offering men a vision of beauty and some consolation in an exceedingly chaotic and cruel time, and some of Persia's greatest poets wrote in the age of the Mongols.

A younger eleventh-century contemporary of Abū Sa'īd ibn Abī Khayr was 'Abdallah al-Anṣārī (died A.H. 481/A.D. 1088), the patron saint of Herat in Khurasan. Pīr-i-Anṣār, as he is better known, composed the earliest Persian devotional poetry known, though not all the verses ascribed to him by later generations are his.

> Thou, Whose breath is sweetest perfume to the
> spent and anguished heart,
> Thy remembrance to Thy lovers bringeth ease for
> every smart.
> Multitudes like Moses, reeling, cry to earth's remotest place
> "*Give me sight,* O Lord," they clamor, seeking to
> behold Thy face.
> Multitudes no man hath numbered, lovers, and
> afflicted all,
> Stumbling on the way of anguish, "Allah, Allah"
> loudly call.
> And the fire of separation sears the heart and burns
> the breast,
> And their eyes are wet with weeping for a love that
> gives not rest.
> "Poverty's my pride!" Thy lovers raise to heaven
> their battle-cry,
> Gladly meeting men's derision, letting all the world
> go by.
> Such a fire of passion's potion Pir-i-Anṣār quaffing
> feels,
> That distraught, like Layla's lover
> through a ruined world he reels.

Oh God, accept my plea,
And to my faults indulgent be.
Oh God, all my days have I spent in vanity,
And against my own body have I wrought iniquity.

Oh God, do Thou bless
for this is not given to any man;
And do Thou caress,
for this no other can.

Oh God, though succory is bitter,
yet in the garden with the rose it blends;
And though ʻAbdallah be a sinner
yet is he among Thy friends.

Oh God, Thou saidst, "Do this," and didst not let me;
Thou badest, "Do this not," and didst permit me.

Small profit was my coming yesterday:
Today life's market's not more thronged or gay.
Tomorrow I shall go unknowing hence.
Far better were it to have stayed away.

Know that God Most High has built an outward Kaʻba out of mud and stone,
And fashioned an inward Kaʻba of heart and soul alone.
The outward Kaʻba Abraham did build,
The inward Kaʻba was as the Lord Almighty willed.

Oh God, in gold and silver the rich take pride:
The poor resign themselves to *We do decide.* (Sūra 43:31)

Oh God, all other men are drunk with wine:
The wine-bearer is my fever.
Their drunkenness lasts but a night,
While mine abides forever.[36]

Farīd al-Dīn ʻAṭṭār: A native of Nishapur, ʻAṭṭār is usually believed to have perished in Genghis Khan's invasion of Khurasan, in A.H. 617/A.D. 1220. He was a druggist, who collected the sayings and teachings of Ṣūfī saints, and is credited with a very considerable literary output. His Persian poems show great story-telling ability, as well as devotion to the memory of al-Ḥallāj and, in common with other later Persian mystic poets, a clear pantheistic bias. It is not always clear how much of this is conviction, and how much poetic license; how much philosophy, and how much edifying literature; the poets and their admirers frequently found it advisable to leave that undefined. The following is the culmination of his long mystical epic, *Manṭiq al-Ṭayr*.

The sun of my Perfection is a Glass
Wherein from *Seeing* into *Being* pass
All who, reflecting as reflected see
Themselves in Me, and Me in them, not Me,
But all of Me that a contracted Eye
Is comprehensive of Infinity.
Not yet *Themselves*; no Selves, but of the All
Fractions, from which they split and whither fall.
As Water lifted from the Deep, again
Falls back in individual Drops of Rain—
Then melts into the Universal Main.
All you have been, and seen, and done, and thought,
Not *You* but *I*, have seen and been and wrought;
I was the Sin that from Myself rebell'd,
I the Remorse that toward Myself compelled:
. . . Sin and Contrition—Retribution owed
And cancelled—Pilgrim, Pilgrimage, and Road,
Was but Myself toward Myself: and your
Arrival but *Myself* at my own Door:
. . . Rays that have wander'd into Darkness wide
Return, and back into your Sun subside.[37]

In this poem, 'Aṭṭār gives a new meaning to the *bilā kayf* of the orthodox—the doctrine that certain mysteries of faith must be accepted "without asking how."

Transcendence

His beauty if it thrill thy heart
If thou a man of passion art
Of time and of eternity,
Of being and non-entity,
    Ask not.

When thou hast passed the bases four,
Behold the sanctuary door;
And having satisfied thine eyes,
What in the sanctuary lies
    Ask not.

The Heavenly Tablet and the Pen
Are certainly thy tongue and brain:
Do thou the pen and tablet know,
But of the Pen and Tablet, O
    Ask not.

Thy breast is the Celestial Throne
And Heav'n the heart that it doth own.
Yet but a cipher are the twain
And what the cipher is, again
    Ask not.

When unto this sublime degree
Thou hast attained, desist to be:
But lost to self in nothingness
And, being not, of more and less
    Ask not.

Be thou a particle of shade
Whereon the sun's light is displayed
And when thou shalt no longer be,

Of happiness and misery
Ask not.

'Aṭṭār, if thou hast truly come
Unto this place, that is thy home,
In thy enjoyment of the Truth
Do thou of anguish and of ruth
Ask not.[38]

Ibn al-Fāriḍ: A contemporary and friend of Ibn al-'Arabi was 'Umar ibn al-Fāriḍ of Cairo (died A.H. 632/A.D. 1235), the greatest mystical poet who wrote in Arabic, the only one who can compare to the great Persian Ṣūfī poets. He was venerated as a saint during his lifetime, and like other mystics is said to have written as the result of ecstatic inspiration. His odes, like those of St. John of the Cross, are tender and rapturous addresses to God as Absolute Beauty; at times, his imagery seems almost Keatsian.

Where eyes encounter souls in battle-fray,
I am the murdered man whom 'twas no crime to slay.
At first look, ere love in me arose,
To that all-glorious beauty I was vowed.
God bless a racked heart crying,
And lids that passion will not let me close
And ribs worn thin,
Their crookedness wellnigh to straightness shaped
By the glow within,
And seas of tears whence I had never 'scaped
But for the fire of sighing!
How sweet are maladies which hide
Me for myself, my loyal proofs to love
Though after woeful eve came woeful dawn,
It could not move
Once to despair my spirit: I never cried
To Agony "begone!"
I yearn to every heart that passion shook

And every tongue that love made voluble,
And every deaf ear stopped against rebuke,
And every lid not dropped in slumbers dull.
Out on a love that hath no melting eyes!
Out on a flame from which no rapture flies!

Though he be gone, mine every limb beholds him
In every charm and grace and loveliness:
In music of the lute and flowing reed
Mingled in consort with melodious airs,
And in green hollows where in cool of eve
Gazelles roam browsing, or at break of morn;
And where the gathered clouds let fall their rain
Upon a flowery carpet woven of blooms;
And where at dawn with softly-trailing skirts
The zephyr brings to me his balm most sweet;
And when in kisses from the flagon's mouth
I suck wine-dew beneath a pleasant shade.[39]

. . . O happy, happy night in which thy vision
I hunted after with my net of waking!
The full moon, being thy copy, represented
To my unslumbering eye thy face's image,
And in such alien form thine apparition
Cooled mine eye's fever: I saw thee, none other,
Thus Abraham of old, the Friend of Allah,
Upturned his eye, what time he scanned the heavens.
Now is the pitchy gloom for us made dazzling,
Since thou thy splendour gav'st me for my guidance;
And when thou from mine eye in outward seeming
Art gone, I cast it inward, there to find thee.
The beauty of all things seen tempted me, saying,
"Enjoy me," but I said "I am beyond thee.
Beguile not me, thyself by my Beloved
Distraught, in whom thou seem'st but an idea.
. . . My heart confessed His love One: then my turning
To thee were dualism, a creed I like not."[40]

Jalāl al-Dīn Rūmī: Rūmī (died 1273), the theologian of Persian poetry, came of an East Persian family which emigrated to Konya, the Saljūq capital of Muslim Anatolia (Rūm), shortly before the Mongol invasions devastated Persia and Iraq. As it passed through Nishapur, the family is said to have visited the aged 'Aṭṭār, who predicted the infant Jalāl al-Dīn's future greatness.

In Konya, Jalāl al-Dīn succeeded his father as professor in a madrasa, or college for training of *'ulamā'*. Already something of a Ṣūfī, he came under the powerful influence of the Ṣūfī Shams al-Dīn Tabrīzī, who visited Konya and who played Socrates to Rūmī's Plato. Rūmī left off teaching and became a changed man. His devotion to this eccentric and enthusiastic friend and master outraged his disciples, and they forced Tabrīzī to leave the city. At the pleading of Rūmī he twice returned, and was finally killed by an angry mob. In acknowledgment of the debt he owed him, Rūmī called his own collection of poems (*Diwān*), *The Diwān of Shams-i-Tabrīz.*

But Rūmī's greatest work is his *Mathnavī*, "The Qur'ān of the Persian Language," a vast poem containing fables, allegories and reflections on Ṣūfī thought. While it has little artistic unity, being apparently written in periods of inspiration over a long space of time, it is a poetic work of unquestioned genius, erudition and deep religious feeling.

Rūmī's disciples formed the Mawlāwī or Mevlevi brotherhood, the "Whirling Dervishes," whose mystical dance in the *samā'*, to recall the order of the heavenly spheres, is a sedate gyrating. Sections of the *Mathnavī* or the *Diwān* such as the superb opening "Song of the Reed Flute," from the *Mathnavī*, which plaintively tells of the soul's longing for God, the Source of its existence, were chanted at these sessions.

Listen to the tale of the reed flute,
Complaining of the pain of separation:
"Since they tore me from the reed-bed,
My laments move man and woman to tears.
O, for a bosom torn like mine with the wound of
severance,
That I may tell it of the pain of longing!
He who is far from his place of origin
Longs for the Day of the Return.
In every company I tell my wailing song.
I have consorted with the unhappy and the joyous;
Each one becomes my friend for his own sake;
None asks the secrets of my heart.
My secret is not far from my plaint,
But eye and ear lack light to discern it."
Body from Soul and Soul from body are not veiled,
Yet to none is it given to see the Soul.
A fire is this noise of the reed-flute!
May whoso has no fire be nought.
The fire of Love has caught the reed;
The ferment of Love has changed the wine.
The reed is comrade to him who has lost his Friend,
Its strains rend the veil from our hearts. . . .
It tells of the mystic path of blood,
It recounts the love of Majnūn for Layla.
In our woe life's days are grown untimely;
My days move hand in hand with anguish.
Though they pass away thus, let them go!
Thou remainest, Incomparable Purity. . . .
Yet he who is raw cannot understand ripeness,
Therefore my words must be brief:
Arise, oh my son, burst thy bonds and be free!
How long wilt thou be fettered with gold and
silver?[41]

From the Diwan of Shams-i-Tabriz

What is to be done, O Moslems? for I do not
recognize myself.
I am neither Christian nor Jew nor Gabr nor
Moslem.
I am not of the East, nor of the West, nor of the
land, nor of the sea;
I am not of Nature's mint, nor of the circling
heavens.
I am not of earth, nor of water, nor of air, nor of
fire;
I am not of the empyrean, nor of the dust, nor of
existence, nor of entity.
I am not of the Kingdom of 'Iraqain, nor of the
country of Khorāsān,
I am not of this world, nor of the next, nor of Para-
dise, nor of hell.
My place is the Placeless, my trace is the Traceless;
'Tis neither body nor soul, for I belong to the soul
of the Beloved.
I have put duality away, I have seen that the two
worlds are one:
One I seek, One I know, One I see, One I call.
*He is the first, He is the last, He is the outward, He
is the inward.*
I know none other except "Yā Hū" [O He!] and
"Yā man Hū."
I am intoxicated with Love's cup; the two worlds
have passed out of my ken.
I have no business save in carouse and revelry.
If once in my life I spent a moment without thee,
From that time and from that hour I repent of my
life.
If once in this world I win a moment with thee;
I will trample on both worlds, I will dance in
triumph forever.

Oh Shamsī Tabrīz, I am so drunken in this world.
That except of drunkenness and revelry I have no
tale to tell.[42]

Up, O ye lovers, and away! 'Tis time to leave the
world for aye.
Hark, loud and clear from heaven the drum of
parting calls—let none delay!
The cameleer hath risen amain, made ready all the
camel train,
And quittance new desires to gain: why sleep ye,
travellers, I pray?
Behind us and before there swells the din of parting
and of bells;
To shoreless Space each moment sails a disem-
bodied spirit away.
From yonder starry lights and through those curtain
awnings darkly blue—
Mysterious figures float in view, all strange and
secret things display.
From this orb, wheeling round its pole, a wondrous
slumber on thee stole:
O weary life that weighest naught, O sleep that on
my soul dost weigh!
O heart, towards thy heart's love wend, and O
friend, fly toward the Friend,
Be watchful, watchman, to the end: drowse seem-
ingly no watchman may.[43]

Jāmī: The Mongols were driven from Iran by the terrible Tīmūr (Tamerlane) in the fourteenth century—a Trans-oxanian Turk who was as great a catastrophe for the Muslim lands he ravaged as the early Mongols had ever been. However, in the fifteenth century his descendants, the Tīmūrī dynasty in Eastern Persia, patronized a brilliant revival of Persian-Islamic culture, the "Tīmūrī Renaissance." One of the chief ornaments of the Tīmūrī court in Herat was the last great mystical poet to write in Persian, Mulla Nūr al-Dīn 'Abd al-Rahmān Jāmī (died A.H. 898/A.D. 1492). By 1507 the wild Uzbeks of Central Asia had destroyed the Tīmūrī power (although a prince of the Tīmūrī line was to found the Great Mughal dynasty of Delhi).

A practicing mystic, deeply influenced by the ideas of Ibn al-'Arabī, Jāmī was also a scholar, a biographer and a poet of great and varied accomplishment.

Notwithstanding his piety and mysticism, Jāmī had a sharp tongue and was ready at repartee. Thus on one occasion he was repeating with fervour the line:

So constantly art thou in my stricken soul and sleepless eye
That whosoever should appear from afar, I should think it was thou.

An irreverent bystander interrupted him with the question, "Suppose it were an ass?" "I should think it was thou," replied Jāmī.[44]

On another occasion, Jāmī thus silenced a poet of the court who had accused his fellow poets of plagiarism.

We poets, Sāgharī maintains,
Steal his ideas and pen them.
It must be true—I've read his poems:
There's not an idea in them.[45]

The following is from his long poem *Yūsuf and Zulaykhā.*

Each speck of matter did He constitute
A mirror, causing each one to reflect
The beauty of His Visage. From the rose
Flashed forth His Beauty, and the nightingale

Beholding it, loved madly. From that Light
The candle drew the lustre which beguiles
The moth to immolation. On the sun
His Beauty shone, and straightway from the wave
The lotus reared its head. Each shining lock
Of Leylā's hair attracted Majnūn's heart
Because some ray divine reflected shone
In her fair face. 'Twas He to Shīrīn's lips
Who lent that sweetness which had power to steal
The heart from Parvīz and from Ferhād life.

His Beauty everywhere doth show itself,
And through the forms of earthly beauties shines
Obscured as through a veil. He did reveal
His face through Joseph's coat, and so destroyed
Zulaykhā's peace. Where'er thou seest a veil,
Beneath that veil He hides. Whatever heart
Doth yield to love, He charms it. In his love
The heart hath life. Longing for Him, the soul
Hath victory. That heart which seems to love
The fair ones of this world, loves Him alone.

Beware! say not, "He is All Beautiful,
And we His lovers." Thou art but the glass,
And He the face confronting it, which casts
Its image on the mirror. He alone
Is manifest, and thou in truth art hid,
Pure Love, like Beauty, coming but from Him,
Reveals itself in thee. If steadfastly
Thou canst regard, thou wilt at length perceive
He is the mirror also—He alike
The Treasure and the Casket. "I" and "Thou"
Have here no place, and are but fantasies
Vain and unreal. Silence! for this tale
Is endless, and no eloquence hath power
To speak of Him. 'Tis best for us to love,
And suffer silently, being as naught.[46]

5. *The Dervishes*

The word *darvīsh* (poor) is simply the Persian for the Arabic *faqīr* (fakir), a word used, along with the North African *marabout,* for Ṣūfī ascetics and mystics. But "dervish" has come to be applied primarily to the adherent of a Ṣūfī order, or *ṭarīqa.*

The earliest Ṣūfī shaykhs had had their circle of disciples, and with the neo-orthodox revival of the eleventh-century Saljūq restoration, the building and endowing of monastic establishments for Ṣūfīs, as well as the orthodox madrasa schools, became a favorite activity of Muslim rulers.

With the thirteenth century A.D. there appeared regular international orders, with daughter chapters, a rule and a prescribed order of *dhikr,* or *samā'.* The first of these was the sober and orthodox Qādirī *ṭarīqa,* founded about A.D. 1200 at Baghdad by 'Abd al-Qādir al-Jīlānī. Others followed: Jalāl al-Dīn Rūmī's Mawlāwī' or Mevlevī order, the Transoxanian Naqshbandīs, with their silent *dhikr* or prayer service, the Shādhilī order of North Africa, the Chishtīya of India, etc.

With the breakdown and transformation of much of organized society following the Mongol invasions, the *ṭarīqas* provided a convenient form of social organization, and undertook such disparate duties as civil defense, public relief and public security. In some areas dervish brotherhoods governed cities, organized revolutions and converted pagan tribes. The brilliant Ṣafavī dynasty of Persia was founded by a family of Ṣūfī shaykhs carried to power in the early sixteenth century by para-military forces organized as a brotherhood among the nomad Turcoman tribes.

At the same time, the orders popularized the teachings of the Ṣūfīs and carried them down to the lowest ranks of the population, though not without some vulgarization and damaging of the original values Ṣūfism had represented, substituting emotional revivalism for interior devotion.

Nevertheless, the *ṭarīqas* deserve great credit: few world religions have tried to teach—or succeeded in teaching—mystical religion to the masses, and the orders provided valuable social services and comforted the common man, besides doing much to color the religious life of later Islam. Professor Gibb puts it succinctly: "Islam in the eighteenth century was like a richly colored tapestry into whose pattern had gone not only Qur'ān and *Ḥadīth*, *shari'ī* puritanism, (non-conformist) *malāmī* ethics, *Hallājī* exaltation, *bāṭinī* (esoteric) interpretation, the monism of Ibn al-'Arabī, the aesthetic sensibility of Rūmī, and the hypnotic or thaumaturgic rituals of the ecstatic orders, but also astrology, divination, wonder-working, and above all, the cult of saints, dead and alive."[47]

Almost every male Muslim belonged to one or more *ṭarīqas*, which took the place of church denomination, social club, Masonic lodge, night school, burial association and marching society. Every guild was affiliated with a *ṭarīqa*, and almost every village supported some resident Ṣūfī holy man.

The core of the *ṭarīqa's* life was the collective *dhikr* at the lodge, or *tekke*, where the dervishes under the leadership of an adept would contemplate, chant or dance in unison until some fell into a trance.

Today these *dhikrs* can still be seen in some areas of the Muslim world; the observer may encounter things which seem to belong in a case book of abnormal psychology, or witness what looks remarkably like demonic possession. But unless he is wholly unsympathetic, he may find also in these sweating ecstatics examples of pure and devoted attendance upon the Holy.

The dervish was not himself an adept, though he might become one; rather, by following the example and practice of the Ṣūfī saints, he attempted to share in their mystical experiences.

While the orders today are everywhere on the retreat, their influence remains. The manuals of prayer used by the humble faithful in all the great centers of Islam today, for instruction in prayer which goes beyond the often mechanical repetition of the official ritual prayers, were once composed for the dervishes.[48]

I have naught but my destitution
To plead for me with Thee.
And in my poverty I put forward that destitution as my plea.
I have no power save to knock at Thy door,
And if I be turned away, at what door shall I knock?
Or on whom shall I call, crying his name,
If Thy generosity is refused to Thy destitute one?
Far be it from Thy generosity to drive the disobedient one to despair!
Generosity is more freehanded than that.
In lowly wretchedness I have come to Thy door,
Knowing that degradation there finds help.
In full abandon I put my trust in Thee,
Stretching out my hands to Thee, a pleading beggar.[49]

[Attributed to 'Abd al-Qādir al-Jīlānī as well as to Abuyad al-Tijānī]

My Master, My Master, if Thou hast shown mercy
to any like me, then be merciful to me. If Thou
hast received any like me, then receive me.
Oh God, Thy pardon of my sin, Thy passing over
my errors, Thy covering of the ugliness of my
doings,
Thy long patience with my many wickednesses
Whether I did them of error or of set purpose, have
Made me ask in hope that to which I have no
right.[50]
['Ali Zayn al-'Abidīn]

O saints of God, lo I am sick, and before you is
medicine and healing.
Then of your favor look on me for treatment, and
grant me of your goodness what is needed.
How many a sick one sought you at your door, and
left it, sickness gone from him in healing.
How many a chronic sufferer have you helped, bed-
ridden, whom your bounty has sufficed.
You are the door, and God is generous.
He then who comes to you finds grace and health.[51]
[Muhammad 'Ali, Muftī al-Jazā'ir]

O Lord of the clear heavens and the light and the
darkness in them;
O Lord of the outspread lands and the creatures
and created things in them:
O Lord of the steadfast mountains:
O Lord of the sweeping winds:
O Lord of the airy clouds balanced between the
heavens and the earth:
O Lord of the stars sent by Thee on their business
and flashing in the air of heaven.[52]
[Prayer for the 27th of Ramadān]

Thy truth, Thy righteousness, Thine excellence, Thy
might, Thy free favor have never failed me for a

moment since Thou didst send me into the abode of experience and reflection and discursive thought, to see what I should bring with me to the lasting abode and the session of the blessed. I am Thy slave: make me, then, to be Thy freedman.[53]

[al-Ḥizb al Sayfī]

O Lord, call down a blessing on Muhammad in the cooing of doves, in the hovering of birds, in the pasturing of cattle, in the excellence of the strong, in the might of the full-grown, in the sleeping of slumberers . . . in the brightening of morning, in the murmur of the winds and in the tramp of cattle, in the girding on of swords and the brandishing of lances and in the health of bodies and spirits.[54]

[al-Ṣalāt li-al-Buṣīrī]

Praise to Thee, glorified be Thy Majesty, while I live, and when I die . . . and when I am brought forth to Thee astounded by the awful cry (calling to) the Assembly, and when I stand dumbfounded in Thy presence at the publishing of the pages of my past life. And when Thou askest me and my very members are witnesses for Thee against me. . . .[55]

[Prayer for the first day of the New Year]

My God and My Lord, eyes are at rest, stars are setting, hushed are the movements of birds in their nests, of monsters in the deep. And Thou art the Just who knoweth no change, The Equity that swerveth not, the Everlasting that passes not away. The doors of kings are locked, watched by their bodyguards; but Thy door is open to him who calls on Thee. My Lord, each lover is now alone with his beloved, and Thou art for me the Beloved.[56]

[Tahārat al-Qulūb]

CHAPTER FIVE

KALĀM: THE STATEMENTS OF THE THEOLOGIANS

The word usually used for scholastic theology—*kalām*—is, like *sharī'a*, the common term for the Law, late in making its appearance. This does not mean that there was no early Islamic theology. Rather, both Law and theology were at first comprised in the term *fiqh* (insight), which embraced right action and right belief. *Fiqh* contrasted with *'ilm* (knowledge), which applied chiefly to the gathering of *Ḥadīth*, biography and history. When it was desirable to make a distinction between *fiqh* as theology and *fiqh* as law, the expressions *fiqh fi-al-dīn* (insight in religion) and *fiqh fi-al-'ilm* (insight in knowledge) were used. The latter term recognizes the close bond between right action—the Law—and *Ḥadīth*, the vehicle of the *sunna*.

The elaboration of theology was greatly accelerated in Islam, as in other religions, by political and social history. During the first two centuries, more than one segment of the Islamic community separated from the main body, at times taking up arms against those who differed. Thus made intensely aware of boundaries, it became necessary for Islamic thinkers to state what the boundaries were.

1. *Abū Ḥanīfa*

We have mentioned earlier that the study of the Law is

more important in Islam than the study of theology. This is true, yet it would appear to be contradicted by the statement below, attributed to Abū Ḥanīfa, that insight in matters of religion is "better" than insight in matters of knowledge. This is to be explained, however, by Abū Hanīfa's *murji'ī* tendency, his reluctance to condemn any professed Muslim—a tendency which led necessarily to a separation of faith and works.

Indeed, such a separation was demanded by the history of early Islam. The Community had had to meet bitter attacks by dissidents, and had also to take cognizance of the fact that within its own ranks there remained self-professed Muslims whose behavior was no credit to it, the Muhammadan Community.

Abū Ḥanīfa was of the party which maintained that if a man called himself a Muslim yet did not behave in an orthoprax or devout fashion, so long as there was any reasonable doubt that he had apostacized he should be left to the judgment of God. (The more extreme proponents of this view (*murji'ism*) went so far as to hold that anyone who called himself a Muslim was saved.) Thus faith and works are in a sense separable, and faith is prior. Abū Ḥanīfa defends this moderate *murji'ism* in the epistle to 'Uthman al-Battī; it is perhaps his only genuine surviving writing. But it is most likely that the creedal statement known as the *Fiqh Akbar I*, the "Greater Fiqh," is also his. It is in the plural "we," indicating that it is a statement on which he and his school agree, and is intended for the guidance of other believers. It affirms predestination (in Article 3) and disavows the position of the Partisans (*Shī'a*) of 'Alī (in Articles 4 and 5), as well as that of the Khārijīs (in Article 1), who held that those who committed a grave sin had apostacized and ceased to be Muslims; it rejects certain other positions. Such a creed, by a revered religious scholar and teacher, had powerful moral authority but nothing, for example, of the power to loose and to bind claimed by the general Councils which formulated the early Christian creeds.

The Fiqh Akbar 1

Article 1. We do not consider anyone to be an infidel on account of sin; nor do we deny his faith.

Article 2. We enjoin what is just and prohibit what is evil.

Article 3. What reaches you could not possibly have missed you; and what misses you could not possibly have reached you.

Article 4. We disavow none of the Companions of the Apostle of Allah; nor do we adhere to any of them exclusively.

Article 5. We leave the question of 'Uthmān and 'Alī to Allah, who knoweth the secret and hidden things.

Article 6. Insight in matters of religion is better than insight in matters of knowledge and law.

Article 7. Difference of opinion in the Community is a token of divine mercy.

Article 8. Whoso believeth all that he is bound to believe, except that he says, I do not know whether Moses and Jesus (peace be upon them) do or do not belong to the Apostles, is an infidel.

Article 9. Whoso sayeth, I do not know whether Allah is in Heaven or on the earth, is an infidel.

Article 10. Whoso sayeth, I do not know (about) the punishment in the tomb, belongeth to the sect of the Jahmites, which goeth to perdition.[1]

The Epistle of Abū Ḥanīfa to 'Uthmān al-Battī

From Abū Ḥanīfa to 'Uthmān al-Battī. Peace be unto you. I extol to you God, than whom there is no other god. As for what follows, I counsel the fear of God and obedience to Him; God suffices as reckoner and compensator. Your letter has reached me, and I have understood your advice in it. You say that you were moved to write it by what I had written to preserve you in the good and to advise you. You mention that it has reached you that I am of the Murji'a, and that I hold a True Believer may err, and that this distresses you, and that there is really no excuse among friends of God for a thing which keeps one apart from God; that there is nothing by which one may be guided in what mere men create and innovate; that moral imperatives (*al-amr*) are only in what the Qur'ān brought and in what Muhammad, on whom be peace and God's blessing, preached and his Companions agreed upon until the people became divided; and that anything beyond this is human innovation and human creation.

Now understand what I am writing to you. Be prudent in your opinion, and take care lest Satan enter upon you; God preserve us both in obedience to Him—we ask the assistance of His mercy for us both. I would inform you that the people were idolators before God, be He Exalted, sent Muhammad, on whom be blessing and peace. Then He sent Muhammad to call them to Islam, and he called them to testify that there is no god but God, the Unique without associate, and to profess what he brought them from God.

He who entered Islam was a Believer, freed of idolatry, and his possessions and blood inviolate, while he was entitled to the rights of a Muslim and the protection of Muslims. One who neglected Islam when called to it became an infidel, free of faith, his possessions and blood lawful to Muslims, from whom nothing could be accepted except his entry into Islam or his death, except for the People of the Book whom God explicitly exempted, who paid tribute-money.

Then the laws (*al-farā'iḍ*) were revealed after this for people who had believed (*ahl al-taṣdīq*), and adoption of them became a work of faith. Thus God says, "Those who have believed and do the good," and "He who believes in God and does good works," and similar expressions in the Qur'ān. Therefore a loss as to works does not involve a loss as to belief, and belief may be attained without any acts. If a loss as to works involved a loss as to belief, one would be taken by a loss in works from the name of faith and its preservation, just as people who lose belief are taken by its loss from the name of faith and its preservation and truth, and revert to their former state of idolatry. One of the ways by which this may be known is the disagreement between act and belief. People do not disagree in belief, and do not excel each other, but they excel each other in acts, and their laws (*farā'iḍ*) differ as well; yet the religion of the People of heaven and the religion of the prophets does not differ. Thus God says, "We have laid down for you as religion what was prescribed for Noah, and what We have revealed to thee, and what We prescribed for Abraham, and Moses, and Jesus." (Sūra 12:13)

Know that guidance in belief in God and His prophet is not like guidance in what is legislated as to acts. And how does this disturb you? You call a man a True Believer for what he believes, and God calls him so in His Book; and you call a man ignorant for what he does *not* know of the laws. He needs only to learn that of which he is ignorant. Shall one who errs in knowledge of God and His prophets be as one who errs about what people learn when they are already True Believers?

God has said in His teaching about the Law: "God explains it unto you for you may err. And God is the Knower of all things." (4:176) And: "If one of you errs, then another one of you will remember. (2:282) And: "I (Moses) did it then, when I was of those who err," (26:20) *i.e.*, among the ignorant. The proof from the Book of God and the *Sunna* for believing this is a thing too clear and too obvious to pose any problem for a man like yourself. Do you not say "a wicked believer," "a sinful believer," "a trespassing believer," "an uncouth believer," "a cruel believer"? Shall one be rightly guided in wickedness or trespass as he is rightly guided in faith?

Or take the speech of the sons of Jacob to our prophet their father, "Lo, thou art in thy old error." (12:95)—Do you think they meant "You are in your old *infidelity*"? God forbid that you should so understand it, who are learned in the Qur'ān. . . .

'Alī was called "Commander of the True Believers," and 'Umar as well—"Commander of the True Believers." Or would you say that means "Commander of those who obey all of the laws"? Again, 'Ali referred to the Muslims of Syria with whom he was at war as "True Believers," in writings on the subject. Or were they rightly guided while he fought them? The Companions of the Messenger of God fought each other (in the civil wars) so both parties could not have been rightly guided in their acts. Who were the oppressors, according to you? By God, I know no sin People of the *Qibla* [those who face Mecca in prayer: Muslims] could commit greater than fighting and shedding the blood of the Companions of Muhammad, on whom be peace and blessing—so what do you call the two factions? They were not both rightly guided: if you assert that, you are guilty of an innovation [heresy]. If you assert they were both in error, you have innovated. If you say one was rightly guided, then what was the other? But if you say "God knows best," you have hit the mark. Understand well what I have written, and know that I say: The People of the *Qibla* are True Believers, and no loss as to act can remove them from Faith.

He who obeys God in all the laws, according to us, is of the People of Paradise. He who leaves both faith and works is an infidel, of the People of the Fire. But one who believes but is guilty of some breach of the laws is a believing sinner, and God will do as He wishes about him: punish him if He wills, and forgive him if He wills.

Also, I say about the disagreements of the Companions of the Messenger of God: God knows best. And I do not think that this is any different from your own opinion about the People of the *Qibla,* for their affair is that of the Companions of the Messenger of God, a matter decided by *Sunna* and *Fiqh.*[2]

2. *Al-Māturīdī*

In the latter part of the second century A.H., there developed a rationalist tendency among some Islamic thinkers —first influenced apparently by Neoplatonic and Aristotelian theological ideas of the Eastern Christians, and later by direct contact with Greek philosophy translated into Arabic—to systematize Islamic religious doctrine. These thinkers called themselves *ahl al-'adl wa al-tawḥīd* (People of the [Divine] Justice and Unity) from two of their most characteristic arguments. God's justice, they held, necessitated that man have free will and moral choice—otherwise God would punish men for His own acts. Moreover, the Divine attributes, such as being on the Throne, seeing and speaking, must be created, otherwise they would be uncreated co-eternal partners with God, destroying His unity. Since God's Word, the Qur'ān, is an aspect of His speaking, it must therefore be created. They bolstered their position with philosophical ideas whose ultimate origins were Greek.

These arguments were wholly unacceptable to the Old Believers, whose spokesmen included Aḥmad ibn Ḥanbal, and who resented what they saw as an attempt to make God conform to the irrelevant ideas of His creatures. They dubbed the rationalists "withdrawers" (Mu'tazila).

Three Caliphs attempted to make the heresy the official school of the empire, but in A.H. 235/A.D. 850, the Caliph al-Mutawakkil decreed the death penalty for any who taught that the Word of God is created—a considerable blow to the Mu'tazila. The attractions of Mu'tazilī rationalism remained strong, however, and with the latter half of the third century A.H. there appeared several champions of the Old Believer position—which in its most intransigent form had refused to allow any place at all to reason, relying exclusively on Qur'ān and *Ḥadīth*—who undertook to defend it with the same logical weapons by which the Mu'tazila had attacked it. Together with the Mu'tazila, they became known as "exponents of *Kalām*" (*mutakallimin*).

One of these champions was the leader of the Ḥanafī school of Samarqand in Transoxania, Abū Manṣūr al-Māturīdī (died A.H. 333/A.D. 944). Few if any of his actual writings have survived, but his teachings and lecture notes were collected and set down by his students. The following selections are from a creed of the school, derived from Māturīdī's teaching, and probably set down one generation later. It contains many propositions found in the brief creed of his master Abū Ḥanīfa, but its far more complex character shows how swiftly Islamic theology had had to develop in the scant two centuries after Abū Ḥanīfa's death.

A Creedal Statement of Al-Māturīdī

1. Those things in which knowledge (*'ilm*) occurs are three: sound perceptions, right intelligence, and information, coming from truthful servants of God. The Sophists held that it does not occur at all, because the data furnished by these sources are self-contradictory; in perception, a squint-eyed man will see one thing as two; as for reason, its activity may hit or miss, while information may be true or false. We reply, we are dealing here with sound perception, so that what you argue is not sound. As to reason, we mean right reason, and as to information, we mean information of the infallible messengers of God, related by consecutive testimony.

2. The World is originated (*muḥdath*), because it is divided into substances and accidents, and accidents are originated, for this is the name given to something which was not, then came to be. Thus we call cloud an occurrence. And substances are never free from accident, so they are also originated, because of their partnership with originated things in existence. If it is established that the World is originated, then it is established that it is occasioned by the action of another than itself, and if it is established that it has a maker, then its maker is eternal, since if he were not eternal he would have to be also originated, and what is originated must necessarily have an originator, and similarly with the second and third events in a regressive causal series, and the causal series cannot be infinite (*wa al-tasalsul bāṭil*).

And according to the materialists the world is originated from Primeval Stuff (*ṭīna qadīma*), that is to say from an eternal source which is matter, for they hold that creation *ex nihilo* (*al-ijād la min aṣl*) is impossible.

3. The Maker must be one, since if there were two they would necessarily either concur or not concur in their creating. Now agreement would be evidence of the weakness of both or either of them, since a free agent does not agree except by compulsion, and if they differed, then either they would each attain their desire—an absurdity— or they would not attain it, which would mean their impotence, and a weakling is not suitable as a Lord. This is taken from God's Word, exalted be He: "If there were gods other than God in heaven or earth, they would both go to ruin." (Sūra 21:22)

The Zoroastrians say that the world had two creators; one of them was good and created good things; he is Yazdān. The other was evil and created harmful things; he is Ahriman. And the creator of evil is purposeless, and not to be connected with Yazdān. We answer that the Creator of evil would only be purposeless if there were no wisdom in His creation (but there is); the least of which is that it brings tyrants low. . . .

8. The Qur'an, the Word of God, is an eternal attribute, subsisting in God's Essence, though not in the form of letters and sounds, and it is one, not divided in sections, neither Arabic nor Syriac, but His creatures express that one attribute with varying expressions, as they do the essence of God, exalted be He. Similarly life, will, and eternal existence, among the attributes of Essence, are expressed with various expressions. The Mu'tazila have held that the Word of God is other than these expressions, and that it is originated, for if it were eternal, then God would eternally have been a Commander and Prohibiter and Informer about non-existent things, and that would be pointless.

We reply, it would only be pointless if, when a command is given, there had to be an immediate response, for priority and posterity are dependent on time and place—and the Word of God is dependent on neither of these.

If it should be said that God—be He exalted—has said, "We have *made* it an Arabic Qur'ān" (Sūra 43:3) and that making is creating, we reply that His word, be He exalted: "They *make* the angels, who are the servants of the Merciful, females" (43:19), does not support them.

The Ash'arīya have said that what is in the text is not the Word of God, but is only an expression of the Word of God, which is an attribute, and the attribute is not to be separated from that to which it is attributed. We say: it *is* the Word of God, but the letters and sounds are created—for we do not say that the Word of God inheres in the text so that there can be any talk of "separating," since when a thing is known with God's knowledge the attribute of knowing is not thereby separated from Him. . . .

14. The sins of man occur by God's will (*irāda*), wish (*mashī'a*), ordinance (*qaḍā'*), and power (*qadr*), but not by His pleasure (*riḍa*), love (*maḥabba*) and command (*amr*), according to His Word, be He exalted: "He whom God wills to send astray, He maketh his bosom close and narrow" (6:125), and His Word:

"Yet ye will nothing, unless God wills it" (76:31). If the creature were able to act by his own will, he could prevail over the will of God—be He exalted. The Mu'tazila have held that God does not will to prevail over man, according to His Word: "I have only created man and the Jinn that they might serve me" (51:57): that is, "I have not created them to disbelieve," so that He does not will it. We reply: the meaning is: He orders them to serve Him—and He has so ordered; its meaning is not: "God does not desire to do injustice to His servants" (40:31). That is true, but there is no discussion of it, and it does not apply here—nor does their saying that in causing sin, God is doing what He himself reprobates; acting lightly. We say to this that it would only be light behavior, if there occurred no proof of God's being free of that. Again, their statement that if God wills sin, man is compelled to commit it, does not apply. Just as man cannot escape God's will, he also cannot escape God's omniscience, and it constitutes no excuse for sin. If they ask "What then does it mean when God says, "Whatever of ill befalls thee it is from thyself' (4:73)?" We answer it means that evil may not be attributed to God outrightly, for considerations of decency, just as one cannot say to God, "O Creator of Swine!" but must be attributed to Him in a general way, as He says: "Say: all comes from God."—(4:78)

15. God created disbelief and willed it, but did not order men to it; rather He ordered the infidel to believe, but did not will it for him. If it should be asked, "Is God's will pleasing to Him or not?", we say it is pleasing. If they then ask, "And why should He punish what pleases Him?" We answer: Rather, He punishes what is *not* pleasing—for His will and providence, and all His attributes, are pleasing to Him, but the act of the unbeliever is *not* pleasing to Him, is hateful to Him, and is punished by Him. . . .

17. A slain man dies in his due term; if he did not, it would mean that God was unable to fulfill his due term, and was ignorant of it. That is infidelity. The Mu'tazila say he does

not die in his due term, because of the (Qur'ānic) necessity for retribution and the payment of compensation. We say these are only necessitated by the act of killing, forbidden by God, and this is part of the general question of the creation of acts. . . .

19. It is not incumbent on God to do what is most salutary for His creatures; we cite: "And we give unbelievers a respite, that they may increase their sins" (3:178). Now a respite to the creature so that he may increase his sins is not what is good for him; though if He did choose to do the most salutary, God would be good and gracious; if He had to, it would invalidate His Word, be He exalted: "God disposes of grace abounding." The Mu'tazila have held that it is incumbent on God, and that He has given as much faith as possible to every man, and as little infidelity, since if He did not, He would be either unjust or ungenerous. . . .

22. According to some, faith and Islam are one, following God's Word, be He exalted: "If anyone desires a religion other than Islam, it will not be accepted of Him" (3:75). According to others, faith and Islam are different, following His Word—be He exalted—"The Beduins say, 'We believe'; say: You have not believed. Say rather, 'We have become Muslims' " (49:14). But the soundest is that which Abū Manṣur al-Māturīdī said, God have mercy on him: "Islam is knowledge of God without modality (*bilā kayf*), and its locus is the breast (*al-ṣadr*). Faith is knowledge of Him in His Godhood, and its locus is the heart (*al-qalb*), inside the breast. Gnosis is knowledge of God in His attributes, and its locus is the inner heart (*al-fu'ād*) inside the heart. True worship of God (*tawḥīd*) is knowledge of God in His Unity, and its locus is the innermost heart (*al-sirr, wa hūwa dākhil al-fu'ād*)." This is the analogy contained in God's word: "The likeness of His light is like a niche in which is a lamp" (24:35). So this is a matter of four knots (*'uqūd*), not one, and there is no contradiction between them. When they are united the sum is a true service of God (*dīnan*).

If a man says, "I do not know who created this world," or "I do not know if prayer is an obligation for me," or "I do not know what an infidel is," or "I do not know what happens to infidels," he becomes an infidel, while any man from the land of the Turks who professes Islam in a general way, and knows nothing of the Religious Laws (*sharā'i'*), nor fulfills any part of them, would still be a True Believer. This indicates the soundness of the faith of the *muqallid* (who believes uncritically), in opposition to the Mu'tazila and the Ash'arīya. What they have taught would imply that God was unwise in the sending of the Prophet (*al-risāla*) for if uncritical belief had not been enough, God's intention would not have been fulfilled. Nonetheless, the stage where one seeks understanding is a higher one, for its faith is more enlightened—as the Prophet, God's benediction and peace be upon him, said: "If the faith of Abū Bakr were weighed against that of all mankind, it would outweigh theirs,"—*i.e.*, as regards its enlightenment (*nūr*), not as regards its quantity, for profession and interior assent do not permit of being greater quantitatively. Now if faith consists of profession and interior assent, then faith is created. Some people have maintained that it is not created, because it occurs by God's assistance (*tawfīq*) which is not created. We reply: No doubt, but thereby the act of the creature still does not become the act of God and it remains a created thing, like fasting and prayer. . . .

27. The obligation to command the good and forbid evil does not obtain for every individual believer in our times, because it (no longer) pertains to equity (*la 'ala wajh al-ḥisba*). Thus it is not permissible for one to rebel with the sword against an unjust ruler, because it leads to mischief and bloodshed. . . .

29. The torments of the grave are a reality, we hold, in opposition to the Mu'tazila and the Jahmīya. They say, "We see and observe that dead bodies do not suffer any suffering by our causing, and similarly in the unseen," and in this connection they also have denied the Praise of God by mineral bodies,

the Scales of Judgment, the Bridge, the Exit of the People of Faith from the Fire and the Ascending Stairway. We say: Reason is weak. The Prophet, God's benediction and peace be upon him, said: "Think about God's creatures, not about their Creator!"—*i.e.* because of the weakness of your intellect. The proof is in God's Word, be He exalted: "We shall chastise them twice"—*i.e.*, in the grave and at the resurrection. Similarly: "Punishments other than those," and again, "We shall make them taste the lower punishments before the greater" (32:21) —*i.e.*, the torment of the grave; (As to their other objections, we cite:) "There is not a thing but hymneth His praise, but you understand not their praise" (17:44); also: "And We set a just balance for the Day of Resurrection" (21:47).

30. People who innovate in religion or do as they please (*ahl-al-bid'a wa-l-ahwā'*) go to Hellfire, in accord with the *Ḥadīth*. . . .

34. It is not permissible to curse Yazid ibn Mu'awiya, because he is a transgressor; perhaps God will forgive him. . . .

36. The miracles (*Karāma*) of the saints are established. As for the objection of the Mu'tazila that if they were possible, human weakness (*'ajz al-nās*) would be unable to distinguish between them and the wonders (*mu'jiza*) of the prophets, we reply: A wonder is what appears at the time of a specific (prophetic) claim, unlike a saint's miracle. Also, their position would lead to denial of the Revelation, where Mary's miracle is mentioned, "Whenever Zacharia entered the sanctuary, he found food with her" (3:38), as well as the miracle of the throne of Bilqīs and the story of 'Umar, God be pleased with him, (how in Mecca he perceived a woman, Sāriya, in difficulties in Persia) and cried "Sāriya! To the mountains! To the mountains!" (and she heard him).

37. Jinns and Mankind are not preserved from mortal sin, except for messengers and prophets, for if they were not so, prophets would not be free of lying. But prophets are not free

of venial sins, so that their intercession will not be weakened, since one who has not been tried cannot pity those who are. The Mu'tazila have held the Prophets preserved from all sin, because they do not admit of any intercession. . . .

39. The errors of the prophets are in the things they did before the revelation, such as the marriage of David to the wife of Uriah, or in leaving the better and inclining to the good, such as Adam's leaving off avoidance of the Prohibited, out of respect for the name of God. [According to one legend, Adam ate the forbidden fruit believing it would bring him eternal life, so that he could remain forever in Paradise.]

41. The especially favored (*khawāṣ*) of Adam's sons, such as the prophets, are nobler than the especially favored of the angels, and the especially favored angels are nobler than ordinary men, while ordinary men are nobler than ordinary angels. As for the Rafiḍīya, they prefer 'Alī to Abū Bakr and the Companions—God be satisfied with them—according to the *Ḥadīth*, that the Prophet said "O God! Bring me the creatures dearest to Thee, to share this fowl with me," and 'Alī came. And also, because he is said to have been bravest of the Companions, the one of them furthest from disbelief, and the one who learned most from the Prophet.

The Sunnīs quote the Prophet, God's benediction and peace be upon him: "Abū Bakr does not surpass the rest of you by much fasting and prayer, but by something which is in his heart."

According to Ibn 'Umar, God be satisfied with him and his father: "We used to say when the Messenger of God was living, the best man of Muhammad's Community is Abū Bakr, then 'Umar, then 'Uthmān, and then 'Alī." As for the *ḥadīth* related about the fowl and the Prophet's praying—God's benediction and peace be upon him—"Bring me the dearest of Thy creatures," if we were to give this due weight, then God should have brought one of His prophets. As for their saying that 'Alī was braver and had learned more, such information would be inaccessible to them. Still, some of the people of the Sunna do prefer 'Alī to 'Uthmān.

'A'isha, God be satisfied with her, was nobler than Fāṭima, God be satisfied with her, because her position was higher with the Prophet. Others have held that Fāṭima was nobler because 'A'isha's rank was only raised due to her proximity to the Prophet —on whom be the benediction of God the Exalted, and peace![3]

3. *Al-Ash'arī*

Among the Shāfi'ī School of Baghdad, Māturīdī's contemporary al-Ash'arī (died A.H. 324/A.D. 935) played the same role Māturīdī had among the Ḥanafīs of Samarqand, and of the two men al-Ash'arī has become the better known. While there were certain disputed questions between the two schools they founded, their aims were basically the same: to refute Mu'tazilī theology and reaffirm the doctrines of the Old Believer Sunnīs with the aid of logical demonstration and philosophic concepts.

Neither Ash'arī nor Māturīdī was the first to thus seek a medial position in the quarrel of the traditionalists and the rationalists: al-Muḥāsibī the mystic had attempted it in the second century A.H. and had been roundly denounced for it by his contemporary Ibn Ḥanbal. But while Muḥāsibī's attempt had been abortive, by the fourth century long debates had helped to prepare a party who would accept a middle way. The core of the fundamentalists, the Ḥanbalīs, remained hostile to this new rationalism and cursed al-Ash'arī, not for his conclusions but for his innovating method.

Nevertheless, with time and official patronage, *kalām* (dialectic theology) became an accepted formulation of Islamic doctrine.

Al-Ash'arī had himself been a Mu'tazilī, the pupil of

al-Jubbā'ī, chief of the Baṣra Mu'tazila. In A.H. 300/A.D. 913, it is said, Ash'arī became convinced that Mu'tazilism could not be reconciled with the sayings of the Prophet, and left the Mu'tazila for the fundamentalists.

Where the Mu'tazila had denied the eternal attributes of God, and had explained as metaphors the references to His face, hands and eyes, and where the Old Believers had insisted that these be taken literally, Ash'arī insisted that God has all these things, but not as men have them; the Qur'ānic references must be accepted, but not in a crudely anthropomorphic sense. The Qur'ān for him is God's uncreated Word, but the writing or sounds by which men have access to it are created things. Man's acts, too, are created by God—but man "acquires" them, by moral responsibility.

In popular legend, al-Ash'arī is usually given credit for "defeating the Mu'tazila." Far from it; the next century was to see gains for them, due to the sympathy of the dictators of the House of Buwayh, who themselves were Shī'īs. Still, al-Ash'arī had founded a school and a method, and with the Saljūq restoration, his school triumphed. The Mu'tazila passed from the scene and their books were burned, but their doctrines have been preserved to a considerable degree among the Shī'ī sects.

To begin with, there are many deviators from the truth among the Mu'tazila and the *ahl al-qadar* [exponents of free will, who believe that men have "power" (*qadr*), to act], whose straying desires have inclined them to the acceptance of the principles (*taqlīd*) of their leaders and their departed forebears; so that they interpret the Qur'ān according to their opinions with an interpretation for which God has neither revealed authority nor shown proof, and which they have not derived from the Apostle of the Lord of the Worlds or from the ancients of the past; and, as a result, they oppose the traditions of the Companions, related on the authority of the Prophet of God, concerning God's visibility to sight, although with regard to it the traditions come from various sources, and the *ḥadīth* upon it have been continuous, and (information) has come down in steady succession.

(1) They deny the intercession of the Apostle of God for sinners, and reject the traditions concerning it that are related on the authority of the ancients of the past. (2) They gainsay the punishment of the grave and the doctrine that the infidels are punished in their graves although the Companions and the Successors have agreed upon this matter unanimously. (3) They maintain the createdness of the Qur'ān; thereby approximating the belief of their brethren among the polytheists, who said, "It is merely the word of a mortal"; and so they think that the Qur'ān is like the word of a mortal. (4) They assert and are convinced that human beings create evil; thereby approximating the belief of the Magians, who assert that there are two creators, one of them creating good and the other creating evil (for the Qadarīya think that God creates good and that Satan creates evil). (5) They think that God may wish what is not, and what He does not wish may be; in disagreement with that upon which the Muslims have unanimously agreed, namely, that what God wishes is, and what He does not wish is not; and contrarily to the words of God "But ye shall not wish except God wish"—He says that we shall not wish a thing unless God has wished that we wish it—and to His words, "If God had wished, they would not have wrangled," and His words, "Had We wished, We had certainly given to every soul its guidance," and His words, "Doer of what He wills," and His statement with reference to Shū'ayb, that he said, "Nor can we return it, except God our Lord wish; our Lord embraceth all things in His ken." Therefore the Apostle of God called them "the Magians [Zoroastrians] of this Community" [according to a spurious *ḥadīth*—Ed.] because they have adopted the religion of the Magians and copied their tenets, and think that there are two creators, the one for

good and the other for evil, just as the Magians think, and that there are evils God does not wish, as the Magians believe. (6) They think that they, and not God, have control over what is hurtful and what is helpful to them, contrarily to the words of God to His Prophet, "Say: I have no control over what may be helpful or hurtful to me, but as God wisheth," and in opposition to the Qur'ān and to that upon which the people of Islam have unanimously agreed. (7) They think that they alone, and not their Lord, have power over their works, and assert that they are independent of God, and attribute to themselves power over that over which they do not attribute power to God, just as the Magians assert that Satan has power over evil that they do not assert God has. Hence they are "the Magians of this Community," since they have adopted the religion of the Magians, hold fast to their beliefs, incline to their errors, cause men to despair of God's mercy and lose their hope of His spirit, and have condemned the disobedient to Hell forever, in disagreement with God's words, "But other than this will He forgive to whom He wishes." (8) They think that he who enters Hell will not come forth from it, in disagreement with the tradition, related on the authority of the Apostle of God, that God will bring forth people out of Hell after they have burned in it and become ashes. (9) They deny that God has a face, notwithstanding His words, "But the face of thy Lord shall abide resplendent with majesty and glory." They deny that He has two hands, notwithstanding His words, "Before him whom I have created with My two hands." They deny that God has an eye, notwithstanding His words, "Under Our eyes it floated on," and His words "That thou mightest be reared in Mine eye." They deny that God has knowledge, notwithstanding His words, "In His knowledge He sent it down." They deny that God has power, notwithstanding His words, "Possessed of might, the Unshaken." (10) They reject the tradition, related on the authority of the Prophet, that God descends each night to the lower heaven, and other traditions among those that the trustworthy have handed down on the authority of God's Apostle. Of like fashion are all the innovators—the Jahmīya, the Murji'a—deviators in their innovations, who dissent from the Book and the *Sunna*, and that upon which the Prophet and his Companions take their stand and the Community have unanimously agreed, as do the Qadarīya, Mu'tazila. . . .[4]

The rational proof of the creation of men's acts is our experience that unbelief is bad, false, vain, inconsistent, and of a certain contrariness, whereas faith is good, toilsome, and painful. Such being the case, unbelief must have a producer who intentionally produces it as unbelief, vain and bad. And its producer can never be the unbeliever, who desires that unbelief be good, right, and true, whereas it is the contrary of that. Likewise faith must have a producer who produces it as it really is, toilsome, painful, and vexatious, and who is not the believer, who, though he strive that faith be contrary to its actual painfulness, toilsomeness, and vexatiousness, has no way to effect that. So if the one who produces unbelief as it really is cannot be the unbeliever, and if the one who produces faith as it really is cannot be the believer, then the intentional producer of both must be God Most High, Lord of the Worlds. For no body can produce them, since bodies can effect nothing in things distinct from themselves.

Question: Why is it that the occurrence of the act which is an acquisition does not prove that it has no agent save God, just as it proves that it has no creator save God?

Answer: That is exactly what we say.

Question: Then why does it not prove that there is no one with power over it save God?

Answer: It has no agent who makes it as it really is save God, and no one with power over it so that it will be as it really is, in the sense that he creates it, save God.[5]

Question: Is God free to inflict pain on infants in the next life?

Answer: God is free to do that, and in doing it He would

be just. Likewise, whenever He inflicts an infinite punishment for a finite sin, and subordinates some living beings to others, God is gracious to some and not to others, and creates men knowing well that they will disbelieve—all that is justice on His part. And it would not be evil on the part of God to create them in the painful punishment and to make it perpetual. Nor would it be evil on His part to punish the believers and to introduce the unbelievers into the Gardens. Our only reason for saying that He will not do that is that He has informed us that He will punish the unbelievers—and He cannot lie when He gives information.

The proof that He is free to do whatever He does is that He is the Supreme Monarch, subject to no one, with no superior over Him who can permit, or command, or chide, or forbid, or prescribe what He shall do and fix bounds for Him. This being so, nothing can be evil on the part of God. For a thing is evil on our part only because we transgress the limit and bound set for us and do what we have no right to do. But since the Creator is subject to no one and bound by no command, nothing can be evil on His part.

Objection: Then lying is evil only because God has declared it to be evil.

Answer: Certainly. And if He declared it to be good, it would be good; and if He commanded it, no one could gainsay Him.[6]

4. *Al-Juwaynī*

In the first part of the fifth A.H./eleventh A.D. century, the Islamic orthodoxy of the 'Abbāsī Empire was everywhere on the defensive, as was the empire itself. There now occurred mass migrations of Central Asiatic Turks into Islamic territory. Fortunately for the settled Muslims, who were unable to effectively resist this virile nomadic people, many of the Turks had already been converted to Islam by Ṣūfīs from Eastern Iran, so that some of them were ready to defend the culture of the settled people against their own tribesmen.

The 'Abbāsī Caliph invited one family of Turkish chiefs, The Saljūqs, to replace the dictatorship of the House of Buwayh, and in 1058 awarded its head the new titles *Sulṭan* (authority) and "King of the East and West." The Sunnīsm of the Saljūqs recommended them to the imperial orthodoxy; they honored the Caliph and kept the nomads in check. Their more troublesome tribesmen they sent to the Northwest Marches, where they made rapid conquests at the expense of the East Christian Byzantine Empire, in what is now Turkey.

Sunnīs, and hospitable to Ṣūfī influence, the Saljūqs at first persecuted as rationalist innovators the followers of al-Ash'arī along with the Mu'tazila. Being themselves illiterate, the Saljūqs were forced to rely heavily on their Persian ministers (*wazīrs*). The greatest of these was the master-statesman Niẓām al-Mulk (died A.H. 485/A.D. 1092) who as regent helped reorganize the crumbling empire politically, militarily, socially and economically. A Shāfi'ī, he supported the Ash'arīya, to enlist their aid in the ideological struggle against the Sunnī Empire's most dangerous foes, the Ismā'īlī Shī'a. The *madrasas* or religious academies he founded also gave the rulers an important method of controlling the religious leaders.

In Nīsāpūr he endowed the Niẓāmīya *madrasa* for the renowned Ash'arī *mutakallim* Abū Ma'ālī 'Abd al-Mālik al-Juwaynī, best known by his title *Imām al-Ḥaramayn* (*Imām* of the Two Holy Places), earned by four years spent teaching with distinction in Mecca and Medina (A.D. 1058–1062) during the early wave of Saljūq persecution of the Ash'arīya in Iran. A very prolific writer of *kalām* and Shāfi'ī *fiqh*, al-Juwaynī died in A.H. 478/A.D. 1085. The following selection is from a creed of his last years, a work dedicated to his patron, the Niẓam al-Mulk.

Prophecy: A group known as the Brahmans believe in the Creator, but deny prophethood. We shall indicate the way in which they delude themselves and answer them briefly and clearly.

Among the things they mention is, that if prophets brought things contrary to reason, they would have to be discarded, and that if they brought what agrees with reason and satisfied it, sending them would be an absurd thing.

We reply: They bring both what reason cannot deny and would not be guided to (independently); provisions of the Law, the Divine promises and threats, on which depend judgments and which reason would not perceive, even though it concurs with all virtuous things. But reason would not concur on all the particulars which the Laws expound.

Thus there is no obstacle in what the prophets bring to what reason makes clear, so that they confirm the data of reason and assist it. (Besides) when one speaks according to the propositions of reason, his words may not be counted as nonsense, even if reason has led to what he is saying. There are (to be sure) in some of the things God has created satisfying proofs as to the existence of the Creator, and none of the wonders of creation may be counted an absurd thing.

Among things the Brahmans say is this: "We find in the laws of your prophets matters permitted and even made obligatory which reason finds hideous, (such as) the sacrificing of animals who have done no harm, and instructions of positions for prostration (in prayer), and running between Safā and Marwa, the fast pace and the pointless throwing of stones."

We shall mention briefly what will cut off this whole argument. We say to the Brahmans: You assert that you have knowledge of the Creator, who acts as He chooses, and then you reject prophethood according to what reason approves and disapproves. All that you call hideous is what He has commanded, and we shall show you the like about the other things God does. As for the sacrifice of animals, God lets them die, occasioning their death, and permits whatever (natural) pains He will. What He does Himself (in nature) is not considered hideous, and it may not be considered hideous when He commands it. As to their disapproving the aspect of a man in the ritual prayers, we say: (Even) if God were to create a man in the attitude of prostration and never enable him to find a rag with which to cover himself, and leave him with his pudenda exposed, God's action could (still) not be disapproved.

Whoever has come this far with us can refute such things as we have mentioned among all the objections they raise, for they have based their whole position on criticizing the acts of God, and as we have said before, one can only criticize the acts of those who are harmed or benefitted thereby—and God is exalted far above that.

So, since we have stated our position and dealt with it in satisfactory terms, if anyone raises objections (to prophethood) which depend on a position similar to theirs, we shall pay no attention to him.

Further, we say that prophethood means that God causes one of His servants to know His order to communicate His message to His servants. This is not a matter which reason finds absurd, so it may be reaffirmed that prophethood is not an absurdity.

We shall now discuss the certification of prophethood and its occurrence, and prophetic wonders and the conditions for them, and then how wonders indicate the truthfulness of the messengers of God, and how a wonder is to be established, and how we may certify the prophethood of our master and lord Muhammad—the benediction of God and peace be upon him.[7]

5. *Al-Ghazālī*

Ash'arī scholasticism won acceptance by the *'ulamā'* in

all but the Ḥanbalī School. While the Turkish Sulṭāns and their Persian *wazīr* were kindly disposed toward Ṣūfīs, and the atmosphere was favorable for rapprochement between the mystics and the legists, the *'ulamā'* maintained an attitude of hostility and suspicion toward the Ṣūfīs. Credit for being the catalyst in the new religious synthesis of the eleventh century A.D. must be given to al-Juwaynī's brilliant pupil, Abū Ḥāmid al-Ghazālī, a man whose intellect, orthodoxy and sincerity were above serious suspicion, and whose arguments were able to disarm hostility. At thirty-three he was appointed by Niẓām al-Mulk as a professor in the Niẓāmīya *madrasa* of Baghdad, teaching Shāfi'ī law and writing polemics against the Ismā'īlīs. Despite his success, he entered a period of profound spiritual crisis, where as he says in his autobiographical work *Deliverance from Error*,[8] "I examined my motive in my work of teaching, and realized that it was not a pure desire for the things of God, but that the impulse moving me was the desire for an influential position and public recognition."[9]

Following a near breakdown in A.H. 488/A.D. 1095, he quit the world to become a wandering Ṣūfī. After eleven years spent in meditation and retirement, he was persuaded by the ruling Sulṭān to teach again, in the Niẓāmīya of Nīsāpūr. The end of his life he spent in retirement with his disciples at a Ṣūfī convent in Tūs, where he died in A.H. 505/A.D. 1111.

He has been regarded as a "Renewer of Islam" and the greatest of its theologians, though not all of the modernists would grant this. In his great work, the *Iḥyā' 'Ulūm al-Dīn* (*The Revivification of the Religious Sciences*) Law and *kalām* are stated in orthodox terms, but reinterpreted with Ṣūfī emphasis on religious experience, sincerity and interior devotion. He actively championed the more sober mysticism of Junayd and al-Muḥāsibī. After Ghazālī, Ṣūfīs and *'ulamā'* drew closer together. While they never fully united, they at least closed ranks against common enemies, and while individuals of one group might remain hostile or unacceptable to the other, each group was now prepared to admit that the other had an important role to fulfill within the Islamic community. Ṣūfīs taught in *madrasas*, and some *'ulamā'* became Ṣūfīs.

Al-Ghazālī's emphasis on direct religious experience as the vital element in religious knowledge led him to criticize the casuistry and authoritarianism of the *fuqahā'*, along with Islamic rationalism. Man's affair was to seek to know God and love Him; intellect's role to know its own limitations in this supremely important task. And in his own highly Aristotelian way he gave to Islamic philosophy, derived from Hellenistic thought and represented by men like al-Fārābī and Ibn Sīnā, a blow from which it was never to recover. It is true, the philosophers' answer to his attack was made in the next century by Ibn Rushd of Spain (Averrhoes, died 1198 A.D.). But by that time, al-Ghazālī's victory had been won.

From the Iḥyā', On the Love of God: Love for God, etc.: Love for God is the furthest reach of all stations, the sum of the highest degrees, and there is no station after that of love, except its fruit and its consequences . . . nor is there any station before love which is not a prelude to it, such as penitence, long-suffering, and asceticism. . . .

Yet some of the *'ulamā'* deny the possibility of love for God, and say that it means nothing more than persevering in obedience to God, be He exalted, while true love of God is impossible except metaphorically or in very unusual circumstances. And, since they deny the possibility of loving God, they also deny any intimacy with Him, or passionate longing for Him, or the delight of confiding in Him, and the other consequences of love. Thus we must of necessity deal with this matter here, and mention in this book the proofs of the Law on love, and propound its reality and its occasioning features. . . .

Whoever loves another than God for other than God's sake does so from ignorance . . . (though to love the Messenger of God is praiseworthy, for it is really loving God) . . . for among men of insight (*baṣā'ir*) there is no true beloved save God most High, and none deserving of love save Him. In order to explain this clearly, we shall turn to the five causes of love which we have mentioned, and we shall show that all of them unite in the truth of God. . . .

As for the first cause of love, it is man's love for himself, and his own permanency, his self-perfection and his continued existence, and man's hatred of perishing and of non-existence, of what diminishes him or destroys his perfection. This is the natural disposition of every living thing, nor can it be imagined that anyone would deviate from it.

Yet this necessarily tends to the deepest love of God, for one who knows himself and knows his Lord knows absolutely that he has no existence of himself, and that his self-existence and continued existence and perfection of existence are all from God and to God and for God, who is his Creator and Sustainer and Perfector. . . . In brief, there is nothing in existence which is self-subsistent, save the Living and Self-sustaining God, in Whom subsist all other things, so that if a knowing man loves himself . . . then of necessity he must love God. . . . If he does not, then it is because of his ignorance of himself and his Lord; for love is the fruit of knowledge. . . .

As for the second cause, it is man's nature to love one who bestows benefits and possessions on him and is kind of speech to him and gives evil to those who are evil to him . . . and if a man had true knowledge, then he would know that his Benefactor is God alone, Whose benefits to all His servants are countless. . . .

Benefits from human beings are not to be imagined, except in a metaphorical way, for the Benefactor is only God. Let us suppose that such and such a man has endowed you with all his treasures and empowered you to dispose of them as you will, and that you then think that these benefits came from that man. That would be a mistake, for the man's good action was only performed by means of himself and his possessions . . . and his motivation to turn them over to you. But who was it who was gracious to His creature, and who created his possessions and his ability to act thus, and who created his will and his motivation? Who caused him to feel affection for you and turn his face upon you? Had it not been for all this, he would not have given you a single grain of his wealth. And inasmuch as it was God who empowered his motives . . . he was overcome and compelled to give his wealth to you, for he was unable to oppose Him. So the Benefactor was He who compelled him for you and employed him. . . . The owner of the hand (which gave) was compelled with the compulsion of a water channel to let water run in it, so that if you believe him to be the benefactor, or thanked him as other than the means, you would be ignorant of the truth of the matter. For doing good cannot be expected of a man, except to himself; as for doing good to someone else, that is impossible for created beings, for they will not give up something that is theirs, except for some selfish motive. . . . A knowing man will not love any but God for doing good, for He alone is worthy of that.

As for the third cause, it is love of a benefactor for himself, even when he does not bring you any benefit, and this love is natural—for if information reached you of a king who was pious, just, wise, gentle with people and kindly to them . . . in a far country, and news reached you of another king, who was cruel, arrogant, corrupt, shameless and wicked . . . you would find in your heart an inclination toward the first which was love, and a repugnance for the second which was hate, and (the first emotion) is love of a benefactor simply because he is good, and not because he is good *to you*. This also necessitates the love of God—nay, it necessitates loving none but God . . . for only He is truly good.

As for the fourth reason, it is to love every beautiful thing for its own beauty, and not for any satisfaction which can come from it. . . . Beauty can be external beauty, which is perceived with the eye of the head, or it may be interior beauty, which is perceived with the eye of the heart. The first sort may be perceived by children or beasts; to perceive the second sort is the special property of men of heart, and none may share in it who know only the life of the lower world. All beauty is beloved by a perceiver of beauty, and if he perceives it with his heart, it becomes his heart's beloved. . . .

So then, what is beautiful is to be loved, and the Absolutely Beautiful is the One, who has no equal; the Unique, who has no opposite, the Eternal, who has no similitude; the Rich, who has no need; the Omnipotent, who does as He wishes, and judges as He will. . . .

As for the fifth cause, it is love for what is related and similar . . . for like inclines to like . . . as experience, report, and history all testify. This too necessitates loving God, because of the inner similarity, which does not go back to resemblances of feature or form, but to inner significance, some of whose meanings we may mention in books, and some of which it is not permissible to write, but which must rather be left under a covering of dust until the traveller stumbles upon them in his path. . . .

What may be mentioned is the nearness of the servant to his Lord in attributes which call for imitation, and patterning himself on the character of the Lord . . . such attributes as knowledge, piety, goodness, kindness, and spreading mercy and good among God's creatures. . . .

As for the things it is not permissible to write in books, they pertain to that special relation of the human (to the Divine) to which God has alluded with His word, be He exalted: "They will ask thee about the spirit; say 'The spirit is a matter for my Lord' " (17:25), since He has thus revealed that it is a Divine matter beyond the bound of created reason. Clearer than this is His word: "When I have shaped man, and breathed My spirit into him, fall you down, and bow before him!" (15:29) And for that the angels prostrated themselves to Adam. And He indicates it again with his word: "We have made thee a vice-regent on the earth" (38:26), which Adam would never have merited except for that relationship, which the Prophet has hinted at in his saying, "God created man in His own image." . . . And this is the greatest of the reasons of Love, and the remotest and rarest of them all . . . and thus the reasonable and accepted view among people of insight is that God alone is worthy of true love. . . .[10]

On the Philosophers: Logic: Nothing in logic is relevant to religion by way of denial or affirmation. Logic is the study of the methods of demonstration and of forming syllogisms. . . . There is nothing here which requires to be denied. Matters of this kind are usually mentioned by the theologians and speculative thinkers in connection with the topic of demonstrations . . . an example of this is their proposition . . . "If it is true that all men are animals, then it follows that some animals are men." They express this by saying that "The universal affirmative proposition has as its converse a particular affirmative proposition." What connection has this with the essentials of religion, that it should be denied or rejected? If such a denial is made, the only effect upon the logicians is to impair their belief in the intelligence of the man who made the denial, and, what is worse, in his religion, inasmuch as they consider that it rests on such denials.

(However), there is a type of mistake into which students of logic are liable to fall. . . . When they come at length to treat of religious questions, not merely are they unable to satisfy (their own) conditions (of demonstration), but they admit an extreme degree of relaxation (of their standards of proof).

Natural Science or Physics: . . . Just as it is not a condition of religion to reject medical science, so likewise the rejection of natural science is not one of its conditions, except with regard to particular points which I enumerate in my book, *The In-*

coherence of the Philosophers. The basis of all these objections is the recognition that nature is in subjection to God most high, not acting of itself but serving as an instrument in the hands of its Creator. Sun and moon, stars and elements, are in subjection to His command. There is none of them whose activity is produced by or proceeds from its own essence.

Theology or Metaphysics: Here occur most of the errors of the philosophers. They are unable to satisfy the conditions of proof they lay down in logic, and consequently differ much from one another here. The views of Aristotle, as expounded by al-Fārābī and Ibn-Sīnā (Avicenna), are close to those of the Islamic writers. All their errors are comprised under twenty heads, on three of which they must be reckoned infidels and on seventeen heretics . . . the three points in which they differ from all Muslims are as follows:

a. They say that for bodies there is no resurrection; it is bare spirits which are rewarded or punished, and the rewards and punishments are spiritual, not bodily. . . . These exist, as well, but they speak falsely in denying the bodily punishments and in their pronouncements disbelieve the Divine Law.

b. They believe that God knows universals but not particulars. This too is plain unbelief. The truth is that "There does not escape Him the weight of an atom in the heavens or in the earth." (Sūra 34:3)

c. They say that the (cosmos) is everlasting, without beginning or end. But no Muslim has adopted any such view on this question.

On the further points . . . their doctrine approximates that of the Mu'tazila; and the Mu'tazila must not be accounted infidels because of such matters (but heretics).

. . . It is customary with weaker intellects thus, to take the men as criterion of the truth and not the truth as criterion of the men. The intelligent man follows 'Ali (God be pleased with him) when he said, "Do not know the truth by the men, but know the truth, and then you will know who are truthful." The intelligent man knows the truth; then he examines the particular assertion. If it is true, than he accepts it, whether the speaker is a truthful man or not . . . for he knows that gold is found in gravel with dross.[11]

The following is from a popular creed designed by al-Ghazālī in the *Iḥyā'* to be learned, like catechism, by children. While it is only the statement of one authority, it is interesting as showing what the *'ulamā'* of his time thought it appropriate for the common people to know of doctrine. This section deals with eschatology.

(And we witness) . . . that God would not accept the faith of a creature, so long as he did not believe in that which the Prophet narrated concerning things after death. The first of that is the question of Munkar and Nakīr; these are two awful and terrible beings who will cause the creature to sit up in his grave, complete, body and soul; and they will ask him, "Who is thy Lord, and what is thy religion, and who is thy Prophet?" They are the two testers in the grave and their questioning is the first testing after death. And that he should believe in the punishment of the grave—that it is a verity, and that its judgment upon the body and soul is just, according to what God wills. And that he should believe in the Balance. . . . In it, deeds are weighed by the power of God most High; and its weights on that day will be of the weight of motes and mustard seeds. . . . And that he should believe that the Bridge is a Verity; it is a bridge stretched over the back of Hell, sharper than a sword and finer than a hair. The feet of the unbelievers slip upon it, by the decree of God, and fall with them into the Fire. But the feet of believers stand firm upon it, by the grace of God, and so they pass into the Abiding Abode. And that he should believe in the Tank to which the people shall go down, the Tank of

Muhammad, from which the believers shall drink before entering the Garden and after passing the Bridge. Whoever drinks of it a single draught will never thirst again thereafter. Its breadth is a journey of a month; its water is whiter than milk and sweeter than honey; around it are ewers in numbers like the stars of heaven; into it flow two canals from the Spring of *al-Kawthar*. And that he should believe in the Reckoning and the distinctions between men in it; him with whom it will go hard in the Reckoning and him to whom compassion will be shown therein, and him who enters the Garden without any reckoning. . . . And that the attestors of God's Unity will be brought forth from the Fire, after vengeance has been taken on them, so that there will not remain in Hell an attestor of God's Unity. And . . . the intercession of the prophets, next of the *'ulamā'*, next of the martyrs, next of the believers—each according to his rank and dignity with God most high. And he who remains from the believers, and has no intercessor, shall be brought forth of the grace of God . . . so there shall not abide eternally in the Fire a single believer, but whoever has in his heart the weight of a single grain of faith shall be brought forth therefrom. . . .[12]

6. *Ibn Taymīya*

The fate of one who resisted the new synthesis of Sunnīsm, Ṣūfism and Scholasticism in which al-Ghazālī had played such an important role is illustrated by the career of Taqī al-Dīn Aḥmad ibn Taymīya (died A.H. 728/A.D. 1328), a Ḥanbalī of Damascus in the Mamlūk Sultanate, following the Mongol invasions of Iran and Iraq.

The Ḥanbalī School, or at least its right wing, had remained aloof from the rationalism of the Mutakallimīn, and Ibn Taymīya came from a family of old Ḥanbalī traditions. At the same time, he considered himself a *mujtahid*, a doctor of the school with a right to form independent judgments from first principles—and this at a time when most of the *'ulamā'* held that the "doors of interpretation" (*ijtihād*) were closed.

He abominated the subservience of the *'ulamā'* of his time, and the growing cult of saints; he held that to make a special visit even to the tomb of the Prophet, let alone some dead Ṣūfī, was an idolatrous innovation. Most of his writings are in the form of controversial tracts attacking the accepted order of things.

Such a man was almost predestined for prison. He spent years in the fortresses of Damascus, Cairo and Alexandria, for intemperate statements about the Ash'arīya, and for Ḥanbalī statements on the nature of God which smacked of the deprecable old anthropomorphism of that school. And he used his confinement to turn out more works attacking and refuting his detractors, until they had him deprived of ink and paper. The blow is said to have killed him within a month.

By school and by conviction, he is a fundamentalist, calling for return to the Qur'ān and the *Sunna*, attacking innovation. But his position is skillfully argued and defended, and at all times his preoccupation is to resuscitate the moral dynamism of Islam. This, and not scholastic argument, is his real concern, skillful polemicist though he was. The earnestness, the conviction of the early Ṣūfīs is his too, and he approves them in his writings. But he sounds always a few leading ideas: God, despite the reality of His attributes, is far above anything man can conceive; *mysterium tremendum.* Contrary to the philosophers, the Ṣūfīs and al-Ghazālī, man's purpose is not to know Him, but to obey Him. Concern with obedience leads him also to a viewpoint less deterministic than the Ash'arīya.

Hence Ibn Taymīya's importance for the Muslim modernists. Almost disregarded in his own days as a crank, he has become the inspiration of the revivalists. His doctrines were behind the rise of the Wahhabi movement which began in the mid-eighteenth century in Arabia and has brought the House of Sa'ūd to power, and they have guided the modern Azharīs, the Salafīya and the Muslim brotherhood. One reason for this is that many modern Muslims see their society as marred today by traditionally sanctioned "backwardness" and superstition. Ibn Taymīya's independence of approach in religious questions sweeps away medieval accretions, whether gracious or graceless. In the following, by restricting *ijmā'* (Consensus, the practice of the Community historically accepted) to only such matters as may be textually backed by Qur'ān or approved *Ḥadīth*, he blandly cuts the nerves of the whole Islamic establishment of his time.

Consensus: The Ṣūfīs have built their doctrine on desire (*al-irāda*) and that is indispensable—but on the condition that it is the desire to serve God alone in what He has commanded. The exponents of *kalām* have built their doctrine on reason, which leads to knowledge, and it is also indispensable—providing that it is knowledge of those things about which the Messenger has informed us, and reasoning about the sure things which he indicated—Divine Revelation. Both of these conditions are indispensable (to right use of desire and knowledge).

Whoever seeks knowledge without desire, or desire without knowledge is in error, and whoever seeks them both without following the Prophet is also in error.

Desire is only profitable if it is the desire to serve God according to the Law He laid down, not with heretical innovation.[13]

It is similar with those who part with the Prophet and follow a way other than that of the believers. Whoever parts with him does not follow their way—and this is obvious. And whoever has followed another way has separated from the Prophet, and exposed himself to the Divine Threat (*wa'īd*). Whoever departs from the consensus of the Muslims has followed another way absolutely, and accordingly exposed himself to the Divine Threat. If it says they are only to blame if they separate from the way of the Prophet, we reply: The two things are bound together, because everything in which Muslims agree must be backed by texts from the Messenger of God, so that whoever opposes them opposes the Messenger, and whoever opposes the Messenger opposes God. It necessarily follows that everything the Muslims agree on was clearly revealed through the Messenger, and that is the truth.

So there is absolutely no question on which they unite which has not been clearly demonstrated by the Messenger, but this has escaped some people, and they know of Consensus and point to it as one would point to a text, without knowing the text. Consensus is a second proof added to the text, like an example. Whatever Consensus indicates is indicated by the Book and the Sunna. All that the Qur'ān indicates also came from the Prophet, since the Qur'ān and the Sunna both came through him, so there can be no question on which Muslims agree not based on a text.

The Companions had an understanding of the Qur'ān hidden from the moderns . . . who now seek for precepts in what they believe about Consensus and Logical Analogy (*qiyās*). Whatever modern says that Consensus is the basis of the greater part of the Law has given himself away, for it is lack of knowledge of the Book and the Sunna which obliges him to say it. Similarly when they hold that new events require use of logical analogy for interpretation, because there is no indication in the texts—that is only the statement of one who has no knowledge of Book or Sunna, with their clear rules for making all judgments. . . .

It is often, or even usually, impossible to know what is Consensus—for who can encompass all the opinions of all religious experts (*mujtahidīn*)? Quite the contrary with the texts; knowledge of these is possible, and easy by comparison. The ancients (*salaf*) judged by the Book first, since the Sunna would not contradict the Qur'ān . . . if there is anything abrogated in the Qur'ān, the abrogation is written there. . . . If an answer is not found in the Qur'ān, one should look in the Sunna, and . . . there is nothing there which is abrogated, by Consensus or anything else . . . for true Consensus cannot contradict the Qur'an and the Sunna.[14]

The Necessity of the Legal Punishments (Ḥudūd): It is not permissible when guilt is established by proof or by witness to suspend the legal punishment, either by remitting it or by substituting a fine or any other thing: the hand (of a thief) must be cut off, for the application of the punishments is one of the acts of cult (*'ibādāt*), like the Holy War in the Way of God, and it must be kept in mind that the application of legal sanctions is one of the acts of God's mercy, so that the ruler must be strict by applying it and let no compassion deter or delay him in the observance of God's religion. Let his goal be to have mercy on God's creatures by deterring men from things rejected by God, and not to discharge his wrath or gratify his desire for power.[15]

The Ḥisba: To bid to good and reject the reprehended is not obligatory on every individual in essence, but is to be carried out as far as is possible, and since the Holy War is its completion, it is exactly like the Holy War. Any man who performs his (other) duties and does not fight the Holy War sins; and every one must act according to his ability, as the Prophet said: "Whoever sees something reprehensible, let him change it with his own hand, and if he is unable, with his tongue, and if he is unable to do that, in his heart."

So if it is thus, it is known that the bidding to good and the rejection of the reprehended, together with its completion, the Holy War, is one of the most important things we are ordered to perform.[16]

Pantheists: God—praises be to Him—is not His own creature, and not a part of His creation or an attribute of it. He is the

Praised and Exalted, set apart in His holy Existence, aloof in His glorious Selfhood from all things He has created, and that is what the Books (of the Prophets) have brought . . . and thus God has created His servants, and thus reason attests.

Often have I thought that the appearance of such as these [pantheist Ṣūfīs] is the chief cause for the appearance of the Mongol Tatars and the disappearance of the Law of Islam, and that they are the vanguard of Antichrist the One-eyed, the Great Liar who shall assert that he is God.[17]

On Philosophy and al-Ghazālī: According to the so-called philosophers, there are three kinds of happiness; sensual, imaginative, and intellectual which is knowledge. . . . Thus they hold that the happiness of the soul consists in the knowledge of eternal things . . . then they imagine that the heavens . . . (are eternal) and that the soul acquires happiness through knowing them.

Abū Ḥāmid (al-Ghazālī) in his works like the *Miʿrāj al-Sālikīn* also suggests this. His statements are a bridge between the Muslims and the philosophers. . . . This is why in his works like the *Iḥyā'* he teaches that the goal of all action is only knowledge, which is also the essence of the philosopher's teaching. He magnifies the renunciation of the world which (preoccupies him more) than *tawḥīd,* which is serving God alone. *Tawḥīd* alone comprises true love of God. . . .

These so-called philosophers magnify the separation of the soul from the material body, which means renunciation of physical desires and of the world. . . . In pursuance of this, Abū Ḥāmid has divided the mystic path into three stages. . . . What he has made the goal of human life, *viz.* the knowledge of God, His attributes, His actions, and angels, in his *Al-Maḍnūn*—which is pure philosophy—is worse than the beliefs of the (old) idolatrous Arabs, let alone of Jews and Christians.[18]

CHAPTER SIX

THE DISSIDENTS OF THE COMMUNITY

Thus far we have dealt with the main body of Muslims, the Sunnīs, or traditionalists. Local and school differences may exist among them with no impairment to their basic conviction that they form one religious community.

However, there exist also among the "People of the *Qibla*" (those who turn toward Mecca) dissident sects who feel that they are set apart from all other Muslims, and who regard the Sunnīs as heretics, or even infidels.

To understand these sects, it is necessary to return to the early days of Islam. The second Caliph, 'Umar, was struck down in the Mosque by a Persian slave bent on avenging the conquest of his people (A.D. 644). The six most distinguished Companions of the Prophet then met to elect one of themselves Caliph. The choice narrowed to 'Alī, the Prophet's cousin, husband of his daughter and father of his grandchildren; and to 'Uthmān, an early convert from the clan of Umayya, the aristocratic Qurayshī family which had led the opposition to the Prophet in Mecca. 'Uthmān had also married a daughter of the Prophet. The other four finally decided upon 'Uthmān, and 'Alī's friends bitterly denounced the "conspiracy" to withhold allegiance from the Prophet's own family.

'Uthmān was personally pious, but it was felt that his family, the Umawīs, had entirely too much influence with him. He gave them high posts, and seemed unwilling to notice their corrupt dealings. He lived more luxuriously than his predecessors, and he allowed his family and the chief Companions to become owners of vast private properties in the conquered lands. At the same time, he antagonized many of the Companions. Discontent grew in the camp cities, where it was felt that all spoils and revenues of the conquests should be divided equally among the community. ʻAlī was known to share this view.

In ʻUthmān's eleventh year as Caliph, an army rebellion demanded his abdication. When he refused, even after being blockaded in his palace, murderers burst in and hacked him to death. The insurgents and two of the chief Companions, Ṭalḥa and Zubayr, then prevailed upon ʻAlī to accept the Caliphate.

Since the murder of ʻUthmān, the Muslim community has never again been fully united; it was confronted with a moral dilemma to which no universally acceptable solution has been found. If one approved of ʻUthmān's acts, he was wrong; if he approved of the murder, he was wrong and any moral neutrality was also felt to be wrong.

Ṭalḥa and Zubayr, together with ʻA'isha, the Prophet's widow, now deserted ʻAlī, accusing him of illegal election and complicity in the murder, and raised an army.

ʻAlī made the new camp city of Kūfa in Iraq his capital, and his followers routed and killed Ṭalḥa and Zubayr. The commander of the army in Syria, Muʻāwiya, cousin of ʻUthmān, then claimed the right of vengeance for the dead Caliph. A diplomat of great skill, he first maneuvered ʻAlī into a situation where he felt obliged to accept arbitration. At this, many of the pietists who had approved of ʻUthmān's death deserted ʻAlī's army, accusing him of repudiation of the Qur'ān, where they found, "If one party rebels against the other, fight against that which rebels" (49:9). Since 'Alī had in this way apostacized, they maintained, all who continued to follow him were infidels. These Khārijīs, or "Seceders," thus became a new sect of Islam, and held that other Muslims were apostates whose blood it was lawful to shed. 'Alī was forced to fight them, but their appeal to the tribal elements was strong, and in A.H. 40/A.D. 661, 'Alī was assassinated by a Khārijī.

'Alī had been a deeply religious man, who had appealed profoundly to the loyalties of his followers, and he had lent his moral authority to social and economic reforms many Muslims desired to see. Very soon he and his descendants were given an almost prophetic prestige; they have even been seen by some of their followers as emanations of the Godhead.

Mu'āwiya became Caliph, and the House of Umayya ruled for ninety years. The Khārijīs and the Faction of 'Alī, the Shī'a, led unsuccessful religious revolts, and even in the remainder of the community dissatisfaction with the Umawīs grew. In A.D. 750 a general revolution by all elements for "an *Imām* of the Prophet's family" toppled the Umawīs, but it was the descendants of the Prophet's uncle 'Abbās who had secretly engineered the revolution and who now seized the power. The Shī'a continued their opposition, and subdivided repeatedly over the claims of 'Alī's descendants, who became the nuclei of new Shī'ī sects.

1. *The Khārijīs*

The Khārijīs soon divided into several sects; from the first they were men who would not and could not compromise. Since their principles frequently led them to fight to the last against overwhelming odds, only the most moderate of these sects, the Ibāḍīs, has survived into modern times.

Khārijī holy wars against other Muslims were always terrifying; even the women and children of their opponents were put to death with religious thoroughness. At the same time, their just dealings with the People of the Book made them many friends among the subject peoples. They were nothing if not sincere men, and in their devotion to the Qur'ān and the Divine Imperative as they understood it, one must admire, even if grudgingly, the harsh, uncompromising righteousness of the Semitic prophets whose followers they were.

While they found followers in the Arabian peninsula, it was North Africa which became "the Scotland of these Puritans of Islam." Here, the warlike Berbers proved willing to accept Islam, but not the dominance or the taxation of the Arab Caliphs. From A.D. 761 to 908, the Berber Ibāḍīs maintained a separate state under their own *Imāms* at Tiaret in Central Algeria. This state was destroyed by the rising Shī'ī Fāṭimī Caliphate, based in Tunisia.

Their descendants fled to the Saharan oases of the Mzab, in Algeria, where they maintain a theocratic community under the *Ṭolba*, the Council of Elders. In addition, there are Ibāḍīs in the Jabal Nafusa of Libya and the isle of Jerba off Tunisia. In South Arabia, the more conservative Ibāḍīs of 'Uman under their *Imām* maintain a running war with the moderates under the Sulṭān of Muscat. The ruling clique of Zanzibar are also Khārijīs.

In all, there are probably no more than half a million Khārijīs in the world today. They look upon themselves as the only Muslims, and have their own legal system and collections of *Ḥadīth*. They are exceedingly puritanical, and forbid tobacco, games, music, Ṣūfism, luxury, celibacy and anger. Concubinage is permitted only with the consent of the wives. Intermarriage with other Muslims is rare, and heavily frowned upon. They maintain the classical Khārijī doctrines, as follows:

The Qur'ān is created, and must be literally interpreted. There will be no beatific vision of God in the hereafter. The *Imāmate* is not obligatory, but if there is an *Imām*, he may be any pious believer, "even an Abyssinian slave." If he commits a major sin he must be deposed. The commission of any major sin by a believer is apostacy, and exposes him to ostracism or death, unless he performs a thorough admission of guilt and public penance.

The following selection is the *khuṭba*, or Friday sermon, of an early Ibāḍī rebel who in A.H. 129/A.D. 747 briefly took Mecca and Medina. It has been preserved in several early collections of rhetoric as an example of Arab eloquence and moral fervor. It was intended to persuade other Muslims to make common cause with the Ibāḍīs, and one finds clearly expressed the Khārijīs' view of Islamic history, and their pious hatred of their opponents.

The Sermon of Abū Ḥamza the Khārijī

Abū Ḥamza the Khārijī entered Medina;[1] he was one of the Khārijī pietists and preachers. He mounted the pulpit leaning on his Arab bow. Mālik ibn Anas said, "Abū Ḥamza preached us a sermon which would have thrown doubt into the most perspicacious and refuted a skeptic." He said:

"I counsel you in fear of God and obedience to Him; to act according to His Book and the Sunna of His prophet—His blessing and peace be on him—and to observe the ties of blood, and magnify the truth of God which tyrants have diminished, and to diminish the falsehood they have magnified; to put to death the injustice they have brought to life, and to revivify the just laws they have let die; to obey God—and those who obey Him disobey others in obedience to Him, for there is no obeying a creature which disobeys its Creator.

"We call you to the Book of God and the Sunna of His prophet, and to equal sharing, and to justice for the subject peoples, and to putting the fifths of the booty in the places God ordained for them.

"As for us, we have not taken up arms lightly or frivolously, for play or amusement, or for a change of government in which we hope to immerse ourselves, or for the revenge that was taken from us; but we did it when we saw the earth had grown wicked, and proofs of tyranny had appeared, and religious propagandists increased, but men did as they pleased, and laws were neglected, and the just were put to death, and speakers of truth treated violently, and we heard a herald calling us to Truth and the Straight Path, so we answered the summoner of God . . . and by His grace we became brethren. . . .

"Oh people of Medina! Your beginning was the best of beginnings—and your end is the worst of endings, for you have hearkened to your readers and your lawyers, and they cut you away from the Book which has no crookedness, cut you away with the exegesis of the ignorant and the pretensions of triflers, so that you strayed from the Truth, and became dead and unfeeling.

"O people of Medina! Children of the *Muhājirīn* and the *Anṣār!* How sound were your roots, and how rotten are your branches! Your fathers were men of certainty and religious knowledge—and you are people of error and ignorance. . . . For God opened the door of religion for you, and you (let it grow choked with rubbish); He locked the door of this world for you, and you forced it open; hasters to temptation and laggards in the way of the Prophet; blind to the demonstrations of Truth and deaf to knowledge; slaves of greed and allies of affliction! How excellent was the legacy your fathers left, had you preserved it, and how miserable will be that of your children if you hold on to it! Them He aided to the Truth—you He deserts in your error. Your ancestors were few and pious, and you are many and malicious. . . . The preachers of the Qur'ān cry out to you, and you are not chidden; they warn you, and you do not ponder. . . .[2]

"Oh ye people, the blessing of God and peace be on our Prophet, who never delayed or hastened save by God's leave, and command, and revelation. God sent down on him a book, in which He showed him what was to come and what was to be feared, and there was no doubt about His religion, and no ambiguity about His command. Then God took him, when he had taught the Muslims the landmarks of religion, and Abū Bakr led them in their prayers. The Muslims entrusted Abū Bakr with the matters of the lower world, since God's messenger had entrusted him with the matter of his religion. He fought the people of apostacy, and acted in accord with the Book and the Sunna, and he passed his way; God have mercy on him!

"Then ruled 'Umar ibn al-Khaṭṭāb, God's mercy on him, and he went in the way of his friend and acted in accord with the Book and the Sunna. He collected the tribute and distributed the shares and . . . gave eighty lashes for drinking wine, and passed his way. God have mercy on him!

"Then came 'Uthmān ibn 'Affān. For six years he walked in the path of his two friends, but he was less than they. And in his last six years he rendered to no avail what he had done in the first six, and then he passed his way.

"Then 'Alī ibn Abī Ṭālib ruled, and he did not attain the goal in truth, and no beacon was given him for guidance, and he passed his way.

"Then ruled Mu'āwiya son of Abū Sufyān, accursed of God's messenger, and son of one accursed. He made farmers of God's servants and possessions of God's property, and a briarpatch of God's religion, so curse him with God's curse!

"Then came Yazīd the son of Mu'āwiya—Yazīd of the wine, Yazīd of the apes and the hunting panthers! Yazīd of the lustful belly and the effeminate arse—and God and His angels curse him!"

And one by one he related the doings of the Caliphs, until he reached 'Umar the Pious, son of 'Abd al-'Azīz, and passed over him without mentioning him. He went on:

"There came Yazīd ibn 'Abd al-Mālik, a libertine in religion and unmanly in behavior, in whom was never perceived right guidance. God has said about the wealth of orphans: 'If you perceive in them right guidance, deliver them their property' (4:6), and the matter of Muhammad's Community was more than any property! He would eat forbidden food, and drink wine, and wear a robe worth a thousand dinars, through which you could see his flesh so that the veil of modesty was rent; an unpardonable dis-robe. And Habāba the singing-girl on his right, and Salāma the singing-girl on his left, both singing—if you had taken drink away from him, he would have rent his garments! And he would turn to one of them and say, 'Shall I fly? Shall I fly?' Aye, he flew. To God's damnation, and the burning Fire, and a painful torment!

"The sons of Umayya are a party of error, and their strength is the strength of tyrants. They take conjecture for their guide, and judge as they please, and put men to death in anger, and govern by mediation, and take the law out of context, and distribute the public moneys to those not entitled to them—for God has revealed those who are entitled, and they are eight classes of men, for He says: 'The freewill offerings are for the poor and the needy, those who work to collect them, those whose hearts are to be reconciled, and slaves and debtors, and those in the "Way of God," and travellers' (9:60). They make themselves the ninth, and take it all! Such are those who rule by what God has not sent down.

"As for these factions [of 'Alī], they are a faction which has repudiated the Book of God to promulgate lies about Him. They have not left the people (of the Community) because of their insight into religion (as we have), or their deep knowledge of the Qur'ān; they punish crime in those who commit it and commit it themselves when they get the chance. They have determined upon tumult and know not the way out of it. Crude in (their knowledge of) the Qur'ān, following soothsayers; teaching people to hope for the Resurrection of the Dead, and then expecting the return (of their *imāms*) to this world; entrusting their religion to a man who cannot see them! God smite them! How perverse they are!"

2. *The Zaydīs*

The Shī'a began as the partisans of 'Alī, but it received its greatest impetus from the violent death of his younger son, al-Ḥusayn. Al-Ḥasan, the eldest, had been proclaimed 'Alī's successor by the partisans, but Mu'āwiya easily persuaded him to exchange his claim for a large pension and retirement in Medina. In A.D. 669, Ḥasan died, of natural causes according to the Sunnīs; the Shī'a hold that he was poisoned. The headship of the family fell now to his brother Ḥusayn. When he refused to acknowledge Mu'āwiya's son Yazīd as Caliph in A.H. 61/A.D. 680, the inhabitants of his father's former capital, Kūfa, offered to make him Caliph. He set out from Medina across the desert to Iraq, but in the meantime Yazīd's viceroy put down the insurrection at Kūfa and set patrols on the approaches to the city. Ḥusayn walked into the trap with his family and a few retainers at Karbala, some twenty-five miles from Kūfa. As the Prophet's favorite and only surviving grandson, he apparently did not expect to be seriously harmed, and refused to surrender, although surrounded and cut off from water. After ten days, the little band was cut down to the last man, and Ḥusayn's head sent to Yazīd in Damascus, who seems to have been genuinely shocked by the affair. Muslims everywhere were appalled, and the "Martyrdom of Karbala" became the rallying point of all who distrusted the Umawīs. With many moving and pitiful details, the story forms the basis of the "passion plays" of the Tenth of *Muḥarram*, celebrated by most Shī'īs and many Sunnīs. Orginally an Arab political faction, the Shī'a came to differ increasingly in doctrines from the Sunnīs.

Of the three major Shī'ī sects surviving today, that of the Zaydīs most preserves its old Arab character and seems to form a bridge between Sunnī and Shī'ī practice. Their name is traced to a grandson of al-Ḥusayn, Zayd ibn 'Alī Zayn al-'Abidīn, who was also killed leading an armed rebellion of the Kūfans, *c.* A.H. 121/A.D. 739. The sect traces its law-school back to Zayd, but the real systematizers were two descendants of al-Ḥasan: Ḥasan ibn Zayd (b. Muhammad b. Ḥasan b. Zayd b. 'Ali b. al-Ḥasan) and al-Qāsim al-Rassī, (died A.H. 246/A.D. 860). Ḥasan ibn Zayd founded a Zaydī state on the mountainous Caspian seacoast of Persia (*c.* A.H. 250/A.D. 864) which at least produced claimants to the *Imāmate* until *c.* A.H. 520/A.D. 1126. At around the same time another Zaydī *Imāmate* was founded in the highlands of Yemen, *c.* A.H. 288/A.D. 901, which with many vicissitudes has endured until the present day, making it the oldest Muslim state.

Like the other Shī'ī sects, the Zaydīs were profoundly influenced by their contacts with the Mu'tāzila, and believe that God has no eternal and uncreated attributes, and that the Qur'ān is created. They also for the most part do not accept predestination.

In law, they hold to a fundamental strictness of observance. Like the other Shī'a, they differ in some ritual matters from the Sunnīs: in the matter of ablutions, and the call to prayer. They are hostile to Ṣūfism, and Ṣūfī orders have been banned in the Yemen. They prohibit mixed marriages; they will not eat meat slaughtered by a non-Muslim and will not pray behind any man not of known piety. They consider their wars against Sunnīs as holy wars, but appear to regard Sunnīs as "rebellious Muslims," rather than apostates.

Most curious is their doctrine of the *Imāmate*, which is midway between that of the Sunnīs and the other Shī'a. The *Imām* may not be a child, or invisible, as in the other Shī'ī sects; he must be able to lead the holy war and defend the community, and must be a *mujtahid*. He may be any descendant of 'Alī, and the *Imāms* of Yemen have included descendants of both Ḥasan and Ḥusayn. He is not impeccable or infallible, and can be and has been deposed. There may be more than one *Imām* at a time (as in two widely separated Zaydī states).

The traditions on the *Imāmate* are taken from one of the chief Zaydī legal works, a commentary on the *Majmū'* ascribed to Zayd ibn 'Alī. The second selection is from one of the early *ḥisba* manuals extant, written by the Zaydī *Imām* al-Nāṣir li-al-Haqq (died A.H. 304/A.D. 917) of the Caspian area. Not all of its provisions would be enforced today, of course. The general picture it gives is of a society which must have seemed excessively puritanical to many Sunnīs of the third century.

Zaydī Traditions on the Imāmate

Zayd ibn 'Alī told me on the authority of his father Zayn al-'Abidīn from his grandfather al-Ḥusayn, peace be upon them all, that he said "Whoever dies with no Imām dies as ignorant carrion, if the Imām (of that time) is just, good, and pious." . . . And Muslim has published a ḥadīth of Abū Hurayra, with one of Ibn 'Abbās, that the Prophet, God's blessing be upon him and his family, and peace, said: "Whoever of you sees something he dislikes in his commander, let him be patient, for there is not one who arbitrarily (*shabaran*) abandons the Community (*jamā'a*) but dies as ignorant carrion." . . . and he said "There is no obeying in what is rebellion against God; obedience is only in the good." . . .

Zayd ibn 'Alī related on the authority of his father and grandfather from 'Alī—peace be upon them all—that he said, "The Imām's duty is to judge by what God sent down and to be just to the subjects. If he does that, their duty is to hearken and obey, and to respond to his call, and if the Imām does not judge by what God sent down, no obedience is due him."

Zayd related . . . from 'Alī that the Messenger of God—His blessing be on him and his family, and peace, said "Wherever any ruler is hesitant to deal with the needs of his people, God will be hesitant to deal with his on the Day of Judgment."

I asked Zayd ibn 'Alī about the Imāmate and he said: "It is among all the Quraysh, and it may not be established without the oath of allegiance of the Muslims. When they have taken allegiance, and the Imām is good and pious, and knowledgeable in what is licit and illicit, then obedience to him is a duty for the Muslims."[3]

Zayd ibn 'Alī told me on the authority of his father and grandfather that 'Alī (peace be upon them all) said: "There are five things for the Imām: the Friday prayer, the Two Feasts (that of Sacrifice and that of Fast-breaking), collecting the alms-tax and the *ḥudūd* (Qur'ānic punishments), and judgment, and retaliation."[4]

The *Muḥtasib* must give orders that the doors of the mosques be not locked, or pictures painted on the mosques, and that they be not decorated with gold or have appointments like churches and synagogues, (*ka al-bī'a*) or have curtains hung in them, or be ornamented with stucco or otherwise, for all that is objectionable. The minarets of the mosques shall not be raised higher than their roofs, and he shall order any crenellations raised above the people's houses to be concealed. It is related that the Prince of Believers, 'Alī—the blessings of God be upon him and his family, and peace—that he said: "The minarets of the mosque shall not be raised above its walls." . . .

The *Muḥtasib* must forbid burial places to be used as mosques, according to the teaching of the Prophet, God's blessing be upon him and his family, and peace: "God has cursed the Jews because they take the tombs of their prophets as mosques." And Ja'far ibn Muhammad relates from his ancestors, from 'Alī—peace be upon him and his family—that he said: "If you see legend-narrators (*qaṣṣāṣ*) in the mosques, then good-bye to Islam (*'ala al-Islām al-salām*)." . . . And no Jew or Christian or Zoroastrian shall enter the mosques, even if the governor is holding hearings there, and menstruating women shall not enter there, or punishments be administered there. And he shall know the insignia of all People of the House (of the Prophet), peace be upon them, and see to it that the people of his district perform the prayers, and say twice at the end of the prayer-call "There is no God but God" and at the beginning of the prayer say it once, and drop the saying of "Amen" and say "Hasten to the best of works" at the prayer-call and the beginning of the prayers, and make them say "In the name of God the Merciful, the Compassionate" out loud, and forbid them the *masḥ 'alā al-khuffayn* [merely wiping the socks instead of washing the feet at the ablution; permitted by some schools.—Ed.] and order them to say "God is most great," five times at funerals [instead of four].

The *Muḥtasib* must also forbid carpenters and turners to make backgammon and chess sets, and sets for "fourteen," as it is a (sort of) lottery. It is mentioned of the Prince of Believers ('Alī), that he would say "Peace be upon thee" to all who passed by him; even boys, and Abyssinians wearing necklaces, but he would not greet the owner of a backgammon-game or a chess-set, and that he once passed some people playing chess and said, "What are these images to which you apply yourselves?" and he ordered the chess-set to be broken and burnt the board on which they played.

And he shall order that they make unto themselves no idol or image or doll for children, and he shall break whatever he finds of such things.

And they shall not take unto themselves hand-drums or pipes or lutes or tambourines or mandolines or timbals or any other musical instrument, and whatever is confiscated of this nature shall be broken; their makers shall be instructed in this, according to the Prophet's instructions, the benediction of God be upon him and his family, to 'Alī: "I send you as God sent me, to break flutes and lutes, and to level heaped-up graves."

Similarly with anything with pictures on it, such as glass or other things; he shall order them to be rubbed out, and if they cannot be rubbed out except by breaking them, break them. Likewise with any pictures on doors or garments; he shall cut off the heads of the pictures. Similarly he shall break coins minted by foreigners on which are pictures. And he shall forbid men to mix with women in the markets and streets.[5]

3. *The Twelvers*

The Twelver Shī'a, or *Ithna-'asharīya*, are numerically the largest of the Shī'ī sects, and exhibit most of the doctrines which became classical with the Shī'a.

Theologically, they are Mu'tazilī rationalists, believing that the Qur'ān is created, and that since God is *essentially* good, He *cannot* do evil. He has created man with free will in order to know Him, and desires man's welfare. It follows that He would not leave man without guidance; thus the books of the prophets have been sent down. Even so, as the sects of Islam attest, confusion arises, so it follows that God has given man in addition to the Prophet an infallible guide in religious matters. This guide is the *Imām*. It is also clear then that the selection of the *Imāms* is a matter which could not be left to human error; they were Divinely appointed from birth. The true *Imāms* are the direct line of 'Alī through al-Ḥusayn. A younger brother of the Zayd ibn 'Alī claimed by the Zaydīs is their fifth *Imām*, since Zayd was a concubine's son.

In common with earlier, now extinct Shī'ī sects, they believe in the doctrines of occultation (*ghayba*) and return (*raj'a*). The twelfth of the line of *Imāms* did not die, as his enemies assert, but like the Qur'ānic Jesus, he was taken by God from human sight, and is in occultation. He will return to earth as the *Mahdī*, the awaited messianic figure who (according to certain *ḥadīths* questioned by many Sunnī scholars) will bring the triumph of religion and herald the last judgment.

They hold that 'Alī was announced by Muhammad as his successor and plentipotentiary (*waṣī*), but that Abū Bakr, 'Umar and 'Uthmān deliberately deprived him of his rights. Repeatedly sinful men defrauded the *Imāms* of the "holy family," who foresaw and accepted their glorious but tragic destiny as the repositories of truth despised.

In law, the Twelvers do not accept *ḥadīths* transmitted by enemies of the *Imāms* such as 'A'isha, and make use also of the saying of the *Imāms*. In addition to the Shī'ī regulations for the prayer call and ablutions, they admit the doctrine of *taqīya* or *katmān*, the propriety or even necessity of hiding one's true beliefs among non-Shī'īs—a legacy from times when they were a persecuted minority—and they retain the peculiar institution of legal temporary marriage between a free man and woman for *mut'a* (pleasure).

Historically, they have been hostile on the whole to Ṣūfism, but they believe in the intercession of the members of the "holy family" and make pilgrimages to their tombs, especially those of the *Imāms*.

The Twelvers were encouraged in Persia under the Mongols, since they had no objection to the destruction of the Sunnī Caliphate, and in A.D. 1502 Twelverism was made the state religion of Persia under the Ṣafavī Shahs. It has become an element in Persian nationalism. Outside Persia, there are large Shī'ī communities among the Arabs of Iraq and Southern Lebanon and in India.

The following selection is from a creed of Ḥaṣan ibn Yūsuf, 'Allāma al-Ḥillī (died A.H. 726/A.D. 1326), an eminent Twelver theologian who flourished under the Mongols in Iraq.

1. Our doctors all agree in considering (obligatory) knowledge of God . . . and what is proper for Him and impossible for Him and Prophecy and the Imāmate and the Return.

72. The Most High is a Speaker (*mutakallim*) by the agreement of all. By speech (*kalām*) is intended letters and sounds which are audible and orderly. The meaning of his being a Speaker is that He brings Speech into existence in some sort of body (*jism*). And the explanation of the Ash'arīya is contrary to reason.

76. . . . The Ash'arīya say that God's speech inheres in the (Divine) essence. Those who say that it is letters and sounds have differed among themselves. The Ḥanbalīs and Karrāmīya say it inheres in His essence. . . . The Mu'tazila and the Imāmīya say (and this is reality) that it is inherent in something else, not in his essence (like the burning bush of Moses). The meaning of His being a Speaker is that He makes Speech, not that He is one in whom Speech inheres. . . .

79. . . . As to the priority or origin of His Speech, the Ash'arīya have said the idea was prior, and the Ḥanbalīs said that the letters were prior. The Mu'tazila said that Speech was an originated thing, and that is the reality, for several reasons. . . .

81. . . . The Most High is veracious, for a lie is necessarily evil, and God is far removed from evil, because it is impossible for Him to have any imperfections.

100. Ocular vision of the Most High is impossible, because

everything which can be seen possesses direction. Then He would be a body, and that is impossible. And there is the word of the Most High to Moses: "Thou shalt never see Me" (7:139) . . . Yet on the Day of Resurrection perfect knowledge will become necessary (though without ocular vision).

118. We are free agents (*bi-al-ikhtiyār*), and reason requires this . . . otherwise our responsibility for a thing would be impossible, and then there would be no sin; and because of the evil in His creating an act in us and punishing us for it, and because of tradition.

123. (Evil is impossible for Him) because He has what deters Him from it; knowledge of evil; and He has no motive, for the motive would be either the need (or the wisdom) of evil, both of which are excluded.

125. . . . The will to do evil is impossible for Him, for that will is evil.

144. Kindness (*luṭf*) is incumbent on the Most High. . . . *Luṭf* is that which brings the creature near to obedience and keeps him far from disobedience. . . . For whenever He who wills an act of another (as when God wills that man perform the Law) knows that he cannot do it without the aid of an act which the Willer can perform without any trouble, then if He does not perform it He would contradict His own aim (for God has an aim, contrary to the Ash'arīya), and reason pronounces that evil. And God is far above that.

176. . . . Men have disagreed on whether the Imāmate is incumbent or not . . . the Imāmīya (Shī'a) say it is incumbent on God by reason; the proof is that it is kindness, and all kindness is incumbent on God. . . . That is the major premise; the minor premise is that it brings men to obedience. Whoever has known dark experiences and examined political principles knows that whenever men have a chief and a guide whom they obey, who restrains the oppressor from his oppression . . . and leads men

to rational principles and religious duties and restrains them from corruption . . . then they will, because of this, draw near to soundness and depart from corruptness . . . this idea is realized by the Imāmate. . . .[6]

These selections on the *imāmate* are from the creed of Ibn Babūya al-Sadūq, one of the greatest early Twelver doctors, who collected traditions and elaborated the doctrine in the Buwayhī period. He died in A.D. 381/A.H. 991.

35. Our belief concerning the number of the prophets is that there have been one hundred and twenty-four thousand prophets and a like number of plenipotentiaries (*awṣīyā*). Each prophet had a plenipotentiary to whom he gave instructions by the command of God. And concerning them we believe that they brought the truth from God and their word is the word of God, their command God's command, and obedience to them obedience to God. . . .

The leaders of the prophets are five (on whom all depends): Noah, Abraham, Moses, Jesus, and Muhammad. Muhammad is their leader . . . he confirmed the (other) apostles.

It is necessary to believe that God did not create anything more excellent than Muhammad and the Imāms. . . . After His prophet, the proofs of God for the people are the Twelve Imāms. . . .

We believe that the Proof of Allah in His earth and His viceregent (*khalīfa*) among His slaves in this age of ours is the Upholder (*al-Qā'im*) (of the laws of God), the Expected One, Muhammad ibn al-Ḥasan al-'Askarī (*i.e.*, the Twelfth *Imām*). He it is concerning whose name and descent the Prophet was informed by God, and he it is who WILL FILL THE EARTH WITH JUSTICE AND EQUITY JUST AS IT IS NOW FULL OF OPPRESSION AND WRONG. He it is whom God will make victorious over the whole world until from every place the call to prayer is heard and religion will belong entirely to God, exalted be He. He is the rightly guided *Mahdī* about whom the prophet gave information that when he appears, Jesus, son of Mary, will descend upon the earth and pray behind him. We believe there can be no other *Qā'im* than him; he may live in the state of occultation (*ghayba*) (as long as he likes); were it the space of the existence of this world, there would be no *Qā'im* other than him.

36. Our belief concerning prophets, apostles, Imāms [in the special Shī'ī sense] and angels is that they are infallible (*ma'ṣūm*); . . . and do not commit any sin, minor or major . . . he who denies infallibility to them in any matter . . . is a *kāfir*, an infidel.

37. Our belief concerning those who exceed the bounds of belief, the *ghūlat* [such as those who ascribe divinity to 'Alī or the other *imāms*.—Ed.] and those who believe in delegation [*mufawwiḍa:* the belief that after creating Muhammad and 'Alī, God rested and delegated all the administration of His creation to their hands.—Ed.], is that they are *kuffār*, deniers of God. They are more wicked than the Jews, the Christians, the Fire Worshippers . . . or any heretics; none have belittled God more. . . .

Our belief concerning the Prophet is that he was poisoned (by Jews) during the expedition to Khaybar. The poison continued to be noxious and (shortening his life) until he died of its effects.

I. Imām: And the Prince of Believers ('Alī), on whom be peace, was murdered by . . . Ibn Muljam al-Murādī, may God curse him, and was buried in Gharī.

II. Imām: Ḥasan ibn 'Alī, on whom be peace, was poisoned by his wife Ja'da bint Ash'ath of Kinda, may God curse (her and her father).

III. Imām: Ḥusayn ibn 'Alī was slain at Karbala. His murderer was Sinān ibn-Anas al-Nakhā'ī, may God curse him and his father.

IV. Imām: 'Alī ibn Ḥusayn, the Sayyid Zayn al-'Abidīn, was poisoned by al-Walīd ibn 'Abd al-Mālik, God curse him.

V. Imām: Muhammad Bāqir ibn 'Alī was poisoned by Ibrahīm ibn al-Walīd, God curse him.

VI. Imām: Ja'far al-Ṣādiq was poisoned by Abū Ja'far al-Manṣūr al-Dawanīqī, may God curse him.

VII. Imām: Mūsa al-Kāzim ibn Ja'far was poisoned by Harūn al-Rashīḍ, may God curse him.

VIII. Imām: 'Alī al-Riḍā ibn Mūsa was poisoned by Ma'mūn ibn Harūn al-Rashīd, may God curse him.

IX. Imām: Abū Ja'far Muhammad al-Tāqī ibn 'Alī was poisoned by al-Mu'tasim, may God curse him.

X. Imām: 'Ali al-Naqī ibn Muhammad was poisoned by Mutawakkil, may God curse him.

XI. Imām: Ḥasan al-'Askarī was poisoned by al-Mu'tamid, may God curse him. . . . And verily the Prophets and Imāms, on whom be peace, had informed (people) that they would be murdered. He who says that they were not has given them the lie and has imputed falsehood to God the Mighty and Glorious.

39. Our belief concerning *taqīya* (permissible dissimulation of one's true beliefs) is that it is obligatory, and he who forsakes it is in the same position as he who forsakes prayer. . . . Now until the time when the Imām al-Qā'im appears, *taqīya* is obligatory and it is not permissible to dispense with it. He who does . . . has verily gone out of the religion of God. And God has described the showing of friendship to unbelievers as being (possible only) in the state of *taqīya.*

And the Imām Ja'far said, "Mix with enemies openly but oppose them inwardly, so long as the authority is a matter of question." He also said, "Diplomacy (*al-rī'ā'*) with a true believer is a form of polytheism, but with a (hypocrite) in his own house, it is worship." And he said "He who prays with hypocrites (*i.e.*, Sunnīs), standing in the first row, it is as though he prayed with the Prophet standing in the first row." And he said, "Visit their sick and attend their funerals and pray in their mosques."

40. Our belief concerning the (ancestors of the Prophet, contrary to the Sunnīs) is that they were Muslims from Adam down to 'Abdallah, father of the Prophet....

41. Our belief concerning the 'Alawīya (descendants of 'Alī) is that they are the progeny of the Messenger of God and devotion to them is obligatory (in) requital of his apostleship....[7]

4. *The Seveners*

A most interesting and historically important sect of Islam has been the division of the Shī'a known as the Seveners. Although they have been divided by many schisms, and given rise to at least one separate religion, they all trace their spiritual parentage of Ismā'īl, eldest son of the sixth *Imām* of the Twelvers, Ja'far al-Ṣādiq. Ismā'īl is said by some Twelvers to have died before his father, by others to have been disowned for a fault ranging from drinking wine to participating in religious activist and revolutionary activities. The Twelvers make his younger brother their seventh *Imām;* the Seveners followed the descendants of Ismā'īl and are often called Ismā'īlīs.

The explication of their doctrine was profoundly in accord with old Hellenistic-Oriental gnostic ideas which still flourished in many isolated parts of the Islamic Empire. It was skillfully and secretly taught as an esoteric system by *dā'īs,* or missionaries, while the whereabouts of the *Imāms* was carefully concealed. In some areas, such as the Syrian mountains, Kurdistan and Central Asia, the doctrine was grafted on to earlier gnostic communities.

In the late third century, the Ismā'īlīs led a series of religious political revolts patterned on that of the 'Abbāsīs, which culminated in the establishment of an Ismā'īlī Caliphate "of the Children of Fāṭima" under their own *Imām* in Tunisia in 909. In 969 these Fāṭimī Caliphs took Egypt and built Cairo as their capital, while trying to expand eastward at 'Abbāsī expense. A curious episode of the Cairene period is that of the Caliph al-Ḥākim, who proclaimed his own divinity and in 1021 disappeared during a palace coup. The Druzes of the Lebanese Mountains accepted his claim, severed their connection with Muslims and hold that he was God Incarnate, now in *ghayba.* With the death of al-Ḥākim's grandson, al-Mustanṣir (A.H. 487/A.D. 1094), the Ismā'īlīs divided. The younger son, al-Musta'lī, became Caliph, and the elder son, al-Nizār, was imprisoned. The followers of the sect in 'Abbāsī territory refused to accept this, and took Nizār's son to one of their mountain fortresses, Alamūt. The Nizārīs, as they became known, were accused of immoderate use of Indian hemp (marijuana) or *hashīsh,* hence the name *hashshāshīn.* Their well-known practice of the carefully planned murder of enemies of the sect was justifiable by their doctrine that opponents of the *Imām* were manifestations of the material world of non-being, and had no "real" existence. (This has given us the word "assassinate.")

The Mongols destroyed the Nizārī strongholds, and for many years the sect was in another period of *taqīya* or concealment. At times they have concealed themselves in the guise of Ṣūfī orders; Seveners have always had a close affinity with some Ṣūfīs, and influenced the teachers of Ibn al-'Arabī. In 1817 the Qajar Shah of Persia gave their *Imām* the title "Aghā Khān." Nizārī *dā'īs* had had considerable success in converting Hindus to their doctrines, and the *Imām* moved to India in the nineteenth century.

The visible line of Musta'lī *Imāms* ended in A.H. 524/A.D. 1130, when Musta'lī's son al-Āmir died. He is said by the sect to have left a son, the infant al-Ṭayyib, who went into occultation; the Musta'lī *Imāmate* is therefore invisible. The Fāṭimī Caliphs who succeeded, not being in the direct line of succession, were not *Imāms*. Even this limited Caliphate was brought to an end by Ṣalāḥ al-Dīn al-Ayyūbī in 1171; the leadership of the sect passed to the *dā'īs* in Yemen, who converted numbers of Hindus in Gujerat in West India, the so-called Bohras.[8] The Musta'līs have split several times.

A good deal of Sevener literature has been published: it appears to be self-contradictory and confusing. This is because all explication of their doctrine was conducted on the sound principle that Truth, while absolute, is necessarily apprehended in a relative way by each individual—that one man's deepest spiritual verity may be another's scandal. Thus there might be many approaches in their propaganda, depending on who was involved, and where, and when. What really mattered, after all, was that one be devoted to the sinless *Imām*, and ready to serve him. There were degrees of knowledge within the sect according to the amount of truth the individual was judged able to bear, though this aspect was much overemphasized by their opponents.

To be sure, the doctrine changed in the forms in which it was presented, and varied from one time or area to another. In India, it might be convenient to explain the avatars of the gods as former prophets, or vice versa. But in all its known forms, the Ismā'īlī doctrine comes from the world of late Hellenistic thought—the metaphysics of Neoplatonism and the physics of Ptolemaeus. God is seen as pure Unity, the One, without attributes, incomprehensible to human thought. He is only to be approached by His emanations. He manifests Himself through prime or spiritual matter; here the Universal Intellect, or *Nous*, is emanated. To it is imparted the Divine knowledge. It then passes this knowledge on to the Universal Soul, or *Pneuma*. At the bottom of the scale of emanations is the physical, material world, but even it bears the stamp of the Divine. The emanation of the Universal Intellect in the world of nature is the *Nāṭiqs*, or greatest prophets, in cycles of seven. The current cycle runs from Adam to Muhammad, the sixth. The emanation of the Universal Spirit is the *Waṣī*, who accompanies each *Nāṭiq*. He is the *Imām*, and may be incarnated in many bodies.

As a religious synthesis of all the science and philosophy available to medieval Islam, Ismā'īlism had an immense intellectual appeal; it was a "scientific" religion. The mystical number seven and the science of the celestial spheres also figure in Ismā'īlī literature.

The following selection is attributed (perhaps wrongly) to Ibn Ḥawshab al-Kūfī, a famous *dā'ī* active in the Yemen in A.D. 266/A.H. 880. In any case, it is a very early Isma'īlī treatise, and shows admirably the system of esoteric interpretation of the Qur'ān (*ta'wīl al-bāṭin*) for which the Seveners were famous. The outcome of its Messianic promise was the Fāṭimī Caliphate.

. . . The first words of the Qur'ān are: "In the name of God, the Merciful, the Compassionate." "In the name of God" is written with seven [Arabic] letters, from which twelve others can be derived, and then the twelve letters of "The Merciful, the Compassionate" follow. This sūra is "The Sūra of Praise" (*ḥamd*), and is seven verses. The seven letters of "In the name of God" refer to the seven *Nātīqs* [spokesmen: for the Universal Reason; used of the greatest prophets.—ED.] and the twelve derived letters indicate the fact that every *Nāṭīq* has twelve intendants (*naqībs*).

Then from the twelve of "The Compassionate, the Merciful are derived nineteen letters, referring to the fact that from each *Nāṭiq* is derived seven Imāms and twelve *ḥujjats*, making nineteen altogether.

The seven verses of the sūra symbolize the seven degrees of religion. The Sūra of Praise opens the Book of God, and similarly the degrees of religion open the door of knowledge in God's religion.[9]

. . . The letter "yā' " (in *Mahdī*) has the numerical value of ten, and the seventh *Nāṭiq* will be the tenth after Muhammad and 'Alī and the seven Imāms of their line. He is the tenth, and he is the seventh *Nāṭiq,* and he is the Eighth after the seven Imāms. . . .

God says, glory be to Him: "We have cleft the earth in fissures" (80:26) (And the earth is the *Waṣī:* 'Alī). And then: "And caused to grow therein grain and the grape, and reeds, and olives, and palms, and dense-tree'd gardens, and fruits, and pasture; and enjoyment for you and your flocks." The meaning of "pasture" (*i.e., āb: i.e.,* "father") is 'Alī, and (referred to here) are his descendants the seven Imāms and the Eighth, who is the *Mahdī,* the Seventh *Nāṭiq.*[10]

The *ḥujjat* (literally: "proof"; a high-ranking Ismā'īlī *dā'ī*, somewhat on a par with archbishop) who organized the Nizārīs of Alamūt (and of chapter strongholds as far west as Syria, where they came in contact with the Crusaders) was Ḥasan ibn Ṣabbāḥ. He probably composed the treatise from which this is taken. It was intended to appeal to non-believers, and its metaphysics would have had an obvious appeal for Christians; the *Imāms* are the Logos, the universe is divinized and God wears a human face.

The Great and Exalted has a manifestation in His own form

for all eternity in this world. . . . He has made a man noble with that form, and all the prophets and friends of God have indicated a man who would be the Great and Exalted among people in the form of a man.

. . . Those who speak the truth call (him) Mawlānā, Our Lord, and they consider this the greatest name of God . . . and further Mawlānā has been called Imām. . . . The Shī'a call Mawlānā *Qā'im of the Qiyama;* some hold to the name Mālik al-Salām (King of Salem: Melchisedek), some say Muhammad the Mahdī, and some say Muhammad ibn Ḥasan al-'Askarī . . . some are sure it is ('Alī's son) Muhammad ibn al-Ḥanafīya. . . .

Who is this person, where does he live, and what is his name? . . . It is known at large and among the elite that the Prophet indicated Mawlānā 'Alī ibn Abī Ṭālib . . . as Qā'im of the Qiyāma. . . .

Above all the Imāms is Mawlānā 'Alī . . . who has no end nor beginning. But relatively to the people he appears now as a son, now as a grandson, now aged . . . now young, now a king, now a beggar . . . he appears in the form of the Imām of the time, today and tomorrow.

Haḍrat Bābā Sayyidna Ḥasan-i Ṣabbāḥ . . . was the greatest *ḥujjat* of the Qā'im of the Qiyāma. . . .

This world from the core of the earth to the zenith of the heaven of heavens is one body (*shakhs*). . . . And the same power which appears in the sun and moon and stars . . . is in a black stone and darkness. But it is necessary to see. And one must treat all opposites analogously. . . .

The divine light first shines from the heavens . . . and (also) rises from the core of the earth. The (Ptolemaic) heavens are called "fathers" and the four humours (hot, cold, dry, and moist) are called "mothers"; minerals, plants, and animals are called "offspring." They (are) nine fathers . . . then the power of divine light causes whatever is subtly alive in fathers and mothers and offspring to become gathered into the body of a man, and in this special form to arrive at Godhood. . . .

In the realm of *sharī'a* its people imagine God conjecturally

... but one must know that in this form of man, the Lord has manifested Himself ... the Lord has made man great and ennobled; regarded relatively He has brought Himself into this special form. ...[11]

This selection, while from a rather late work, displays clearly several characteristic Ismā'īlī arguments of the past; the central doctrines of Islam are made part of an elaborate theosophical allegory; the Law becomes a mere exterior form for the uninstructed, who do not have the gnosis imparted by the *ḥujjat*. It is taken from *Kalām-i Pīr*, one of the holiest manuals of the Central Asian Nizārīs, attributed wrongly to Nāṣir-i Khusraw (died *c.* A.H. 480/A.D. 1087), a great Persian *dā'ī* and poet. It comes from a time when the *imām* was in concealment, and the *ḥujjat* took his place. The Nizārīs of today, it should be remarked, do not take the duties of Islam lightly, and are a very progressive community. Such treatises as these are a part of the historic Nizārī past.

... In the nature of man are diabolical as well as angelic and human elements ... it is necessary for a prophet to explain the devil-like and brutal in concrete similes ... thus he tells (men) that the place for sinners is Hell ... full of fire with snakes, scorpions and poisonous plants. And he explains the meaning of the angelic qualities in man in concrete forms, telling them that the place for the good is Paradise, a garden full of good food and drink, pretty girls and boys. A prophet must always explain his teaching in such primitive similes, devised ... for the understanding of all grades of intelligence. Primitive people do not understand ... anything beyond this, but intelligent people will at once grasp the purport of the simile.

... But the conditions of mankind are always changing, under the influence of the stars and peculiarities of different periods, and thus the Law must change. ... Thus the (book of a prophet) must be allegorical and its teachings expressed in similes. . . . Primitive people . . . understand (nothing) beyond the outward meaning, the *ẓāhir;* they should follow the outward side of the Prophet's instructions, similar to straw or bark. Those capable of understanding the inner meaning, the *bāṭin* . . . can perceive the meaning of the commandments . . . the *ẓāhir* must be continually changing, while the . . . *bāṭin* is concerned with the world of reality . . . or divinity, and is unchangeable. . . .[12]

The meaning of the fast is *taqīya* or dissimulation . . . the Feast of Fast-breaking is the Day . . . of the Great *Qiyāma* [the triumph of the religion].

The meaning of the *zakāt* or religious tax is teaching the religion and making it to reach the faithful . . . (according to) their capacity to understand it . . . the distributor is the *Ḥujjat,* who conveys as much as one can stand. . . .

Running in the pilgrimage means hastening toward the Imām.

Prostration . . . means this: if a believer who is fully initiated (*ma'dhūn*) or a *dā'ī,* commits a mistake, he must return to the higher knowledge which is with the *Ḥujjat* . . . .[13]

The treatise on the "Recognition of the Imām" was probably written for the Nizārīs of Badakhshān in the early part of the sixteenth century. It was written for the instruction of a small and isolated community at a time when the *Imām* was concealed, and the only connection was the *ḥujjat,* to whom much importance is given here; a time which must have seemed on the whole a gloomy one. The language has changed somewhat; the *Imām* is now the manifestation of the Creative Act, the Word. The expectation of the promised deliverer is as strong as ever.

This is on the recognition of the Imām, who is the *maẓhar* (manifestation) of the Divine Creative Act; and on his *Ḥujjat,* who is the (manifestation) of the Universal Reason; on the Dā'ī; on the senior initiate (*ma'dhūn*) and the junior initiate (*ma'dhūn-i asghar*) and the neophyte or *mustajīb*, who are altogether the (manifestation) of the Universal Soul; and on (how to recognize) the "opponents" of the religion) who are the (manifestation) of the Universal Body.

I begin with the recognition of the Imām . . . he may be known (directly) in his own person, and at another time through his *Ḥujjat*. It is possible to recognize him directly only on the day of the "Sabbath of Faith" . . . each "day of faith" is one thousand years . . . on the (seventh) the Sun of Faith, the Imām, becomes manifested.

[Each thousand year period belongs to a *Nāṭiq*; the thousand years after the Hijra, toward the end of which this was written, was therefore the "Day of Muhammad."—Ed.] . . . in the other six days . . . called the "Night of Faith," the Law (*sharī'a*) is a veil for the Imām . . . but as there is the moon to take the place of the sun (at night) so the *Ḥujjat* takes the place of the Imām when he is not manifest. . . .

(While) in the 6000 years of the "night of faith" the Imām becomes manifest occasionally . . . these manifestations are not in his full glory. . . . But it would be absurd to think he would leave the "Chosen" without the possibility of recognizing him; for the purpose of their acquiring this knowledge the world was created. . . . Therefore the moon must exist in this night of faith. . . .[14]

REFERENCES AND NOTES

Chapter One

1. H. A. R. Gibb, *Mohammedanism* (2nd ed.; New York, 1953), p. 37.
2. A. J. Arberry, *The Koran Interpreted* (New York, 1955).
3. Since all who submit themselves to God's will are Muslims, Abraham and the twelve apostles are Muslims. It would appear preferable to call those Muslims who have followed Muhammad by the earlier term "Muhammadans," were it not that they resent the term as implying some sort of idolatrous relationship with their prophet.
4. Louis Gardet, "Allah," *Encyclopedia of Islam* (2nd ed.).
5. These verses are usually held to apply to female and male deviates.
6. In later times, this has been held to apply to heretics and social revolutionaries, as well as to brigands.
7. These verses refer to human conception and gestation.

Chapter Two

1. Wilfred Cantwell Smith, "Some Similarities and Differences Between Christianity and Islam," in Kritzeck and Winder, *The World of Islam* (New York, 1959).
2. "By this he meant Gabriel": al-Tabari.
3. Alfred Guillaume, *The Life of Muhammad* (Oxford, 1955), pp. 105–107. Translation of Ibn Ishaq, *Sirat Rasūl Allah.*
4. *Ibid.*, p. 111.

5. *Ibid.*, pp. 114, 115.

6. However, on this cf. Montgomery Watt, *Muhammad at Mecca* (Oxford, 1953), pp. 109 ff.

7. Guillaume, *op. cit.*, pp. 150–152.

8. Cf. Dom Miguel Asin Palacios, *La Escatologia Musulmana En ia Divina Comedia* (2nd Ed.; Madrid-Granada, 1943). Translated to English and Abridged in H. Sunderland, *Islam and the Divine Comedy* (London, 1926).

9. Guillaume, *op. cit.*, pp. 181–186 (here abridged).

10. *Ibid.*, p. 191.

11. *Ibid.*, pp. 197–198.

12. *Ibid.*, pp. 212–222 (here abridged).

13. *Ibid.*, pp. 223–228 (here abridged).

14. Falāh, usually translated as "salvation." Professor Guillaume suggests very plausibly that it is an Arabicization of the Syriac *pulhānā*, used by Aramaic Christians and Jews of the period for "divine service" worship.

15. Guillaume, *op. cit.*, pp. 235–236.

16. *Ibid.*, pp. 678–683.

17. *Ibid.*, pp. 685–687.

18. Al-Bukhārī, ed. Krehl & Juynboll, *Kitāb al-Jāmi'al Sahīh* (Leyden, 1868–1908), p. 445. The *Sahīh* has also been translated into French by O. Houdas and W. Marcais (Paris, 1903–1914).

19. *Ibid.*, Vol. IV, p. 115.

20. *Ibid.*, Vol. IV, p. 139.

21. *Ibid.*, Vol. IV, p. 139.

22. *Ibid.*, Vol. IV, p. 302.

23. *Ibid.*, Vol. IV, pp. 300, 309.

24. *Ibid.*, Vol. IV, p. 298, several versions.

25. *Ibid.*, Vol. IV, p. 308.

26. *Ibid.*, Vol. III, p. 413.

27. *Ibid.*, Vol. IV, p. 114.

28. *Ibid.*, Vol. IV, p. 431.

29. *Ibid.*, Vol. III, p. 403.

30. *Ibid.*, Vol. IV, p. 117.

31. *Ibid.*, Vol. IV, p. 121.

32. *Ibid.*, Vol. IV, p. 139.

33. *Ibid.*, Vol. IV, p. 431.

34. *Ibid.*, Vol. III, pp. 410, 411.

35. *Ibid.*, Vol. III, p. 448.

36. *Ibid.*, Vol. III, p. 506.

37. *Ibid.*, Vol. IV, p. 368.

38. *Ibid.*, Vol. III, p. 122.

39. *Ibid.*, Vol. IV, p. 43.

40. Cited in *Forty Ḥadīths* of al-Nāwāwī also. Cf. G. H. Bousquet, *Classiques de l'Islamologie* (Algiers, 1950).

41. Al-Bukhārī, *op. cit.*, Vol. IV, p. 123.

42. Ibn Khaldūn, *The Muqaddimah* (New York, 1958), translated by Franz Rosenthal, Vol. II, pp. 447–457, *passim.*

Chapter Three

1. Wilfred Cantwell Smith, *Islam in Modern History* (Princeton, 1957), p. 20.

2. Muwaffaq al-Dīn ibn Qudāma, *Kitāb al-'Umda fī Ahkām al-Fiqh*, pp. 1–14. Translation of Henri Laoust as: *Le Précis de droit d'Ibn Qudama* (Beirut, 1950).

3. *Ibid.*, p. 17.

4. *Ibid.*, pp. 19, 20.

5. Ibn Abī Zayd al-Qayrawānī, *Al-Risāla* (4th ed.; Algiers, 1952), with French translation by L. Bercher, pp. 56–68.

6. Muḥammad Fu'ad 'Abd al-Bāqī, *Al-Muwatta'* (Cairo, 1951), Vol. I, p. 222 ff.

7. Abū Ishāq al-Shīrāzī', *Kitab al-Tanbīh.* Abridged from French translation of G. H. Bousquet (Algiers, 1949).

8. Muhyī al-Dīn al-Nawawī, *Minhāj al-Tālibīn*, Vol. I, "Kitab al-Ṣiyām," abridged from pp. 279–291. With a French translation by L. W. C. Van Den Berg (Batavia, 1882).

9. Ibn Abī Zayd al-Qayrawānī, *op. cit.*, pp. 141–147.

10. Burhān-al-Dīn al-Marghinānī, *Al-Hidāya* (2nd ed.; London, 1870), translated by Charles Hamilton, pp. 25–33. From reprint of 2nd ed. (Lahore, 1957).

11. *Ibid.*, p. 34.

12. *Ibid.*, p. 36.

13. *Ibid.*, pp. 44, 45.

14. *Ibid.*, p. 66.

15. *Ibid.*, p. 72.

16. Al-Māwardī, *Al-Ahkām al-Sultānīya* (Cairo, 1909), pp. 3, 4.

17. Ibn Khaldūn, *The Muqaddima,* Vol. I, pp. 387, 388.

18. Al-Marghinānī, *op. cit.*, pp. 587–588.

19. *Ibid.*, pp. 592–594.

20. *Ibid.*, pp. 609–610.

21. Ibn al-Ukhūwa, *Ma'alim al-Qurba*, ed. by R. Levy. Arabic text with English abstract (Gibb Memorial Series; London, 1938), p. 79, Arabic text.

22. *Ibid.*, p. 143.

23. *Ibid.*, pp. 163, 164.

24. *Ibid.*, pp. 195, 196.

25. Al-Marghinānī, *op. cit.*, pp. 618–621.

26. *Ibid.*, pp. 607, 608.

27. Paul Horster, *Zur Anwendung des Islamischen Rechts im 16. Jahrhundert* (Stuttgart, 1935), p. 67.

28. *Ibid.*, pp. 70, 71.

29. *Ibid.*, p. 75.

30. *Ibid.*, p. 78.

31. *Ibid.*, pp. 77, 78.

Chapter Four

1. Louis Massignon, *Lexique Technique de la Mystique Musulman* (2nd ed.; Paris, 1954), p. 15.

2. Abū Nu'aym al-Isfahānī, *Hilyat al-Awliyā'* (Cairo, 1933), Vol. II, pp. 132–140.

3. A. J. Arberry, trans., *Ṣūfism* (London, 1950), pp. 33, 35, here abridged.

4. Cf. Massignon, *op. cit.*, p. 172.

5. Al-Sulamī, *Ṭabaqāt al-Ṣūfīya* (Cairo, 1953), p. 30. Somewhat different version translated by Arberry in *Ṣūfism*, p. 37.

6. Story translated in Arberry, *Ṣūfism*, p. 37.

7. Margaret Smith, trans., *The Persian Mystics: Attār* (Wisdom of the East Series; London, 1932), p. 39.

8. Arberry, *Ṣūfism*, p. 37.

9. Ibn Yazdānyār, *Rawdat al-Murīdīn* (Mss. Princeton, Paris, Berlin, Cairo, Istanbul).

10. Quoted by Margaret Smith, *Rābi 'a the Mystic* (Cambridge, 1928), p. 11.

11. *Ibid.*, p. 99.

12. *Ibid.*, p. 100.

13. *Ibid.*, p. 101.

14. *Ibid.*, p. 22.

15. Quoted by Margaret Smith, *Readings from the Mystics of Islam* (London, 1950), pp. 15, 16.

16. Al-Isfahānī, *op. cit.*, Vol. 10, p. 74. Quoted also in M. Smith, *An Early Mystic of Baghdad* (London, 1935), p. 9.

17. Arberry, *op. cit.*, p. 50.

18. Quoted by al-Ghazālī in Margaret Smith, trans., *Readings from the Mystics of Islam*, p. 35.

19. *Ibid.*, p. 36. This is not a quote from the Qur'ān, but a so-called *Ḥadīth Qudsī*, attributed to one of the prophets.

20. Ibn Yazdānyār, *op. cit.*

21. *Ibid.*

22. Al-Hallāj has been carefully studied in a series of works by Professor Louis Massignon.

23. R. A. Nicholson, trans., *The Legacy of Islam* (London, 1939), p. 218.

24. Massignon and Kraus, eds., *Akhbār al-Hallāj* (Paris, 1936), pp. 7, 8, Arabic.

25. For his biography, see R. A. Nicholson, *Studies in Islamic Mysticism* (Cambridge, 1921).

26. Cf. R. A. Nicholson, "Legacy of Islam," *op. cit.*, p. 220.

27. Margaret Smith, *Readings from the Mystics of Islam*, p. 49.

28. Editor's translation. The *rubā'iyāt* of Abū Sa'īd have been edited by Ethe.

29. Margaret Smith, *Readings from Mystics of Islam*, p. 52.

30. *Ibid.*, p. 54.

31. Editor's translation.

32. Smith, *Readings from Mystics of Islam*, p. 53.

33. Editor's translation.

34. R. A. Nicholson, ed. and trans., *Tarjumān al-Ashwāq* (London, 1911).

35. Smith, *Readings from Mystics of Islam*, p. 99.

36. A. J. Arberry, *Islamic Culture* (India, 1936), pp. 369–389.

37. Edward Fitzgerald, *Mantiq al-Tayr* in Collected Works, p. 196.

38. 'Attār, *Dīwān*, trans. by A. J. Arberry in *Immortal Rose* (London, 1948), pp. 32, 33.

39. From his *Dīwān*, trans. by Nicholson in *Studies in Islamic Mysticism*, pp. 175, 176.

40. *Ibid.*, p. 174.

41. Editor's translation.

42. R. A. Nicholson, ed. & trans., *Dīwānī Shamsi Tabrīz* (Cambridge, 1898), p. 125.

43. *Ibid.*, Appendix II.

44. E. G. Browne, *Literary History of Persia* (Cambridge, 1928), Vol. III, p. 511.

45. Quoted in Browne, *op. cit.* Editor's translation.

46. E. G. Browne, *A Year Amongst the Persians* (Cambridge, 1926, 1950), pp. 137 ff.

47. Gibb and Bowen, *Islamic Society and the West* (London, 1957), Vol. I, Part II, p. 201.

48. Cf. Constance C. Padwick, *Muslim Devotions* (London, 1961).

49. *Ibid.*, p. 218.

50. *Ibid.*, p. 203.

51. *Ibid.*, p. 242.

52. *Ibid.*, p. 250.

53. *Ibid.*, p. 253.

54. *Ibid.*, p. 257.

55. *Ibid.*, p. 280.

56. *Ibid.*, p. 219.

Chapter Five

1. Wensinck, trans., *The Muslim Creed* (Cambridge, 1932), pp. 103, 104.

2. *Kitāb al-'Alim wa al-Muta'allim* (Cairo, 1949).

3. Arabic in *Islam Akaidine Dair Eski Metinler*, with Turkish paraphrase by Y. Z. Yörükän (Istanbul, 1953).

4. W. Klein, trans., *Kitāb al-Ibāna 'an Usul al-Diyāna* (New Haven, 1940), pp. 47–49.

5. R. J. McCarthy S.J., trans., *Kitāb al-Luma'* (Beirut, 1953), pp. 55, 56.

6. *Ibid.*, pp. 99, 100.

7. *al-'Aqīda al-Nizāmīya* (Cairo, 1948), pp. 47, 48. Also in German translation by H. Klopfer as *Das Dogma des Imam al-Haramain al-Djūwainī* (Cairo, 1958).

8. Montgomery Watt, *The Faith and Practice of al-Ghazālī* (London, 1953).

9. *Ibid.*, p. 56.

10. *Ihyā 'Ulūm al-Din* (Cairo, 1939), Vol. IV, Book 26.

11. Watt, *op. cit.*, pp. 35, 38.

12. D. B. MacDonald, *Development of Muslim Theology, Jurisprudence and Constitutional Theory* (New York, 1903), pp. 305–307.

13. *Ma'ārij al-Wusūl*, in *Majmū' al-Rasā'il al-Kubra* (Cairo, 1905), Vol. I, p. 193. Also in French translation by H. Laoust (Cairo, 1939).

14. *Ibid.*, pp. 215–216.

15. *Al-Siyāsa al-Shar'īya* (Cairo, 1955), p. 98.

16. *Al-Ḥisba*, in *Majmū' al-Rasā'il al-Kubra, op. cit.*, p. 66.

17. *Majmū' al-Rasā'il wa al-Masā 'il* (Cairo, 1922), Vol. I, pp' 179–180.

18. F. Rahman, *Prophecy in Islam* (London, 1958), pp. 101–102.

Chapter Six

1. According to Isfahānī and Ibn 'Abd Rabbihi; but al-Jāhiz places the khutba in Mecca. Very likely there was more than one, and they have been confused.

2. Thus far translated from *al-'Iqd al-Farīd* of Ibn 'Abd Rabbihi (Cairo, 1944), Vol. IV, pp. 144–146. The section following is taken from the account by al-Jāhiz in *al-Bayān wa al-Tabyīn* (Cairo, 1948–1950), Vol. III, p. 95.

3. From *al-Rawd al-Nādir* (Cairo, 1928–1930), Vol. V, pp. 6–11.

4. *Ibid.*, Vol. III, p. 457.

5. From "A Zaydi Manual of Hisba of the 3rd Century," ed. by Serjeant in *Rivista degli Studi Oriental* (1953), Vol. 28, pp. 16, 17.

6. *Al-Bābu-l-Hādī 'Ashar*, trans. by W. E. Miller (London, 1958).

7. A. A. A. Fyzee, ed. and trans., *A Shi'ite Creed* (London' 1942).

8. Much interesting information is to be found in J. N. Hollister, *The Shi'a of India* (London, 1953).

9. Translated from edition of Arabic text by Kamil Hussein in *Collectanea of the Isma'ili Society* (Leiden, 1948), Vol. I, p. 189. A translation of a defective text was made earlier, by W. Iwanow, in *Studies in Early Persian Isma'ilism* and published by the Isma'ili Society (Bombay, 1948).

10. *Ibid.*, p. 199.

11. Marshall G. Hodgson, trans., *The Order of Assassins* (The Hague, 1955), pp. 284–313.

12. W. Iwanow, ed. and trans., *Kalām-i Pīr* (Bombay, 1935), p. 49.

13. *Ibid.*, pp. 92, 93.

14. W. Iwanow, trans., *On the Recognition of the Imām* (Bombay, 1947), pp. 17–20.

GUIDE TO PRONUNCIATION OF TERMS

The system of transliteration used in this volume for rendering Arabic and Persian words in Latin letters closely follows standard modern international practice.

The sounds thus represented may be approximated as follows in standard English:

Vowels

Short "a": between the vowel sounds of "hat" and "fur."

Long "a": (ā): like the *a* in "hard."

Short "i": as in English "pit."

Long "i" (ī): like the vowel sound in "feet."

Short "u": as in "hook," or "put."

Long "u" (ū): as in "clue," or the vowel sound in "food."

Consonants

Glottal stop, or hamza, *represented by* ('): can be found in between two English words ending and beginning with vowels, as: "Iowa apples," or where the "t's" should be in "bottle," as it is pronounced by many New Yorkers.

ʿayn, *represented by* (ʿ): a sort of twang of the vocal cords preceding or following another letter.

(*q*), *the Arabic* qāf: made by a "k" far back in the throat, at the uvula.

(*ḥ*), *Arabic* ḥā: a strongly aspirant "h," made in the throat area above the windpipe.

(*ṣ*) (*ẓ*) (*ṭ*) (*ḍ*): each is made by darkening the sound of the corresponding undotted letter. When these dotted consonants are made, the tongue should lie flat and broad in the mouth, behind the lower front teeth. The consonant sound will also slightly alter the quality of any vowel which immediately precedes or follows it.

(*gh*), *Arabic* ghayn: it is made by a sort of dry gargling like the Parisian (r).

(*kh*), *Arabic* khā': much like German "*ch*" in "nicht" or "Nacht," or the Greek *chi*.

INDEX

'Abbāsīs, 108, 110, 129, 179, 217
Abraham, 12–14, 24, 53, 61
Abū Bakr, 51, 58–59, 62–65, 91, 92, 203, 211
Abū Ḥamza al-Khārijī, 201–205
Abū Ḥanīfa, 104, 105, 159–65, 166
Abū Sa'īd ibn Abī Khayr, 136–38
Abū Yūsuf, 104, 105, 106, 117
Adam, 1, 6, 8–9, 138, 173, 220
Aghā Khān, 218
'Alī, 50, 64, 161, 173, 197–99, 203, 204ff
al-amr bi al-ma'rūf, 111–115 (see *ḥisba*)
al-nahī 'an al-munkar
al-Anṣari, 'Abdullah, 142–143
Antinomianism, 135–41, 237
Asceticism, 123–30
al-Ash'arī, 174–79
Assassins, 218
al-'Aṭṭār, 143–146
Averrhoes (see Ibn Rushd)
Avicenna (see Ibn Sīnā)

Bohras, 219
Brahmans, 181, 182
Buddha, 126
Bukhārī, 68–74, 76, 77
Buwayhīs, 108, 175, 180, 214

Circumcision, 114
Clergy, 80
Community, the, 59, 66, 66–77, 79, 160, 177, 178, 193, 197
Consensus, 45, 193–195

Dante, 53, 138
Dervishes, 148, 154–58
Dhikr, 154–56
Divorce, 104, 107–108
Druzes, 218

Ebū Su'ūd, 118–21
Ecstatics, 130–35, 146, 156
Eschatology, 38–43, 171–72, 176, 190–91, 211
Evil, 138, 167, 168–69, 178–79, 182, 212, 213

Fasting, 31–32, 98–101, 224
Fāṭima, 64, 174, 217
Fāṭimīs, 108, 217–219, 220
Fātiḥa, xiii, 86, 89, 90, 220
Fatwa, 118–121
Fiqh, 78–121, 160, 181
al-Fīrūzābādī, 94–98
Fosterage, 104
Free Will, 26, 160, 165, 169, 175–76, 178, 210, 213
Funeral Rites, 90–94
Fuṣūṣ al-Ḥikam, 121, 138–41

Gabriel, 48, 53–55
Garden of Eden, 6
Ghayba, 211
al-Ghazālī, 182–191, 192, 196
Gnosticism, 217

Ḥadīth, 44–77, 79, 90–94, 159, 166, 173, 200, 211
Ḥajj (see Pilgrimage)
al-Ḥallāj, 133–35, 136
Ḥanafīs, 80, 104–105, 113, 115–18, 119–21
Ḥanbalīs, 80, 81–86, 174, 191, 212
Ḥaram, 115
al-Ḥasan al-Baṣrī, 124–26
Ḥasan ibn al-Ṣabbāḥ, 221–23
Ḥasan ibn Zayd, 206
Hell, 5, 7, 37–43, 171–172, 177, 190, 223